OECD
Economic Surveys

Korea

2008

OECD

ORGANISATION FOR ECONOMIC CO-OPERATION AND DEVELOPMENT

The OECD is a unique forum where the governments of 30 democracies work together to address the economic, social and environmental challenges of globalisation. The OECD is also at the forefront of efforts to understand and to help governments respond to new developments and concerns, such as corporate governance, the information economy and the challenges of an ageing population. The Organisation provides a setting where governments can compare policy experiences, seek answers to common problems, identify good practice and work to co-ordinate domestic and international policies.

The OECD member countries are: Australia, Austria, Belgium, Canada, the Czech Republic, Denmark, Finland, France, Germany, Greece, Hungary, Iceland, Ireland, Italy, Japan, Korea, Luxembourg, Mexico, the Netherlands, New Zealand, Norway, Poland, Portugal, the Slovak Republic, Spain, Sweden, Switzerland, Turkey, the United Kingdom and the United States. The Commission of the European Communities takes part in the work of the OECD.

OECD Publishing disseminates widely the results of the Organisation's statistics gathering and research on economic, social and environmental issues, as well as the conventions, guidelines and standards agreed by its members.

Also available in French

Table of contents

This book has...

StatLinks

A service that delivers Excel® files from the printed page!

Look for the *StatLinks* at the bottom right-hand corner of the tables or graphs in this book. To download the matching Excel® spreadsheet, just type the link into your Internet browser, starting with the *http://dx.doi.org* prefix.
If you're reading the PDF e-book edition, and your PC is connected to the Internet, simply click on the link. You'll find *StatLinks* appearing in more OECD books.

BASIC STATISTICS OF KOREA

THE LAND

Area (thousand km^2)	100	Major cities, 2007 (million inhabitants):	
Agricultural area (thousand km^2)	14	Seoul	10.4
Forests (thousand km^2)	65	Pusan	3.6
		Incheon	2.7
		Taegu	2.5

THE PEOPLE

Population, 2007 (million)	48.5	Civilian labour force, 2007 (million)	24.2
Per km^2, 2007	49.1	Civilian employment	23.4
Annual rate of change of population, 2007	0.3	Agriculture, forestry, fishing	1.7
		Industry	4.2
		Construction	1.9
		Services	15.6

PRODUCTION

GDP, 2007 (trillion won)	901.2	Origin of GDP, 2007 (per cent of total):	
GDP per head (US$)	20 045	Agriculture, forestry, fishing	3.0
Gross fixed investment, 2007 (trillion won)	259.4	Industry	30.5
Per cent of GDP	28.8	Construction	8.9
Per head (US$)	5 755	Services	57.6

THE GOVERNMENT

			Number of seats
Public consumption, 2007 (per cent of GDP)	15.1	Composition of the National Assembly, April 2008:	
Central government revenue, 2007, consolidated basis (per cent of GDP)	27.0	The Uri Party	81
		The Grand National Party	153
Central government budget balance, 2007, consolidated basis (per cent of GDP)	3.8	Other	65
			299

FOREIGN TRADE

Commodity exports, 2007, f.o.b. (per cent of GDP)	38.5	Commodity imports, 2007, c.i.f. (per cent of GDP)	39.6
Main exports (per cent of total exports):		Main imports (per cent of total imports):	
Light industry products	7.4	Consumer goods	10.4
Heavy industry products	83.7	Industrial materials and fuels	56.5
Electronic products	34.2	Crude petroleum	16.9
Cars	9.3	Capital goods	33.1

THE CURRENCY

Monetary unit: Won	Currency unit per US$, average of daily figures:	
	2004	1 145
	2005	1 024
	2006	952
	2007	929

Executive summary

Korea has been hard-hit by the commodity price shock and the global financial crisis, which have slowed economic activity and pushed up inflation. The terms-of-trade loss reduced national income, thus damping domestic demand, while the slowdown in world trade has moderated Korea's export growth. Moreover, the sharp exchange rate depreciation and the intensification of the global financial market crisis have further dimmed the outlook. Although the recent fiscal stimulus is likely to help support growth, an economic rebound depends on a recovery in the world economy. In addition to these short-term difficulties, Korea faces a number of challenges to sustaining economic growth over the medium term, notably tax reform, enhancing service sector productivity growth and reforming the labour market and education system.

Macroeconomic policy has a difficult role to play. In the near term, monetary policy should focus on supporting activity and financial-market stability. Foreign exchange market intervention to support the won is likely to be costly and ineffective in the face of global financial turmoil and should therefore be limited to smoothing operations. As conditions stabilise, monetary policy will need to give more weight to the risk that inflation may become entrenched well above the 2.5% to 3.5% target zone. While tax cuts and additional spending are helping cushion the downturn, fiscal policy in the medium term should focus on maintaining a strong government financial position in light of future spending pressures. Given planned tax cuts, this will call for reining in public outlays, which have grown rapidly in recent years.

A comprehensive tax reform is essential. Government spending is one of the lowest in the OECD area, reflecting Korea's relatively young population. However, the population is projected to age faster than in any other OECD country, putting considerable upward pressure on public expenditures in the long term. Tax reform is thus needed to meet the demand for higher revenue while, at the same time, promoting economic growth, addressing rising income inequality and relative poverty and improving the local tax system to provide more autonomy for local authorities. To achieve these goals, reform should rely primarily on higher consumption taxes and base broadening of income taxes for additional revenue, an in-work tax credit to meet distributional objectives and more use of local property-holding taxes to finance local authorities. Keeping direct tax rates low will promote growth.

Enhancing service sector productivity is essential to sustain growth. Weak productivity gains in services – 60% of the economy – have been a major drag on growth. Boosting productivity requires strengthening competition by accelerating regulatory reform, focusing on removing entry barriers, and upgrading competition policy. Greater openness to international competition, by improving the climate for foreign direct investment and including services in free trade agreements, would also help, as would addressing the problems in small and medium-sized enterprises. Industry-specific reforms are needed in key services, including telecommunications and financial and business services.

Labour market and education reforms are also essential for growth. Labour market dualism, driven by the rising share of temporary workers, has negative implications for human *capital formation. Reducing dualism would improve efficiency and equity. To mitigate the impact of population ageing, labour force participation needs to be increased, particularly for women and youth. Expanding the availability of childcare and maternity leave is a priority for the former, while reducing dualism would promote the participation of both groups. Low youth employment rates are partly due to the mismatch between the education system and the labour market, making it important to reform all levels of education. For older workers, the age of retirement from firms should be raised by abolishing mandatory retirement, reducing the importance of seniority in setting wages and phasing out the retirement allowance.*

ISBN 978-92-64-05425-7
OECD Economic Surveys: Korea
© OECD 2008

Assessment and recommendations

An adverse world economic environment has slowed growth and boosted inflation...

The Korean economy has faced a number of shocks in 2008, including higher commodity prices, slowing world trade and the global financial crisis. The terms-of-trade shock – Korea is the world's fifth-largest oil importer – weakened the won and heightened inflationary pressures, which have squeezed household income and corporate profits, damping private consumption and investment. In addition, housing market policies contributed to a 5% decline in residential investment over the past year, while the deceleration in world trade took a toll on Korean export growth. With weaker domestic demand and exports, output growth fell from 5% in 2006-07 to 3% in the first three quarters of 2008, at a seasonally-adjusted annual rate. Intensified financial turbulence in September 2008 has further dimmed the economic outlook by accelerating the depreciation of the won and tightening credit conditions. The timing of the rebound depends on an improvement in the world economy, which may not occur until well into 2009. In that event, economic growth is projected at around 3% on a year-average basis in 2009 before rising back to around 4% in 2010.

... creating a difficult task for macroeconomic policies

Faced with a marked slowdown, the government is implementing a supplementary budget and tax rebates totalling almost 1% of GDP, to be followed by cuts in personal and corporate income tax rates in 2009-10. In November, the government submitted revisions to the 2009 budget proposal, adding further stimulus measures. Concerned about high inflation, the Bank of Korea hiked interest rates by ¼ per cent in August 2008, but then reversed course in October as the global financial crisis worsened, cutting rates by a cumulative 125 basis points by early November. The government announced in October that it would guarantee banks' foreign borrowing up to a total of $100 billion. In addition, the authorities intervened in the foreign exchange market in July to stabilise the won and arranged a $30 billion currency swap with the US Federal Reserve in October. Between June and October 2008, Korea's foreign exchange reserves fell by $46 billion, to $212 billion. The won continued to depreciate, falling by 26% in trade-weighted terms between early July and the end of November. Foreign exchange market intervention is likely to be costly and ineffective in the face of global financial turbulence that is driving the won's depreciation and should therefore be limited to smoothing operations. This would also limit any further decline in foreign exchange reserves, which provide a cushion against Korea's short-term foreign debt, which soared from $66 billion at the end of 2005 to $189 billion in September 2008.

Monetary policy faces large challenges

In 2008, inflation significantly exceeded the upper limit of the 2.5% to 3.5% target zone for the first time since the introduction of inflation targeting in 1998. In October, headline consumer prices were up by 4.8% (year-on-year) and core prices (excluding energy and food) by 5.2%, pointing to second-round effects from the commodity price shock. Going forward, with lower commodity prices and slow growth, inflation is projected to fall back within the target zone in the course of 2009. Against this backdrop, monetary policy should for now focus on financial-market stability and supporting activity, until conditions normalise, and then shift its priority to achieving the inflation target. Vigilance is warranted, however, given the sharp depreciation of the won and the fact that the growth slowdown only influences inflation with a sizeable time lag. The course of monetary policy will depend on the extent and duration of the economic downturn, which in turn will be influenced, among other factors, by the amount of fiscal stimulus.

With the strong fiscal position deteriorating…

The implementation of the supplementary budget and tax rebates in the fourth quarter of 2008 may boost output growth by as much as ¼ percentage point in 2009. The budget includes spending to build roads and subsidise utility companies, although this distorts energy prices and encourages excessive consumption. Taking account of the supplementary budget, the central government consolidated budget excluding the social security surplus would record a deficit of around 1½ per cent of GDP in 2008 following a small surplus in 2007. In addition, the stimulus measures planned for the 2009 budget will further boost outlays. It is essential that fiscal stimulus be timely, targeted and temporary. Looking ahead, the government plans to cut personal income tax rates by 2 percentage points by 2010 and the national corporate income tax rate from 25% (close to the OECD average) to 20%. The authorities expect that this will reduce tax revenue by around 2% of GDP. Over the medium term, the priority should be to maintain a strong fiscal position, given future spending pressures associated with population ageing and the development of the social insurance system.

… it is important to restrain the growth of public spending in coming years to prepare for population ageing…

Korea faces a major fiscal challenge with rapid population ageing. The share of the elderly in the population is projected to rise from 10% to 14% by 2018, at which point the working-age population will begin to decline. Korea's elderly dependency ratio, now the third lowest in the OECD, is expected to be the fourth highest by 2050. The limited coverage of the public pension system, which has levelled off at about one-third of the working-age population, and the low level and duration of contributions, especially among the self-employed, creates concerns. The means-tested benefit introduced in 2008 may need to be expanded to limit poverty among elderly people. In addition, greater economic co-operation with

North Korea may boost government spending. Preparing for these future spending pressures requires maintaining the strong fiscal position by achieving a balanced budget, excluding the social security surplus, over the medium term. Given the tax cuts, this calls for reining in government spending, which has risen by 9% per annum (excluding the cost of financial-sector restructuring) since 2002. It is also essential to implement the October 2008 plan to privatise 38 public institutions and abolish three, while merging 38 into 17.

... and implement a comprehensive tax reform, which would boost revenue through consumption taxes in the longer term...

Government spending, currently one of the lowest in the OECD area as a share of GDP, is likely to rise significantly over the medium term, given the long-term spending pressures, thus requiring additional tax revenue. However, such increases will impose larger economic costs, underscoring the need for a comprehensive reform that sustains Korea's growth potential, addresses rising income inequality and relative poverty and improves the local tax system. The most efficient way to boost revenue is through consumption taxes, which impose fewer distortions than direct taxes. Korea has considerable scope to hike its value-added tax (VAT) rate of 10%, which is well below the OECD average of 18%. At the same time, the base should be broadened by scaling back the scope of exemptions and the special treatment of small and medium-sized enterprises (SMEs). The complicated system of individual consumption taxes on 20 items should be simplified, in part as an effort to reduce the role of earmarked taxes, which account for 14% of tax revenue. Excises should be limited to products with negative health or environmental effects, such as tobacco, liquor and energy. In particular, greater use of environmentally-related taxes would increase efficiency.

... and a broadening of corporate and personal income tax bases

---

In addition, direct tax bases should be broadened. Cutting corporate tax expenditures, which remain large at about one-fifth of corporate tax receipts, would help to offset the revenue impact of the planned rate cuts, while reducing distortions in the allocation of investment. Introducing a tax expenditure budget, as planned in 2010, and enhancing transparency would help identify tax expenditures whose costs exceed their benefits. In addition, the low rate paid by SMEs does not appear to be effective in addressing the challenges faced by small firms and should therefore be phased out. The relatively minor role of personal income taxes – among the lowest in the OECD area at 4% of GDP – reflects large exemptions and deductions for employees aimed at levelling the playing field with the self-employed. Only half of wage income is taxed, well below the OECD average of 84%, and only half of employees pay income taxes. However, the proportion of self-employed paying income tax has risen from 40% to 63% over the past decade, suggesting scope to cut the exemptions and deductions granted to wage income, while avoiding increases in marginal rates.

*The earned income tax credit should be the major
tool to address rising income inequality and
relative poverty*

Increasing the share of workers paying income taxes would have a negative effect on income distribution and relative poverty, which has trended up during the past decade. By the mid-2000s, the rate of relative poverty – defined as a disposable income below 50% of the median – had risen to 15% in Korea, the seventh highest OECD-wide. In 2008, the government introduced an earned income tax credit (EITC), which is likely to boost employment by making work pay for low-skilled persons. However, the EITC will initially cover less than 2% of households. Expanding the credit, which could be financed by broadening the personal income tax base, requires further enhancing transparency about the income of the self-employed. In addition, taxing fringe benefits as individual income would improve equity.

*Local property taxes can enhance local
government autonomy*

The Comprehensive Property Tax (CPT), a highly progressive nationwide tax on property that is paid by 2% of households, aims at redistributing income and stabilising house prices. Its introduction in 2005 was accompanied by a scaling back of the local property tax. However, local governments' tax powers should instead be expanded to allow them to better respond to the preferences of local citizens and help ensure fiscal discipline by making the cost of local services more visible. Property taxes are well-suited for local governments as they are visible, impose discipline on the quality of services and are relatively resistant to tax-base flight. The government should, therefore, follow through on its plan to scale back the CPT by raising the threshold at which it applies and reducing the tax rates, as a first step toward merging it with the local property tax. Greater reliance on local property holding taxes would enhance local government autonomy and facilitate a streamlining of the complicated local tax system, which includes 16 different taxes and thus raises compliance costs. In particular, the heavy reliance on property transaction taxes, which have lock-in effects that reduce the supply of housing, should be reduced.

*Direct tax rates should be kept low to sustain
output growth*

A comprehensive tax reform, which relies primarily on consumption taxes for additional revenue, the EITC for income redistribution and property-holding taxes for local government, would limit the rates of direct taxes, thus promoting growth. OECD experience shows that taxes on personal and corporate income tend to reduce saving and investment, labour supply and demand, inflows of foreign direct investment (FDI), entrepreneurship and education. The government's reforms to reduce direct taxes are in line with international trends and will help support competitiveness. The planned cut in the corporate tax rate should be accompanied by a reduction in quasi-taxes, which include a wide range of administrative fees and user charges, as well as a number of contributions that tend to be levied on firms in a discretionary and non-transparent manner.

Promoting growth also requires measures to boost
productivity in the service sector…

With the slower expansion of the working-age population, sustaining growth depends primarily on increasing productivity, which is currently only 34% of the US level. The large gap mainly stems from Korea's service sector, where productivity has fallen to 60% of that in manufacturing. The problems in services are closely related to the difficulties facing SMEs, which account for 91% of service-sector employment. Extensive public support for SMEs, including financial assistance, has blunted competitive pressure, slowed the pace of restructuring, in contrast to large firms, and reduced the efficiency of resource allocation. Over the longer run, the wide range of government programmes, which numbered 163 in 2007 and cost 0.7% of GDP, should be scaled back and streamlined. Other support, notably policy loans and credit guarantees, should also be cut. Remaining support should be focused more on start-ups than on existing firms. While recent government measures have moved in this direction, more efforts should be made in the longer term to scale back and streamline support for SMEs.

… through regulatory reform and competition
policy…

Faster labour productivity growth also requires strengthening competition through regulatory reform and competition policy. Despite progress during the past decade, around one-third of business lines in the service sector remain subject to entry barriers (on top of registration and declaration requirements). International comparisons indicate that entry barriers and product market regulations are relatively high in Korea. The newly-created Presidential Council on National Competitiveness should focus on the key barriers that restrict competition. In addition, competition policy should be further strengthened. *First*, although financial penalties have risen, their deterrent effect is still weaker than in most other OECD countries, indicating a need for further increases. In addition, criminal penalties, which are rarely applied, should be used more frequently. *Second*, the investigative powers of the competition authority, the Korea Fair Trade Commission, need to be expanded. *Third*, the number of exemptions from the competition law, including for SMEs, should be further scaled back.

… and increased openness to international
competition…

Greater openness to the world economy is another priority to boost productivity in services. The stock of FDI in Korea is the third lowest in the OECD area and inflows have fallen since 2004. Moreover, the share of inward FDI in services is the third lowest OECD-wide. Consequently, foreign affiliates accounted for only 8% of service-sector turnover and 4% of employment in 2004, well below the OECD averages of 19% and 10%, respectively. Strengthening international competition requires reducing barriers to FDI, including foreign ownership ceilings in key services, and liberalising product market regulations. In addition, it is important to foster a foreign investment-friendly climate by enhancing the transparency of tax and regulatory policies and reforming the labour market. Moreover, the incentives for foreign investment in the Free Economic Zones should be extended more broadly within the service sector. In the area of trade, Korea is negotiating Free Trade Agreements with the European Union, Canada and Mexico. These agreements should be broad-based, including services as well as goods.

... while addressing barriers in key service industries

It is important to address factors limiting productivity in key services that are expanding rapidly:

- *Telecommunications*: the new Korea Communications Commission (KCC) is a step toward separating the ministry setting industrial policy from the organisation charged with fostering competition. The independence and transparency of the KCC's regulatory decisions should indeed be safeguarded in practice in line with the law. It is also necessary to relax entry barriers and foreign-ownership ceilings and to introduce auctions and broaden secondary markets for spectrum.

- *Financial sector*: Korea is introducing a "big bang" in 2009 to reduce segmentation in the securities industry, with a view to becoming a financial hub for Asia. It is critical to ensure that enhanced supervisory capacity, with a functional emphasis, precedes market growth and innovation. Caution is called for in easing ownership restrictions on banks that separate industrial and financial capital.

- *Business services*: constraints on entry, form of practice, advertising and foreign participation have limited the size of this sector and should be relaxed. For example, the decision to cap total enrolment in law schools at 2 000, despite the fact that the number of lawyers per capita in Korea is only a quarter of the OECD average, restricts competition and keeps prices high.

Potential growth also depends on reducing labour market dualism...

The sharp increase in the share of non-regular workers, who now account for more than one-third of employees, has negative consequences for both growth and equity. Such dualism is largely explained by the rising share of temporary workers, from 17% of employees in 2001 to 26% in August 2008, almost double the OECD average. Not surprisingly, temporary workers receive less firm-based training than permanent workers, thus slowing human capital formation and productivity growth. Lower wage costs encourage firms to hire non-regular workers, who earn 30% less per hour than regular workers, with productivity differences explaining only part of the gap. The cost advantage is magnified by the low coverage of non-regular workers by the social insurance system. While three-quarters of regular workers were covered by national health and pension insurance in 2007 in their workplace, the share was only around 40% for non-regular workers. Firms also hire non-regular workers to achieve greater employment flexibility, given the relatively strict employment protection for regular workers. Dualism thus creates equity concerns as a significant portion of the labour force works in precarious jobs at relatively low wages and receives less protection from social insurance.

... by liberalising employment protection
for regular workers and extending the coverage
of the social insurance system...

Reducing dualism requires weakening the incentives that encourage firms to hire non-regular workers. One priority is to liberalise employment protection for regular workers so that firms can achieve the necessary flexibility without depending as much on non-regular workers. A second priority is to increase the coverage of non-regular workers by the social safety net, thus improving equity and narrowing the gap in labour costs. The government has introduced reforms to harmonise the collection practices of the four social insurance systems, but the key to greater coverage is to create a unified collection agency. To reduce the use of non-regular workers, a new law, which is being gradually phased in since mid-2007, prohibits "unjustifiable discrimination" against them and states that workers with fixed-term contracts are considered to be regular employees after two years. However, there is a risk that this law will decrease total employment. In fact, the number of non-regular workers has declined since 2007. The law should be closely monitored and revised as necessary as its full impact becomes apparent.

... and increasing labour inputs by boosting
the labour force participation rate of women...

Raising the female participation rate would help sustain output growth in the face of a declining working-age population. Although it is on the rise, the rate for women in the 25-to-54 age group is still the third lowest in the OECD area. The measures recommended above to reduce labour market dualism, as well as to move away from seniority-based wages, would support female employment by creating better job opportunities for women who interrupt their careers for family responsibilities. Greater availability of high-quality childcare would help as well. This would require phasing out price controls that discourage private-sector suppliers. Lengthening maternity leave and ensuring that eligible persons are able to take such leave, as well as parental leave, is also important. Another factor discouraging female employment is the extremely long working hours in Korea, which make it difficult to combine employment with family responsibilities. Encouraging the development of family-friendly workplaces would boost female employment and the fertility rate, which currently stands at only 1.3 children per women.

... and youth...

The employment rate of youth between the ages of 15 to 29 has been falling and is well below the OECD average. In addition, the proportion of youth who are neither in education nor training is relatively high, especially for those with higher education, who account for the majority of youth. Labour market dualism is again a factor, as it reduces wages below the reservation wage of many youth. In addition, active labour market policies should focus on facilitating the school-to-work transition, while avoiding employment subsidies, which tend to have high deadweight costs.

... in part by upgrading the education system

Perhaps the key problem for youth employment is the degree of mismatch between skills provided in tertiary education and those required in the labour market. Around 30% of graduates of tertiary education do not find jobs in their field of study. It is important to increase links between universities and companies and to strengthen competition between educational institutions through regulatory reform and more transparency about their performance. In addition, public support for tertiary education could be increased from its exceptionally low level. However, the scope for additional outlays is limited by the fact that education spending is already the third highest OECD-wide, even without including the 2% of GDP spent on private tutoring institutes (*hakwon*). Increasing the quality of education at all levels would lower the demand for such institutes, thus easing the pressure on students and the financial burden on families. Allowing universities more autonomy in the student selection process would also reduce the importance of the standardised exams that make private tutoring useful.

It is also essential to promote the employment of older workers

Finally, it is important to raise the age at which employees leave firms, which is typically around 55, well before the pension eligibility age. Early retirement reflects the seniority-based wage system, which makes older workers expensive for firms. Abolishing mandatory retirement would help to flatten the wage-seniority profile, given that firms accept seniority-based wages on the condition that they can force older workers to leave, and thereby extend the length of employment. In addition, it is important to phase out the mandatory lump-sum retirement allowance, which increases the cost of keeping older workers. The government launched a company pension system in 2005, but less than 9% of firms have adopted it thus far. One stumbling block is that employers and employees must agree on whether to introduce a defined-benefit or a defined-contribution scheme. The generous tax treatment of the retirement allowance system should be reformed to accelerate its phasing out and encourage the introduction of defined-contribution schemes, which would also enhance labour market mobility.

OECD ECONOMIC SURVEYS: KOREA – ISBN 978-92-64-05425-7 – © OECD 2008

ISBN 978-92-64-05425-7
OECD Economic Surveys: Korea
© OECD 2008

Chapter 1

Facing the key challenges ahead in Korea

Korea has been adversely affected by soaring oil and commodity prices, which led to a spike in inflation and slowed the pace of economic activity. Moreover, the global financial crisis accelerated the depreciation of the won and clouded the economic outlook. Output growth is likely to remain subdued until the world economy improves, which may not happen until well into 2009. Korea faces a number of challenges, both in the short and long run. This chapter looks at four key challenges: i) setting an appropriate macroeconomic policy to cope with the severe external shocks; ii) raising additional tax revenue as rapid population ageing puts upward pressure on public spending; iii) promoting the development of services, where productivity growth and levels lag significantly behind manufacturing; and iv) reforming the labour market and the education system to address the growth and equity problems related to labour market dualism and population ageing.

With output growth at an annual rate of 4.4% between 2002 and 2007, Korea's per capita income has risen to two-thirds of the OECD average (Figure 1.1). While Korea remains one of the fastest-growing economies in the OECD area, the performance over the past five years was a marked slowdown from the 6.4% rate during the period 1999 to 2002 (Table 1.1). In terms of the composition of growth, the external sector accounted for nearly one-half between 2002 and 2007, while domestic demand was relatively subdued. The combination of buoyant exports and sluggish domestic demand has exacerbated a number of imbalances in the economy; i) export-led growth has primarily benefited the manufacturing sector, thereby widening the productivity gap with services; ii) the gap between large companies and small and medium-sized enterprises (SMEs), which are predominant in services, has also widened; and iii) labour market dualism has become more entrenched, with the share of non-regular workers rising to more than a third, leading to higher income inequality and relative poverty.

The government that took office in February 2008 is committed to raising potential growth through "business-friendly policies", thereby accelerating the doubling of per

Figure 1.1. **Korea's per capita income is converging to the OECD average**

Gross domestic product per capita in 2007 purchasing power party exchange rates

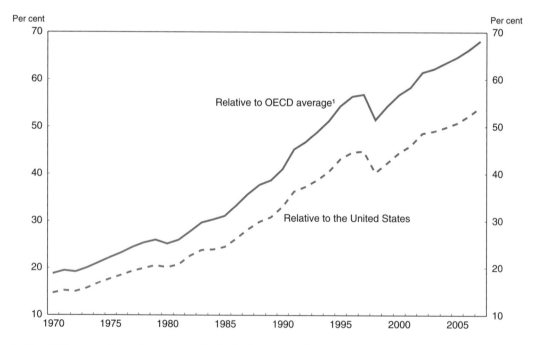

1. The OECD average is based on 26 countries (excluding the Slovak Republic, Poland, Czech Republic and Hungary) from 1970 to 1990, 29 countries (excluding the Slovak Republic) from 1991 to 1992 and all 30 countries from 1993.

Source: OECD Economic Outlook Database.

StatLink http://dx.doi.org/10.1787/512881427013

Table 1.1. **Economic growth trends in Korea**

	Average annual growth rates		Contribution to growth	
	1999-2002	2002-07	1999-2002	2002-07
Private consumption	7.1	2.2	3.8	1.1
Government consumption	4.1	4.9	0.5	0.6
Residential investment	4.5	2.0	0.2	0.1
Business investment	6.8	4.1	1.4	0.8
Public investment	4.4	0.4	0.2	0.0
Gross fixed capital formation	6.1	3.2	1.8	0.9
Final domestic demand	6.4	2.8	6.2	2.7
Stockbuilding	–	–	0.0	–0.2
Total domestic demand	6.4	2.7	6.2	2.5
Exports	9.5	13.5	0.1[1]	1.9[1]
Imports	9.8	10.9		
GDP	6.4	4.4	6.4	4.4

1. Contribution of net exports.
Source: Bank of Korea.

capita income from its current level of $20 000 (at market exchange rates) to $40 000.[1] However, short-term growth prospects have been dimmed by the oil shock and the global financial crisis, while rising inflation, slowing employment growth and high household debt have undermined consumer confidence. This chapter first discusses the economic outlook through 2010 and then examines Korea's growth potential over the longer term, taking into account expected demographic changes. The following sections outline the key challenges facing Korea – macroeconomic policy, tax reform, enhancing productivity in the service sector and reforming the labour market and education system.

The current economic situation and outlook

The pace of output growth slowed markedly from 6.4% during the latter half of 2007 to 3% in the first three quarters of 2008 at a seasonally-adjusted annual rate, indicating that the economy had slowed markedly even before the global financial crisis intensified in mid-September. The main factor was the terms-of-trade shock, which resulted in a spike in consumer price inflation, the first time since the introduction of inflation targeting in 1998 that inflation has significantly surpassed the target zone, which has been set at 2.5% to 3.5% since 2004 (Figure 1.2). In October 2008, headline consumer prices were up 4.8% (year-on-year), and core prices by 5.2%, pointing to second-round effects from higher import prices. In contrast, core inflation in the OECD area as a whole has not accelerated from a rate close to 2% despite a pick-up in headline inflation similar to that in Korea. The oil price hike also put the current account on track for a deficit in 2008 for the first time since the 1997 crisis (Figure 1.3). The deficit, combined with net outflows of both direct and portfolio investment, has increased downward pressure on the won, further intensifying inflationary pressures. Moreover, with the intensification of the global financial crisis in September 2008, won depreciation quickened. By the end of November, the effective exchange rate was down 36% compared with the beginning of the year.

Higher inflation has squeezed household income, thus damping private consumption. Indeed, national income in real terms declined by 1% in the first half of 2008 (Figure 1.3, Panel B). Although wage growth for regular workers picked up to 7.5% in nominal terms in the second quarter of 2008, it has slowed in real terms. At the same time, employment growth has decelerated in 2008, further constraining household income. Weaker income

Figure 1.2. **Inflation targets and outcomes**
Year-on-year percentage changes

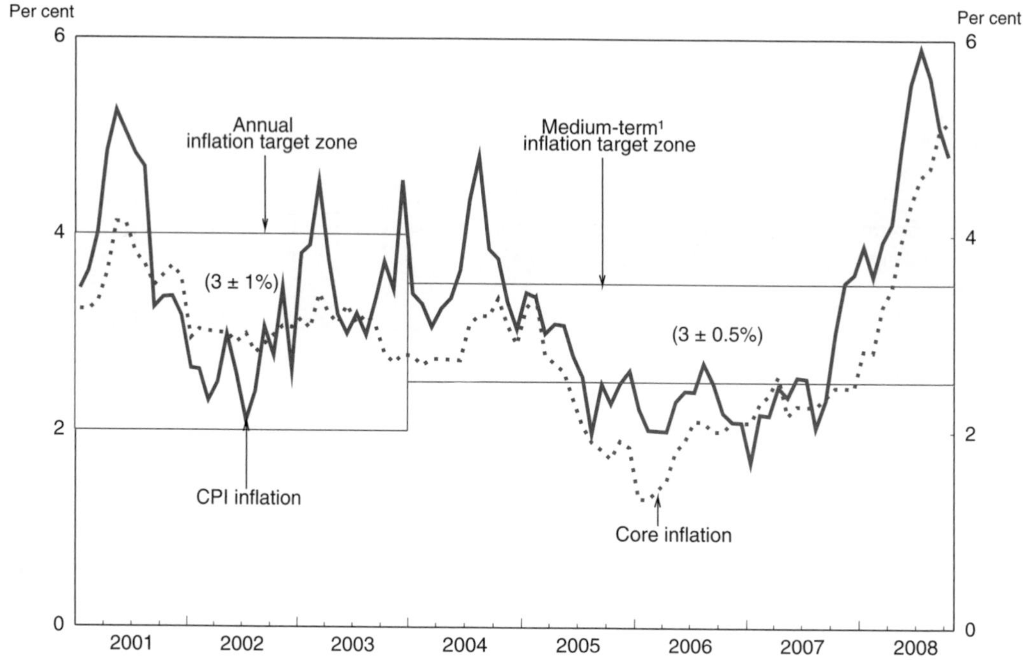

1. Since 2004, the target has been a medium-term objective and, in 2007, it was changed from core to overall CPI.
Source: Bank of Korea.

StatLink ⟶ http://dx.doi.org/10.1787/513033235540

growth, combined with negative wealth effects from the declining stock market, in part due to net capital outflows, and a steep drop in consumer confidence (Figure 1.4), slowed private consumption growth to a 0.5% annual rate in the first three quarters of 2008.

The terms-of-trade shock also squeezed corporate profits. Combined with a marked decline in business confidence (Figure 1.4, Panel B) and a deceleration of exports, this slowed fixed investment growth to less than 0.5% at an annual rate during the first three quarters of 2008. Residential investment has also been a drag on output, reflecting the impact of past government housing policies. During 2005-07, the authorities introduced five policy packages, which imposed price ceilings on new apartments, reduced the price of publicly-built housing, raised taxes on capital gains and property holding and limited bank lending for mortgages (*OECD Economic Surveys: Korea*, 2007). While real estate prices have been stable, residential construction has declined 9% in volume terms since the first quarter of 2007, and the stock of unsold homes has reached a record high. Moreover, in the first half of 2008, the area of new housing starts fell more than 50% from a year earlier. In sum, the weakness in private consumption and residential and business-sector investment slowed domestic demand growth to around 1% in the first three quarters of 2008.

The slowdown in world trade led to a moderation in Korean export growth to 3% in the first three quarters of 2008. Exports were sustained by strong demand from China and ASEAN – which account for nearly one-half of Korea's total – with growth of 34% (in value terms, year-on-year) and the Middle East. In contrast, exports to the OECD area were subdued. At the same time, import growth was close to zero, thereby maintaining the positive contribution from net exports to economic growth.

Figure 1.3. **The terms-of-trade shock in Korea**

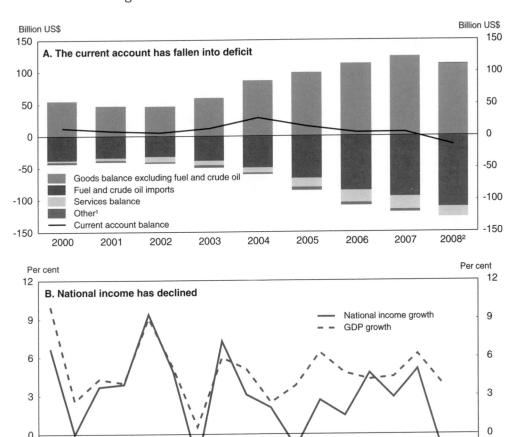

1. Investment income and transfers.
2. Through September.
Source: Bank of Korea and *OECD Economic Outlook Database.*

StatLink ᘓᘔ *http://dx.doi.org/10.1787/513047622110*

Prospects through 2010

The global financial crisis is sharply depressing activity as the large depreciation of the won squeezes income and undermines confidence, and as credit conditions tighten and losses from hedging contracts mount. As a result, GDP growth may fall below 3% in 2009 (Table 1.2), despite some fiscal stimulus. Tax rebates in the fourth quarter of 2008 will boost household disposable income by about 0.4% of GDP, which is likely to support private consumption even though some of the additional income may be saved in the context of weak confidence, high household debt and the low household saving rate. In addition, the September 2008 supplementary budget includes additional spending of 0.5% of GDP. Cuts in personal and corporate income tax rates beginning in 2009 will also cushion the downturn in domestic demand. Moreover, in November 2008, the government announced a package of measures to overcome the economic downturn (see Box 1.1). Nevertheless, output growth is likely to remain subdued during the global crisis, helping to

Figure 1.4. **Consumer and business confidence has declined significantly**

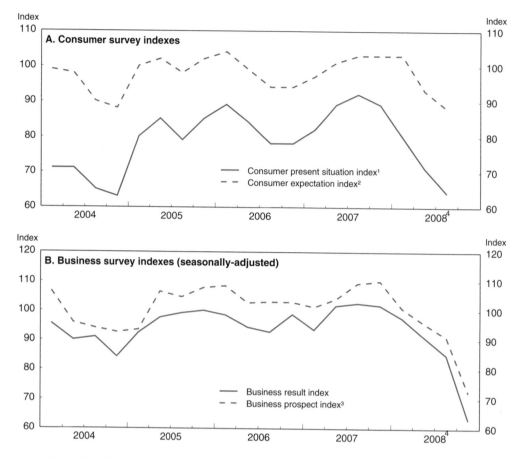

1. A score below 100 indicates that the current situation is worse than that six months ago.
2. A score below 100 indicates that a deterioration is expected over the next six months.
3. A score below 100 indicates that a decline in production is expected during the following month.
4. For the consumer surveys, the third quarter of 2008 is the average of July and August. For the business surveys, the prospect index for the fourth quarter of 2008 is the average of October and November and the business result index is October.

Source: Bank of Korea and Federation of Korean Industries.

StatLink ᝫ http://dx.doi.org/10.1787/513061056582

bring inflation back to the target zone during 2009 and pushing the current account balance back into surplus.

Growth is projected to pick up to slightly above 4% in 2010. Assuming that the won remains at its current level, Korea would be well-placed to expand its share of world trade as the global economy rebounds. A projected return to double-digit export growth in 2010 would make for a gradual pick-up in investment and household income. In addition, the recent measures to boost the housing market, by reducing taxes on capital gains and property holding, may end the decline in residential investment.

However, the economic outlook is highly uncertain given the severity of the shocks to Korea and the problems facing the world economy. Although the large depreciation of the won may lead to a sharper and earlier-than-expected upturn led by buoyant exports, most of the risks to this outlook are on the downside. Continued world financial stress may undermine the health of Korean financial institutions, resulting in a credit crunch in the corporate sector.

Table 1.2. **Short-term economic outlook for Korea**[1]

Percentage changes, volume (2000 prices)

	2005	2006	2007	2008	2009	2010
Private consumption	3.6	4.5	4.5	1.7	−1.1	0.4
Government consumption	5.0	6.2	5.8	3.8	3.8	3.7
Gross fixed capital formation	2.4	3.6	4.0	0.6	0.2	1.1
Final domestic demand	3.4	4.4	4.5	1.7	0.0	1.1
Stockbuilding[2]	−0.2	−0.2	−0.4	0.5	0.0	0.0
Total domestic demand	3.2	4.2	4.1	2.3	0.0	1.1
Exports of goods and services	8.5	11.8	12.1	9.1	6.4	11.3
Imports of goods and services	7.3	11.3	11.9	6.8	2.7	8.3
Net exports[2]	1.3	1.3	1.3	2.1	2.7	3.2
GDP at market prices	4.2	5.1	5.0	4.2	2.7	4.2
Memorandum items						
Consumer price index	2.8	2.2	2.5	5.0	3.9	2.9
Core consumer price index	2.3	1.8	2.4	4.3	4.2	3.0
Unemployment rate	3.7	3.5	3.2	3.2	3.6	3.6
Household saving ratio[3]	4.7	3.4	2.5	3.7	4.2	4.7
Current account balance[4]	1.9	0.6	0.6	−1.1	0.8	1.0
Exchange rate (won per dollar)	1 024	952	929	1 091	1468	1468
Export market growth[5]	9.9	10.0	7.8	5.3	3.9	6.9

1. OECD projections published in *Economic Outlook* No. 84 in November 2008, based on exchange rates of 28 October. This projection was finalised on 31 October 2008, and thus does not include the fiscal stimulus package and other measures announced in Korea in November 2008 (Box 1.1).
2. Contributions to changes in real GDP (percentage of real GDP in previous year).
3. As a percentage of disposable income.
4. As a percentage of GDP.
5. Weighted import growth in volume terms in Korea's trading partners.
Source: OECD *Economic Outlook Database* and Bank of Korea.

Box 1.1. **Measures announced in November 2008 to overcome the economic downturn**

The Korean authorities have responded to the financial crisis and the economic slowdown with a broad range of policy measures, including macroeconomic stimulus and regulatory reform.

Fiscal policy

The government announced a 14 trillion won (1.4% of GDP) fiscal package, which includes 11 trillion won of additional public expenditure in 2009. The biggest increase in spending will be for public infrastructure (4.6 trillion won), with about 90% allocated to help regional economies. The expenditure package also contains 3.4 trillion won for SMEs, farmers and fishermen, 1.1 trillion won for local governments and 1 trillion won for low-income households. In addition, public enterprises will expand their investment by 1 trillion won. The package also provides 3 trillion won in tax reductions by extending the Temporary Investment Tax Credit until the end of 2009. The fiscal stimulus measures will be submitted to the National Assembly by the end of 2008.

Monetary policy

The Monetary Policy Committee of the Bank of Korea reduced its policy interest rate by 25 basis points, from 4.25% to 4%, on 7 November, the third cut in a period of one month. As a result, the policy rate has fallen by 125 basis points from its level at the beginning of October (see Chapter 2). The cuts are aimed at preventing "a sharp contraction of real economic activity against the backdrop of large swings in the exchange rate and stock prices" and a domestic credit crunch. The central bank also intends to provide additional liquidity to financial institutions through open market operations, which will be broadened to include bank bonds and certain public corporation bonds, including the Korea Housing Corporation.

Box 1.1. **Measures announced in November 2008 to overcome the economic downturn** *(cont.)*

Policies to revitalise specific sectors

Some of the restrictions imposed on real estate in recent years will be eased. In particular, regulations on the reconstruction of apartment buildings will be relaxed and the number of "speculation zones" will be sharply reduced. At present, there are 92 such zones covering 37% of Korea's regional districts. Housing purchases in the zones are strictly monitored by the government and the loan-to-value ratio on bank lending for housing is subject to a 40% ceiling. The government will also provide tax benefits for the purchase of homes outside metropolitan areas, ease capital gains taxes and provide additional liquidity to construction companies. As part of its effort to improve the current account balance, the authorities will strengthen policies to promote exports, in particular by expanding the limit on export insurance. The government is also planning a number of initiatives to ease the financial distress of SMEs (see Chapter 4).

Regulatory reform

The government has announced a number of policy changes intended to promote investment and employment:

- The government has announced a comprehensive plan to ease regulations on building and expanding industrial complexes in the capital region.

- Environmental regulations "deemed excessive compared to those of competing countries will be reviewed and streamlined".

- The government will also make efforts to enhance labour market flexibility, in part by improving the system for temporary and dispatched workers (see Chapter 5).

- The government "plans to encourage new investments and facilitate job creation through service sector regulatory reform" (see Chapter 4).

There is also a risk that high inflation will become entrenched, eventually requiring forceful and costly monetary policy tightening to bring it back within the target zone.

Another risk is related to household debt, which has risen to 158% of disposable income (Figure 1.5), above the US level (142%) and close to that in the United Kingdom (185%). Rising debt reflects a number of factors, including falling real interest rates on loans to households and the expanded use of credit cards. In addition, the decline in borrowing by large firms as they reduced debt levels following the 1997 crisis prompted banks to expand lending to households, as well as to SMEs. Household interest payments climbed from 6% of disposable income in 2004 to 9% in 2007, despite declining interest rates. Most debt is at variable rates, shifting risk from financial institutions to households. The high leveraging of the household sector makes it more vulnerable to the global credit crunch. However, the risk of a sharp downturn in private consumption is mitigated by the increase in household financial assets in line with debt. In addition, the high level of bank capitalisation and low level of non-performing loans suggest that banks are well-prepared for some increase in bad loans from the household sector.[2] Moreover, mortgages account for only 40% of household liabilities, compared to the US and UK shares of around 75%, making Korean households and banks less vulnerable to a decline in housing prices. Nevertheless, the high level of debt poses a downside risk as it could affect private consumption. In addition, business investment could weaken as the high level of household debt is partly related to business-related borrowing by the self-employed.[3]

Figure 1.5. **Household financial assets and liabilities**

As a per cent of household disposable income[1]

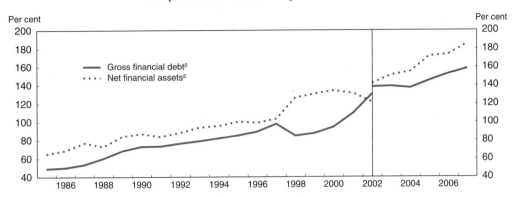

1. For the "Individual Sector" in the Bank of Korea's flow of funds data.
2. Based on SNA68 until 2002 and SNA93 thereafter.
Source: Bank of Korea and *OECD Economic Outlook Database.*

StatLink http://dx.doi.org/10.1787/513082155703

Korea's growth prospects over the longer term

Labour inputs in Korea are very high, at 20% above the US level (Figure 1.6). In contrast, labour productivity per hour worked is only 34% of the US level, suggesting significant scope for continued productivity gains. Indeed, the OECD projects that potential labour productivity growth will increase 3½ per cent a year through 2014, well above the OECD average of 1½ per cent (Table 1.3). The slowing growth of the working-age population, however, is projected to reduce Korea's potential growth from 4¾ per cent over the period 2005 to 2009 to 4¼ per cent between 2010 and 2014. Looking further ahead, the working-age population will begin to shrink from 2018, further pushing down output growth.

Table 1.3. **Potential output growth**

Annual averages, percentage points

	Potential GDP growth		Potential labour productivity growth[1]		Potential employment growth	
	2005-09	2010-14	2005-09	2010-14	2005-09	2010-14
Australia	3.2	2.8	1.1	1.4	2.0	1.4
Canada	2.8	2.0	1.2	1.4	1.6	0.6
Japan	1.5	1.2	1.9	1.9	−0.3	−0.7
New Zealand	2.7	2.2	1.0	1.4	1.7	0.7
United Kingdom	2.7	2.1	1.8	1.9	0.9	0.3
United States	2.5	2.1	1.8	1.7	0.7	0.4
Euro area	2.0	1.7	1.1	1.3	0.9	0.4
Korea	**4.7**	**4.3**	**3.5**	**3.7**	**1.2**	**0.6**
OECD total[2]	2.3	1.9	1.5	1.6	0.7	0.3

1. Output per employee.
2. Excluding Czech Republic, Hungary, Luxembourg, Mexico, Poland, Slovak Republic and Turkey.
Source: OECD, *Economic Outlook 83* (June 2008), OECD, Paris.

Figure 1.6. **Explaining differences in income**

Percentage point differences in GDP per person in USD (PPPs) relative to the United States in 2007[1]

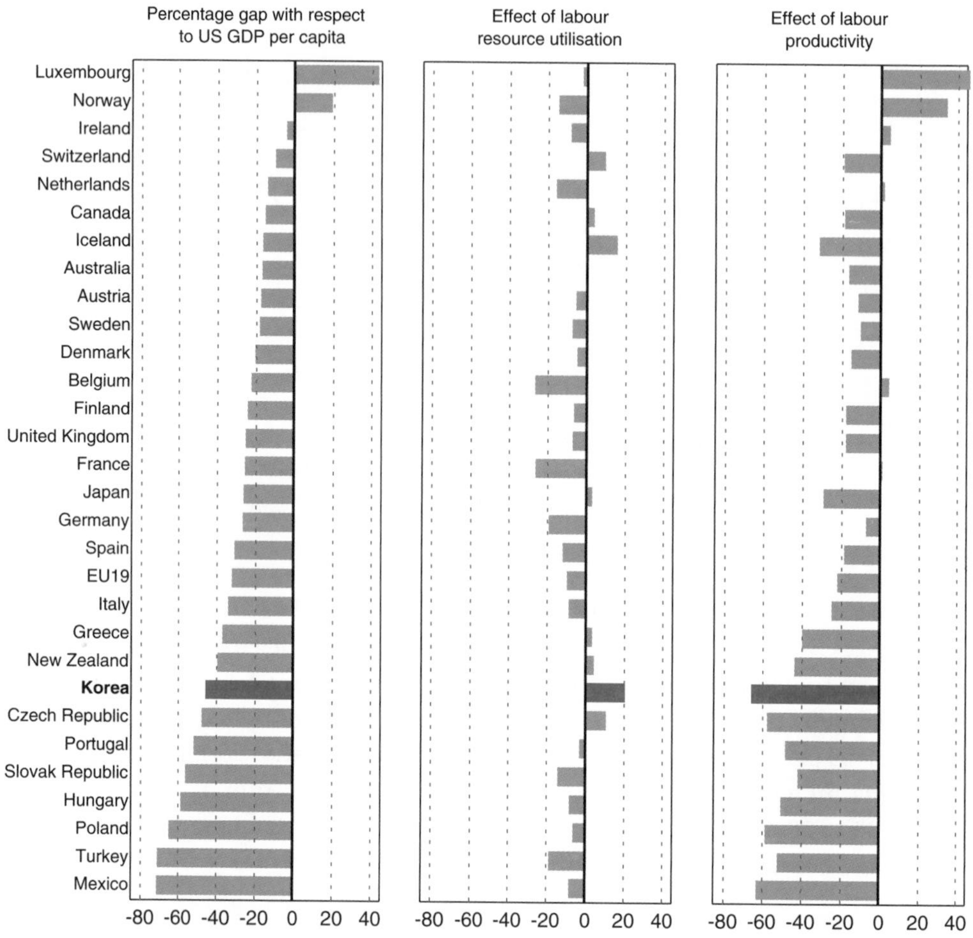

1. The gap in GDP per capita is equal to the sum of the two components shown. The effect of labour utilisation is based on total hours worked per capita. Productivity is measured on a per-hour basis.
Source: OECD (2009), *Going for growth*, OECD, Paris.

StatLink ⬛ http://dx.doi.org/10.1787/513114377472

Rapid population ageing in Korea

Korea's population is projected to peak at 50 million in 2020 and then decline about 15% by 2050 (Table 1.4). The share of Korea's total population over the age of 65 is expected to double from 7% in 2000 to 14% by 2018, a transition that is likely to take at least 40 years in European countries, and to reach 20% by 2026 (Table 1.5). The rise in the elderly dependency ratio between 2007 and mid-century will be the highest in the OECD area, boosting it from the third lowest to the fourth highest (Figure 1.7). Population ageing is driven by the increase in life expectancy by 21 years, from 55.3 in 1960 to 75.9 in 2000 (Table 1.4), the largest in the OECD area. A second factor is the fall in the fertility rate from six in 1960 to 1.1 in 2005, before edging up to 1.3 in 2007. The low rate can partly be ascribed to heightened economic uncertainty since the 1997 financial crisis. Fearing that the fall in the fertility rate will have negative consequences in the long term, the government set an objective of raising it to the OECD average of 1.6.

Table 1.4. **Population indicators and projections for Korea**[1]

	Population (in millions)	Growth rate (Per cent)[2]	Fertility rate[3]	Life expectancy (in years)	Median age (in years)	Share of elderly[4] (Per cent)
1960	25.0	2.3	6.0	55.3	19.9	2.9
1970	31.5	1.8	4.5	63.2	19.0	3.1
1980	37.4	1.5	2.7	65.8	22.2	3.8
1990	43.4	0.6	1.6	71.3	27.0	5.1
2000	46.1	0.6	1.5	75.9	31.8	7.3
2010	49.2	0.1	1.2	79.1	37.9	10.9
2020	50.0	−0.1	1.2	81.0	43.7	15.7
2030	49.3	−0.5	1.3	81.9	49.0	24.1
2040	46.7	−1.0	1.3	82.6	53.1	32.0
2050	42.3	..	1.3	83.3	56.2	37.3

1. Projections by the Korea National Statistical Office for the period 2005 to 2050.
2. The annual average growth rate for the decade. The figure in 1960, for example, shows the rate for the decade 1960 to 1970.
3. The average number of children that a woman can expect to bear during her lifetime.
4. The number of persons over the age of 65 as a percentage of the total population.
Source: Korea National Statistical Office.

As a result of these demographic changes, the labour force is projected to peak in 2020 and then fall to 18 million – 24% below its current level – by 2050 if participation rates for each age group were to remain at their current levels (Figure 1.8). In contrast, if the rate for women were to increase to the same level as for men by mid-century, the labour force would fall by only 9%. Moreover, the 24% decline could be limited to 18% if the participation rate for the 50-to-64 age group were to increase to the maximum level recorded in the OECD area in 2000. On the other hand, the labour force would decline 36% from its current level if the participation rate for older workers were to decrease to the OECD average. Immigration, which was discussed in detail in the 2007 *OECD Economic Surveys: Korea*, is another important means of coping with population ageing.

Table 1.5. **Speed of ageing in selected OECD countries**

Country	Year when the share of elderly (over 65) makes up:			Years elapsed	
	7% of population	14% of population	20% of population	7 to 14%	14 to 20%
Korea	**2000**	**2018**	**2026**	**18**	**8**
Japan	1970	1994	2006	24	12
Germany	1932	1972	2012	40	40
United Kingdom	1929	1976	2021	47	45
Italy	1927	1988	2007	61	19
United States	1942	2013	2028	71	15
Sweden	1887	1972	2012	85	40
France	1864	1979	2020	115	41

Source: United Nations.

Figure 1.7. **Population ageing in OECD countries**
Population aged 65 and over, relative to the population aged 20-64

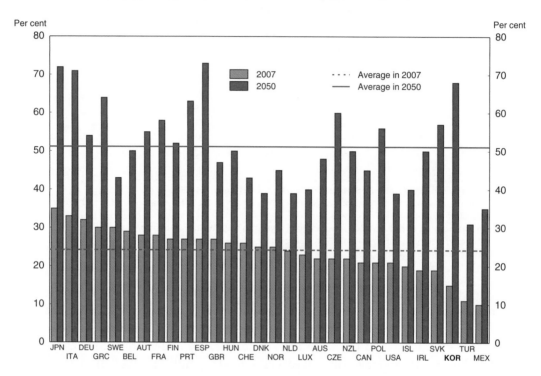

Source: OECD (2006), *Society at a Glance: OECD Social Indicators*, OECD, Paris.

StatLink http://dx.doi.org/10.1787/513116264248

Figure 1.8. **Long-term projections of the labour force**

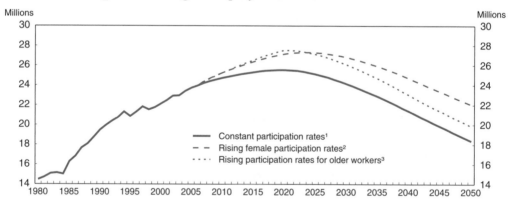

1. The participation rates for men and women remain at their current levels for each age group.
2. Female participation rates reach current male rates in each age group by 2050.
3. The participation rates converge by 2030 to the maximum value in the OECD for each gender and age group over 50, while the rates for younger workers remain at their current levels.

Source: OECD calculations based on population projections by the Korea National Statistical Office.

StatLink http://dx.doi.org/10.1787/513155281372

Key challenges to sustaining rapid growth

Korea faces a number of challenges, which are addressed in the following chapters, to sustain its high growth potential:

- In the short run, Korea faces difficult macroeconomic policy choices in the context of the global financial crisis and the sharp depreciation of the won (Chapter 2).

- Rapid ageing and the development of the social insurance system will put long-term upward pressure on public spending, creating a need for greater tax revenues. Reforming the tax system to promote growth while expanding its revenue-generating capacity is thus a priority (Chapter 3).

- The level and growth of productivity in the service sector lags significantly behind manufacturing. Sustaining high output growth requires measures to boost productivity in services, given that they account for three-fifths of the economy (Chapter 4).

- The high share of non-regular workers creates both efficiency and equity concerns. In addition, raising the participation rate is essential to mitigate the impact of population ageing. In particular, the low youth employment rate points to the need for education reform (Chapter 5).

Implementing appropriate macroeconomic policies

Faced with inflation well above the target zone, Korea hiked the policy interest rate in August 2008. This was reversed beginning in October in the context of cuts in many countries troubled by the financial crisis. In addition, the authorities intervened in the foreign exchange market in July to stabilise the won and arranged a $30 billion currency swap with the US Federal Reserve in October. Between June and October 2008, Korea's foreign exchange reserves fell by $46 billion, to $212 billion. However, they remain significantly above Korea's short-term foreign debt, which has soared from $65 billion at the end of 2005 to $189 billion (21% of GDP) in September 2008. Around 45% of this debt belonged to the local branches of foreign banks. The won continued to depreciate, falling by 26% in trade-weighted terms between early July and the end of November.

On the fiscal side, the September 2008 stimulus package amounted to almost 1% of GDP. Still, it does not threaten Korea's strong public finance position, based on one of the lowest levels of government spending in the OECD, a sizeable general government budget surplus and low public debt. Moreover, Korea is one of three OECD countries in which the government is a net creditor, with net financial assets amounting to a quarter of GDP. Nevertheless, the consolidated central government budget, excluding the social security surplus, is projected to record a deficit of around 1½ per cent of GDP in 2008. Moreover, the reductions in tax revenue resulting from the planned cuts in personal and corporate income tax rates are expected to lower revenue by 2% of GDP by 2012. Maintaining a sound government financial position by balancing the central government budget (excluding social security) is essential in light of future spending pressures related to population ageing and the potential cost of economic integration with North Korea.

Improving the tax system to promote economic growth and cope with population ageing

While government outlays and tax revenue are low as a share of GDP, the rising spending pressures noted above create a need for higher taxes. Reform should address a number of challenges:

Supporting economic growth in the context of rapid population ageing and globalisation

A number of studies, including by the OECD, suggest that raising the overall tax burden can reduce growth.[4] In addition, the structure of the tax system determines its effect on economic choices and the size of its burden on the economy. In particular, a high tax wedge on labour can price low-skilled persons out of employment, thus reducing labour inputs and discouraging human capital formation, thereby slowing technological progress. Similarly, firms have become more sensitive to cross-country variations in the corporate tax system in the context of globalisation and heightened competition. High tax rates on corporate income make a country less attractive as a location for investment and for reporting profits.

Meeting the long-term need for additional revenue

The small government in Korea reflects limited public social spending, which at 7% of GDP is the lowest in the OECD area (Figure 1.9). This is due to the relatively recent launch of a social safety net and Korea's comparatively young population. However, population ageing will put upward spending pressure on the National Pension Scheme, National Health Insurance and Long-Term Care Insurance. According to OECD simulations, Korea's public spending on health and long-term care might rise by 6 to 9 percentage points of GDP by 2050, the largest increase in the OECD area (Oliveira Martins and de la Maisonneuve, 2006), while pension outlays could add another 8 percentage points or more.[5] In addition, the cost of greater economic co-operation with North Korea may also call for more revenue. Economic deterioration and chronic food shortages in the North during the past decade suggest that the cost of integration may be enormous. Indeed, it is likely to be far heavier than in the case of Germany, given that the population of North Korea is half that of the South, while its per capita income is only about 6% as large.[6] Early action on the revenue side would limit the long-term cost from the higher fiscal burden.[7]

Figure 1.9. **Public social spending in Korea remains low relative to other OECD countries**

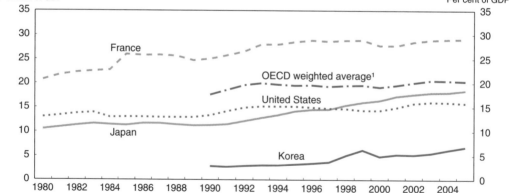

1. The OECD average does not include Hungary and the Slovak Republic for lack of data. The national data are converted to US dollars using 2005 PPP exchange rates.
Source: OECD Social Expenditure Database.

StatLink 🔗 http://dx.doi.org/10.1787/513165553453

Coping with widening income inequality and rising relative poverty

Korea has experienced a significant rise in income inequality since the 1997 crisis. The ratio of the top income quintile to the bottom one rose from 4.1 in 1997 to 5.7 by 2006 and the Gini coefficient has been trending up (Table 1.6). The increase in income equality since 1997 is related to the expanding share of non-regular workers, who are paid about 30% less than regular workers, to more than one-third of employment (see below).

Table 1.6. **Income inequality in Korea has trended up**
For urban salary and wage-earner households[1]

	Gini coefficient[2]	Quintile ratio[3]
1990	27.4	4.1
1995	26.8	4.1
1996	27.2	4.2
1997	26.8	4.1
1998	29.5	4.9
1999	30.3	5.1
2000	28.6	4.6
2001	29.9	4.9
2002	29.8	4.9
2003	29.5 (30.4)	5.1 (5.5)
2004	30.1 (31.0)	5.2 (5.6)
2005	30.4 (31.3)	5.4 (5.8)
2006	31.3 (32.0)	5.7 (6.1)

1. Data for the entire population, available since 2003, are shown in parentheses.
2. The Gini coefficient is defined as the area between the Lorenz curve (which plots cumulative shares of the population, from richest to poorest, against the cumulative share of income that they receive) and the 45-degree line, taken as a ratio of the whole triangle. The values, which range from 0 in the case of perfect equality to 1 in the case of perfect inequality, are multiplied by 100 to give a range of 0 to 100.
3. The ratio of the top to the bottom quintile.
Source: Korea National Statistical Office.

Rising inequality has contributed to an increase in the rate of relative poverty to 14.6% in the mid-2000s, the sixth highest in the OECD area and well above the OECD average of 10.6% (Figure 1.10).[8] As in other countries, population ageing and changes in household structure – more single-person and female-headed households – have played a role. However, increased poverty among families headed by a couple accounted for most of the rise, suggesting that higher income inequality was the key factor. High relative poverty also reflects the weak impact of the public sector: the tax and social welfare systems reduced the relative poverty rate only slightly in Korea, from 17.5% to 14.6% in the mid-2000s (Panel B). In contrast, the average reduction in the OECD area was 16 percentage points. This suggests a need to use the tax system, together with a further rise in social welfare spending, which has quadrupled in absolute terms since 2000, to reverse these trends. However, strengthening the redistributive function of the tax system needs to be weighed against any negative impact on work incentives, which would reduce potential growth. The challenge is to devise a tax reform that addresses income inequality while minimising the negative impact on growth.

Figure 1.10. **International comparison of relative poverty**[1]

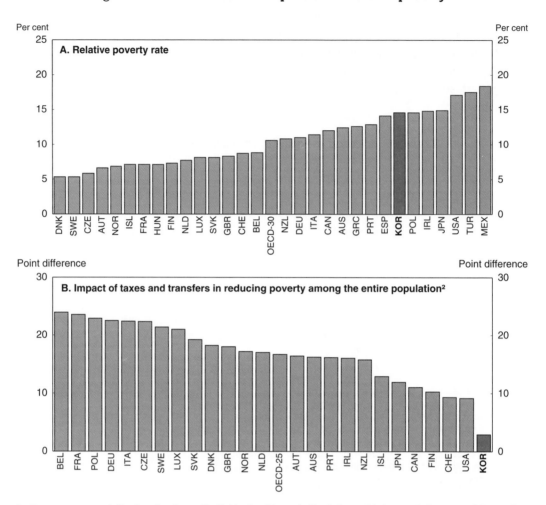

1. Poverty rates are defined as the share of individuals with equivalised disposable income below 50% of the median for the entire population.
2. In percentage points. In Korea, taxes and transfers reduced the relative poverty rate from 17.5% to 14.6%.
Source: OECD (2008b).

StatLink ⟨⟩ http://dx.doi.org/10.1787/513172720643

Improving the local tax system

Local governments account for about a third of government expenditure, and local educational governments, which are independent of local governments, account for another 15%. Despite their size, local autonomy is limited, reflecting the legacy of centralised control. The functions of central and local governments are not clearly defined by law and many policy decisions are made at the central level (KRILA, 2007). With tax and non-tax revenues covering only half of their outlays, local governments rely heavily on transfers from the central government. The Local Share Tax, a general grant set at 19.2% of national "internal tax" revenue (excluding earmarked taxes and customs duties), funds about one-fifth of local expenditure and earmarked grants account for another fifth. The detailed conditions attached to earmarked grants give the central government effective control over a wide array of local policies.

Aligning revenues with spending responsibilities would allow local governments to better respond to the preferences of local citizens and help ensure fiscal discipline by making the cost of local services more visible for local taxpayers. Increasing local autonomy, however, is complicated by wide regional variation in the financial autonomy of local jurisdictions. While Seoul is virtually self-financing, 12% of local governments cannot even fund the salaries of local officials from their own revenues. Reforms that increase local autonomy would therefore tend to boost regional inequality unless they were accompanied by a re-allocation of central government transfers, which would limit local government autonomy. A major challenge, therefore, is to provide local governments with sufficient revenue-raising autonomy to make them accountable to local citizens and encourage fiscal discipline, while ensuring that all have sufficient revenue capacity to provide at least a minimum level of core public services.

The complicated local tax system, which accounts for about 20% of total tax revenue, encompasses 16 local taxes, thus compounding compliance and administrative costs. This contrasts with much leaner local tax systems in the Nordic countries for example – at most four local taxes in Finland, Iceland, Norway and Sweden. The local tax system has a number of other weaknesses. *First*, the heavy reliance on local property transaction taxes acts as a barrier to liquid property markets and efficient land use. Moreover, the volatility of this tax source undermines the stability and predictability of local revenues. *Second*, local governments rarely use their power to change tax rates, although they are allowed to adjust 11 of them by as much as 50% above or below the standard rate. This reflects the reluctance of local governments to diverge from norms set by the national authorities. It is believed that lowering tax rates would lead to reductions in grants, although there is no direct link between them, according to the central government (*OECD Economic Surveys: Korea*, 2005). When local authorities want to raise expenditures, they tend to ask for increases in intergovernmental grants because it is politically easier than raising taxes.

Boosting productivity in the service sector

Labour productivity growth in services slowed from an annual average of 2.6% during the 1980s to 1.2% between 1997 and 2007 (Table 1.7). In contrast, it has risen by nearly 9% per annum in manufacturing since 1990. Services accounted for only a quarter of the growth of value added per person employed between 2000 and 2006, compared with the OECD average of 39% (Figure 1.11). The poor performance of services has widened the

Table 1.7. **Labour productivity growth in manufacturing and services**

A. Annual growth rate of value added per employee in per cent				
Industry	ISIC code	1980-1990	1990-1997	1997-2007
Manufacturing	15 to 37	6.4	8.7	8.7
Market services	50 to 74	4.3	1.6	2.6
Non-market services	75 to 99	–0.2	1.7	–2.0
Total services	50 to 99	2.6	1.5	1.2
Total economy	1 to 99	5.5	4.4	3.3
B. Output growth by sector				
Industry	ISIC code	1980-1990	1990-1997	1997-2007
Manufacturing	15 to 37	11.9	7.5	7.7
Market services	50 to 74	9.5	8.1	4.1
Non-market services	75 to 99	5.7	5.0	2.7
Total services	50 to 99	7.9	7.1	3.7
Total economy	1 to 99	8.5	6.8	4.3

Source: Bank of Korea, National Accounts.

Figure 1.11. **Contribution by sector to growth in OECD countries**

Contribution to growth of value added per person employed in percentage points during 2000-06

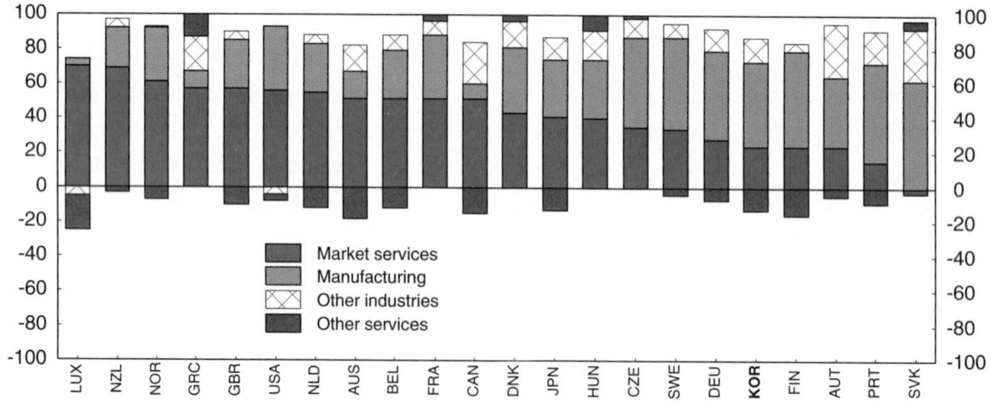

Source: OECD (2008c), *OECD Factbook 2008*, OECD, Paris.

StatLink ▄▅▆ http://dx.doi.org/10.1787/513181350030

labour productivity gap between sectors; productivity in services fell from 76% of that in manufacturing in 1997 to 60% in 2005, the largest gap in the OECD area, where productivity in manufacturing and services is roughly equal.

The problem in services is linked to the weakness of SMEs, which play a dominant role in this sector, accounting for 79% of output and 91% of employment, with particularly high shares in such areas as hotels and restaurants (97%), wholesale and retail trade (95%) and personal services (95%). SMEs have consistently lagged behind large firms in terms of profitability and other financial indicators. By 2005, productivity per employee at SMEs in services was only 45.2% of that of large companies (Table 1.8).

Table 1.8. **Value-added per person employed in the service sector by firm size**

In 2005 in million won

	Average	SMEs	Large firms	Productivity in SMEs as share of large firms (%)	Share of SMEs in output (%)
Wholesale and retail trade	38.1	35.5	89.2	39.8	95.2
Hotels and restaurants	17.7	17.2	51.3	49.9	97.2
Telecommunications	180.2	160.9	377.8	42.6	91.1
Financial intermediation	133.8	72.9	175.6	41.5	40.7
Business services	35.0	34.1	37.6	90.7	74.2
Education	22.6	21.8	33.1	65.9	93.0
Healthcare and social services	36.2	36.0	38.2	94.2	89.7
Personal services, etc.	20.9	20.4	31.9	63.9	95.6
Service sector	**32.6**	**29.4**	**65.1**	**45.2**	**91.1**

Source: Korea Federation of SMEs (2008) and Korea National Statistical Office, *National Statistics.*

Reforming the labour market and improving the education system

A major problem in the labour market is the rising degree of dualism: the share of non-regular workers exceeds one-third of employees (Table 1.9). The largest category of non-regular employment is temporary workers (Panel B), despite long-standing restrictions on fixed-term contracts. The increase in the share of temporary workers, from 16.6% of employment in 2001 to 29.7% in 2004, was the fastest in the OECD area and

Table 1.9. **Non-regular and temporary workers in Korea**

A. Non-regular workers as a per cent of total employment by age and gender in 2005							
	15-19	20-29	30-39	40-49	50-59	60 and over	Total
Males	78.3	32.0	25.3	29.2	35.0	60.0	31.5
Females	64.1	33.4	40.1	46.7	55.2	75.7	43.7

B. Temporary workers as a per cent of total employment							
	2001	2002	2003	2004	2005	2006	2007
Workers with a fixed-term contract of:							
Less than one month	5.6	5.2	6.7	5.6	5.5	5.2	3.2
Between one month and one year	2.8	2.7	4.9	4.7	4.8	4.9	4.7
One year	1.5	1.9	3.3	4.4	5.3	5.0	5.4
Between one year and three years	0.6	0.6	1.3	1.7	1.8	1.7	1.4
Over three years	0.5	0.6	0.7	0.8	0.8	0.9	1.2
Sub-total	11.0	10.9	17.0	17.1	18.2	17.7	15.9
Workers with open-ended contract but who could be dismissed against their own will	2.9	3.8	4.3	7.6	5.9	5.9	6.4
Temporary agency workers (dispatched workers)	1.0	0.7	0.7	0.8	0.8	0.9	1.1
On-call workers	2.2	2.9	4.2	4.6	4.8	4.3	5.3
Total[1]	16.6	18.1	25.9	29.7	29.4	28.3	28.2
Ratio of fixed-term contract workers to total	66.3	60.2	65.6	57.6	61.9	62.5	56.4
Total wage workers (1 000 persons)	13 540	14 030	14 149	14 584	14 968	15 351	15 882

1. The total is adjusted for overlapping between sub-categories. Hence, it is not equal to the sum of the sub-categories.
Source: Korea National Statistical Office, EAPS Supplementary Survey by Type of Employment (every August).

its share was the second highest in the OECD in 2007 (Figure 1.12). The high proportion of temporary workers is a drag on growth as it increases worker turnover and hence reduces firm-provided training, which plays a very important role in Korea (Chung and Lee, 2005). It also raises equity issues as non-regular workers face precarious jobs, wage discrimination and less social protection.

Figure 1.12. **International comparison of temporary employment**
As per cent of total employment in 2007[1]

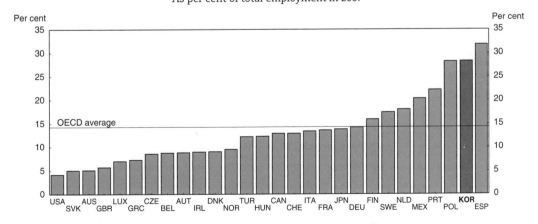

1. Reference year is 2004 in Mexico, 2005 in the United States and 2006 in Australia.
Source: OECD Employment Outlook Database.

StatLink http://dx.doi.org/10.1787/513184173086

The participation rate for prime-age women (25 to 54) is the third lowest in the OECD area, at 62%, and well below the OECD average of 70% (Figure 1.13). Moreover, female employment rates lag behind those for males in each category, leading to an employment gender gap that is the seventh highest in the OECD area. Boosting female employment is a key to mitigating the impact of rapid population ageing. The total female participation rate rose from 49% in 1990 to 55% in 2007, mainly due to the changing behaviour of younger women. In particular, the rate for the 25-to-29 age group has doubled from 32% for women born during the first half of the 1950s to 65% for women born during the second half of the 1970s, reflecting the trend toward later marriage. However, the female participation rate is limited by the fact that a significant share of women withdraw from the labour force at the time of marriage or childbirth, although many later return, resulting in an M-shaped participation curve. A related issue is the significant drop in the fertility rate, which has fallen as the participation rate for young women has risen.

Figure 1.13. **International comparison of female labour force participation rates**
Rates in 2007 for women aged 25 to 54

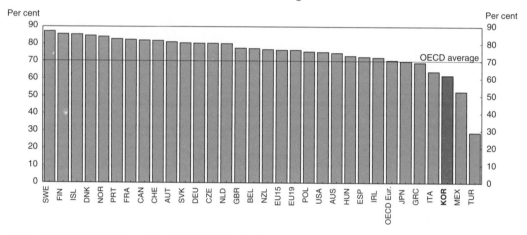

Source: OECD (2008a), *Employment Outlook 2008*, OECD, Paris.

StatLink http://dx.doi.org/10.1787/513260630623

The fall in the youth employment rate, from 51% in 1995 to 47% in 2007, has focused attention on their integration in the labour market. Indeed, the rate for young men in 2007 was the lowest in the OECD area (Figure 1.14). This is explained to some extent by high enrolment in tertiary education, limited possibilities to combine school and work and the 30-month military service obligation for men. The problem is most severe for persons with less educational attainment. Only 53% of those with less than an upper secondary education and 68% of upper secondary graduates could find jobs within a year of leaving school, as against 81% of tertiary graduates. In addition, more than half of new employees between the ages of 15 and 29 quit their first job during the first year and another third quit before the end of three years. One reason for the low employment rate is the mismatch between the skills provided by tertiary education and those needed by firms. Some 35% of university graduates in natural and social sciences do not find jobs in their field of study. More generally, there is a need to upgrade the quality of university education, which has not kept pace with its rapid quantitative expansion.

The unemployment rate for youth (7.5%) is below the OECD average (9.6%). However, this reflects weak incentives for unemployed youth to remain in the labour market, given

OECD ECONOMIC SURVEYS: KOREA – ISBN 978-92-64-05425-7 – © OECD 2008

Figure 1.14. **International comparison of employment and participation rates for young people**

As a per cent of youth aged 15 to 29 by gender in 2007[1]

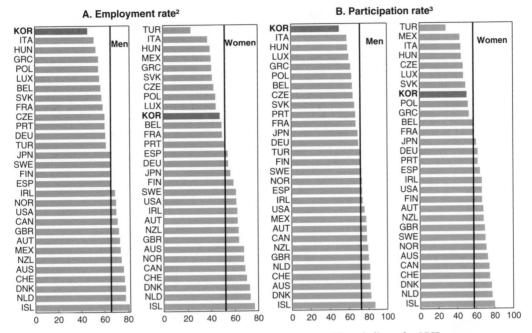

1. For France and Germany, data are available only for 2006. The vertical lines indicate the OECD average.
2. Employed as a percentage of the population in the age group.
3. Labour force as a percentage of the population in the age group.

Source: OECD Employment Outlook Database.

StatLink http://dx.doi.org/10.1787/513261838248

that there are few welfare benefits for individuals without a record of social security contributions. Moreover, a large number of youth are neither in employment nor in education or training (the so-called NEETs). In 2004, NEETs accounted for 17% of the 15-to-29 age group, slightly above the OECD average. The share of NEETs among youth with tertiary education is around three times higher than the OECD average, while the rate among youth with less than upper secondary education is significantly below.

Conclusion

Korea remains one of the most dynamic economies in the world with high levels of investment in fixed capital, R&D and education and a comparative advantage in many high-technology areas. While its potential growth rate is one of the highest in the OECD area, demographic changes will exert more and more of a drag on economic growth. Further progress in reform is key to sustain growth and promote the convergence of per capita income to levels in the most advanced countries (Annex 1.A1). In addition, Korea needs to meet specific challenges related to the global financial crisis, tax reform, enhancing productivity in the service sector and reforming the labour market and education system. The following chapters analyse these challenges.

Notes

1. Using purchasing power parity exchange rates, per capita GDP is around $25 000, 55% of the US level.

2. According to a stress test of household debt by the IMF, a 100 to 300 basis-point rise in interest rates would boost distressed household debt by 8.5 to 17 percentage points, while a drop in housing prices by 10% to 30% would add another 4 percentage points (IMF, 2008).

3. The self-employed account for one-third of total employment in Korea, the fourth highest in the OECD.

4. An increase of about one percentage point in the tax-to-GDP ratio could be associated with a direct reduction of about 0.3% in output per capita in the long run. If the investment effect is taken into account, the overall reduction would be between 0.6% and 0.7% (Bassanini and Scarpetta, 2001). Given that Korea has an exceptionally low tax-to-GDP ratio, the impact may be less.

5. For example, the government's *Vision 2030* plan in 2006 projected that public social spending would rise from 6% of GDP in 2004 to the current OECD average of 21% by 2030.

6. In contrast, East Germany's population was only a third of the West's at the time of German re-unification, while the per capita income gap was significantly smaller, with that in the East around half of the West.

7. If capital markets perceive that the government has not done enough to address the rising revenue needs, Korea may face lower debt ratings and higher capital costs than otherwise. This may outweigh the negative impact of early increases in tax rates.

8. Korea National Statistical Office reported a relative poverty rate of 15.2% for 2005.

Bibliography

Bassanini, A. and S. Scarpetta (2001), "The Driving Forces of Economic Growth: Panel Data Evidence for the OECD Countries", *OECD Economic Studies*, No. 33, OECD, Paris.

Chung, Jaeho and Byung-Hee Lee (2005), "Flexibility, Turnover and Training", *Korea Labor Institute Issue Paper*, No. 41, Seoul.

International Monetary Fund (2008), *Republic of Korea: Selected Issues*, September, Washington, D.C.

Korea Federation of SMEs (2008), *Statistics of Small and Medium Enterprises*, Seoul (in Korean).

KRILA (Korea Research Institute for Local Administration) (2007), *Local Government in Korea*, Seoul.

Oliveira Martins, J. and C. de la Maisonneuve (2006), "Projecting OECD Health and Long-Term Care Expenditures: What Are the Main Drivers?", *OECD Economic Studies*, No. 42, OECD, Paris.

OECD (2005), *OECD Economic Surveys: Korea*, OECD, Paris.

OECD (2006), *Society at a Glance: OECD Social Indicators*, OECD, Paris.

OECD (2007), *OECD Economic Surveys: Korea*, OECD, Paris.

OECD (2008a), *Employment Outlook*, OECD, Paris.

OECD (2008b), *Growing Unequal? Income Distribution and Poverty in OECD Countries*, OECD, Paris.

OECD (2008c), *OECD Factbook*, OECD, Paris.

OECD (2009), *Going for growth*, (forthcoming), OECD, Paris.

ANNEX 1.A1

Taking stock of structural reforms

This annex reviews actions taken on structural policy recommendations in the 2007 OECD Economic Surveys: Korea. Recommendations made in this Survey are shown in the boxes at the end of each chapter.

Recommendations in the 2007 Survey	Actions taken or proposed by the authorities
A. HOUSING AND REGIONAL POLICIES	
Housing policy	
Phase out policies aimed at controlling short-term price fluctuations, such as price caps and the requirement to disclose construction costs.	Price regulations will be eased by broadening the scope of allowable costs used for setting prices of residential and commercial buildings and privately-owned housing.
Maintain the focus on increasing the supply of housing, particularly in the capital region.	The government announced a plan in September 2008 to build an average of 0.5 million new homes annually for the next ten years, of which 0.3 million units, supplied by both the public and private sectors, will be in the capital region.
Reduce regulations on construction and land use to facilitate a stronger private-sector response to demand.	Procedures for reforming land-use restrictions have been eased, while continuing the transfer of urban planning authority to local governments.
Focus the role of the public sector on making more land available for private-sector housing projects.	The amount of land supplied for housing by the public sector rose 41% in 2007 to 65 km^2 (0.1% of Korea's area).
Phase out restrictions on the reconstruction of existing apartments to upgrade their quality or size, particularly in areas where prices are rising.	The government's August 2008 plan will ease restrictions by halving the reconstruction period to 18 months and allowing owners to sell their homes during that period.
Relax regulations on mortgage lending by the private sector without undermining prudential supervision.	The maximum loan-to-value ratio on unsold apartment units in non-speculation zones was boosted from 60% to 70% if the price is reduced.
Encourage the development of the private-sector mortgage market, in part by developing the long-term bond market.	The amount of mortgage-backed securities (MBS) issued by the Korea Housing Finance Corp. and banks has risen and other financial institutions will be able to issue MBS.
Continue to lower property transaction taxes.	The special deduction from the capital gains tax for long-term ownership will be increased from 4% to 8% every year (up to a maximum of 80%).
Hike property holding taxes, while not using such taxes to control property prices or redistribute income.	The government plans to scale down the comprehensive property tax and to gradually merge it with the local property tax.
Avoid high taxes on capital gains to limit the extent of distortions and lock-in effects.	The price at which the owner of a single house is subject to the capital gains tax was raised from 600 million won to 900 million won and the rates will be cut in line with the income tax.
Regional policy and fiscal decentralization	
Transform regulations that limit construction in the capital region into market-based instruments.	No action taken.
Streamline initiatives aiming at balanced regional development and give local government more autonomy in local development plans.	No action taken. The construction of three additional enterprise cities is planned in 2009.
Further pursue fiscal decentralisation by granting greater autonomy to local governments, including more responsibility for providing local services.	The central government has transferred authority on 201 items to local governments since 2007.

Recommendations in the 2007 *Survey*	Actions taken or proposed by the authorities
B. PUBLIC SOCIAL SPENDING IN THE CONTEXT OF AGEING	

Remove obstacles that limit the fertility rate

Recommendations in the 2007 *Survey*	Actions taken or proposed by the authorities
Reduce reliance on private tutoring institutions and lower the out-of-pocket education costs for families.	A March 2007 plan included a number of measures such as creating centres in schools and TV programmes to teach English and expanding after-school programmes.
Promote fertility and female employment by ensuring an adequate supply of high quality childcare and encouraging more family-friendly policies in firms.	Parental leave, available for those with children up to one year of age, was extended to the age of three. A certification system for firms with family-friendly policies was developed.
Encourage private-sector supply of childcare, in part by removing price caps on private-sector suppliers.	Price caps have not been removed. The government plans to introduce an electronic voucher system for childcare services.

Encouraging labour force participation

Increase female employment by reversing the trend toward greater non-regular employment and the importance of seniority in determining wages.	The government has been promoting a shift to performance-based pay systems by providing information to workers and employers.
Promote the participation of older workers by raising or eliminating mandatory retirement ages.	The government introduced a subsidy to firms that increase their retirement age by one year or more to age 56 or above.
Replace employment subsidies with high deadweight costs by more emphasis on lifelong education.	The government has launched a detailed analysis of the effectiveness of subsidy programmes to guide reform.

Ensuring adequate income for elderly persons

Raise the means-tested benefit from 5% of the average wage to reduce poverty among the elderly, given the low coverage of the NPS.	The share of elderly receiving the benefit is to be raised from 60% to 70% in 2009 as planned.
Reform the pension schemes for the civil service, military and private-school teachers to cut public subsidies and introduce portability with the NPS.	A civil service pension reform plan with higher contributions and lower benefits was announced in September 2008.
Accelerate the transition from the lump-sum retirement allowance to company pensions and promote the use of defined contribution schemes.	No action taken.

Improving the healthcare system

Avoid overall cuts in co-payment rates to limit the rise in public healthcare expenditures.	The lump-sum co-payment of 3 000 won for fees of less than 15 000 won was changed to a 30% co-payment.
Lower the ceiling on co-payments over a six-month period in order to ensure greater access for low-income persons and patients with chronic illnesses.	The government lowered the ceiling on the amount of co-payments over a six-month period from 3 million won to 2 million won in July 2007.
Reduce the burden on the working-age population by requiring the elderly to contribute more to the NHI.	No action taken.
Allow domestic and foreign for-profit firms to provide healthcare and permit a greater role for private insurance for services not covered by the NHI.	No action taken.
Make the unified NHI a more effective purchaser of healthcare and consider payment systems other than fee-for-service to limit spending pressure.	The daily flat-rate has been applied to long-term care beds from 2008.
Promote "healthy ageing" to avoid longer periods of disability as life expectancy increases.	The government has expanded screening of the elderly to identify health problems as part of the Health Plan 2010.
Improve the framework for the provision of pharmaceuticals to reduce their relatively large share in healthcare spending.	The number of insured drugs was decreased, cost-benefit analyses for drugs were introduced in April 2007 and drug prices are now determined by negotiation.

Providing long-term care for the elderly

Expand the capacity for long-term care, thus lowering the burden on the healthcare system.	The government established 224 and 183 long-term facilities in 2007 and 2008, respectively, bringing the total to 1 428.
Reduce reliance on public-sector institutions by encouraging the entry of private-sector suppliers.	The Long-term Care Insurance introduced in July 2008 will encourage the participation of the private sector.
Control the increase in demand for long-term care by ensuring an effective gate-keeping function and favouring home-based care.	The co-payment rate for institutional care is 20% compared to 15% for home-based care services.

Addressing rising inequality and relative poverty

Expand the National Basic Livelihood Security System to ensure that all households have an income that at least matches the minimum cost of living.	The minimum cost of living for a family of four was increased by 5% in 2008.
Increase the coverage of non-regular workers by the social insurance programmes for pensions (NPS), health (NHI) and employment (EIS).	A 2008 law will raise the coverage of EIS at firms with less than ten workers. The conditions under which daily construction workers can be covered by the NPS at workplaces were eased in 2007.
Ensure that the new labour law provisions to prevent discrimination against non-regular workers do not discourage the hiring of such workers.	No action taken.

Recommendations in the 2007 *Survey*	Actions taken or proposed by the authorities
Reduce employment protection for regular workers to reverse the rising proportion of non-regular workers.	The legal procedures against employers violating provisions against dismissing regular workers were replaced by a fine.

C. INCREASE THE INTEGRATION OF KOREA IN THE WORLD ECONOMY

Removing obstacles to inflows of foreign direct investment (FDI)

Foster a foreign investment-friendly environment.	Korea has adopted a number of measures, including reducing corporate taxes and the time required to establish an industrial complex and simplifying immigration procedures.
Develop the M&A market, including cross-border M&As, by relaxing related regulations.	No action taken. Measures against predatory M&As are being considered.
Further liberalise FDI restrictions, in particular by reducing or removing foreign ownership ceilings.	No action taken.
Reduce product market regulation, especially in services, to encourage FDI.	The Presidential Council on National Competitiveness was established in 2008 to take the lead on regulatory reform.
Phase out the regulations on construction in the capital region.	Foreign investors have been allowed to construct high-tech plants in the capital region since December 2007. In November 2008, the government announced a plan to ease regulations on building and expanding industrial complexes in the capital region.
Enhance the transparency of tax and financial supervision and limit the scope for discretionary interpretation, application and enforcement.	Measures to improve the use of administrative guidance and provide interpretations and explanations on financial laws and regulations have been introduced.
Resolve the issues in the labour market, including labour-management relations, which discourage FDI.	The Ministry of Labour has initiated several programmes to help foreign companies deal with labour–related matters.
Extend the regulatory reforms introduced in the Free Economic Zones (FEZs) to other parts of the country.	The government designated three new FEZs in April 2008.
Streamline the various zones created to encourage FDI inflows and provide equal treatment of the manufacturing and service sectors.	Responsibilities for the zones were merged into one ministry (Ministry of Knowledge Economy) in March 2008.
Increase transparency by limiting the scope of special incentives, such as cash grants, for foreign firms.	No action taken.
Avoid preferential fiscal and regulatory treatment, which distorts the locational decisions of foreign investors.	All local governments are represented on the "Foreign Investment Committee", to prevent the distortion of location decisions. The central government plays the role of mediator.
Do not allow the emphasis on special zones to distract the authorities from the fundamental objective of improving the business climate.	The government has created the Presidential Council on National Competitiveness to address the key problems facing firms and advance regulatory reform.
Review special zone schemes regularly to ensure that the economic benefits exceed the costs.	No action taken.

Improving the climate for international trade

Pursue the liberalisation of trade barriers through multilateral trade negotiations.	Korea is actively participating in all negotiation groups, including market access, at WTO/DDA negotiations.
Further harmonise regulations and standards with international standards to reduce barriers to imports.	The share of Korean standards harmonised with international standards rose from 58.8% in 2006 to 61.4% in 2007.
Pursue WTO-consistent regional free trade agreements (FTAs), covering substantially all products.	Korea signed a FTA on services with ASEAN in July 2007 and a CEPA with India in September 2008. FTA negotiations with the Gulf Co-operation Council were launched in 2008.
Strengthen market principles in the agricultural sector, in part by reducing market price supports.	The Korea-US FTA will lead to the eventual liberalisation of all agricultural products except rice.
Limit moral hazard in policies used to support industries and workers negatively affected by FTAs.	No firms have qualified for such support thus far.

Promoting the inflows of human resources

Reform the Work Permit System (WPS) to reduce the number of unregistered workers and allow a sufficient number of foreign workers to ease labour shortages.	The number of unregistered workers is to be cut from 19% of total foreign workers to 10% in five years. The number of foreign workers is to be set every year to meet labour demand.
Allow low-skilled foreign workers to be employed in the service sector, in addition to manufacturing.	No action taken.
Increase the inflow of high-skilled workers by improving the immigration control system, as well as the business and living environment.	The maximum residence period for professionals was extended from two to five years in July 2008. Work permits for professionals were introduced in September 2008.

ISBN 978-92-64-05425-7
OECD Economic Surveys: Korea
© OECD 2008

Chapter 2

Priorities for macroeconomic policy

Macroeconomic policy faces difficult challenges in responding to the shocks from the global financial crisis. In the near term, the monetary authorities should focus on supporting activity and financial-market stability. While inflation is well above the target zone, it is expected to slow significantly over the next year as output growth decelerates, despite the depreciation of the won. Given that the won's fall is driven by international financial-market turbulence, foreign exchange market intervention is likely to be costly and ineffective and should therefore be limited to smoothing operations. Fiscal stimulus has a role to play in cushioning the downturn. Over the medium term, the priority should be on maintaining a strong fiscal position given future spending pressures associated with population ageing. Slowing the growth of outlays is necessary to achieve the medium-term target of a balanced budget, excluding the social security surplus.

Korea achieved output growth of more than 4% between 2002 and 2007 while keeping inflation in its target zone. However, growth slowed to 3% in the first three quarters of 2008 at a seasonally-adjusted annual rate, while inflation was well above the 2.5% to 3.5% target.[1] In addition, the depreciation of the won since the end of 2007 accelerated in mid-2008 in the context of the global financial crisis. Korea's response thus far has included cuts in the policy interest rate, intervention to support the won and fiscal stimulus. This chapter will consider the appropriate monetary, exchange rate and fiscal policy responses in this challenging macroeconomic environment. Recommendations are summarised in Box 2.1 in the concluding section.

Monetary policy

The rise in inflation has been testing the credibility of the inflation-targeting framework adopted in 1998. With inflation peaking at 5.9% (year-on-year) in July 2008 (Figure 2.1), the Bank of Korea raised the policy interest rate by 25 basis points to 5¼ per cent in August. Most countries have experienced a spike in inflation in the wake of the oil and commodity price shock, with consumer prices up almost 5% in the OECD area by the summer of 2008. However, in Korea, core CPI inflation (excluding energy and food) exceeded 5% in September 2008, in contrast to the relatively stable OECD average of close to 2%, pointing to significant second-round effects from the terms-of-trade shock (Panel B). Higher underlying inflation boosted consumers' expectations of inflation for the coming 12 months from 4% in August to 4.4% in September,[2] even though oil prices have fallen in recent months.

Figure 2.1. **Inflation**[1]

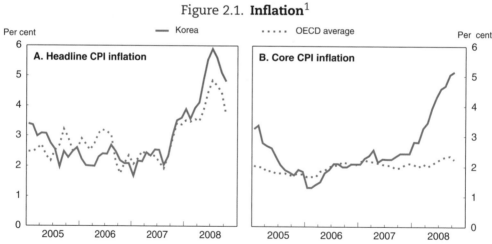

1. Year-on-year changes.
Source: OECD Main Economic Indicators and Analytical Database.

StatLink http://dx.doi.org/10.1787/513301471824

The interest rate hike in August also reflected concern that a number of factors will exacerbate inflationary pressures: *i)* the depreciation of the won is further increasing import prices;[3] *ii)* nominal wages for regular employees accelerated from 5.6% in 2007 to 7.5% (year-on-year) in the second quarter of 2008; *iii)* adjustment in utility prices has been delayed; and *iv)* the rise in producer prices has not yet been fully reflected in consumer prices. Despite the higher policy interest rate, money and credit growth remain robust (Figure 2.2).

Figure 2.2. **Trends in liquidity and lending**

Year-on-year percentage change

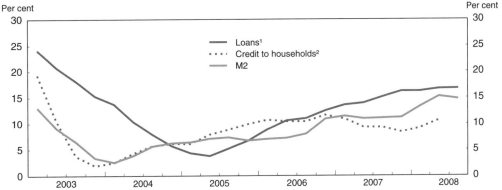

1. Total loans and discounts of commercial and specialised banks.
2. From all financial institutions, as well as credit from department stores, automobile companies, etc.
Source: Bank of Korea.

StatLink ᕕᓕ http://dx.doi.org/10.1787/513352061681

However, the economic outlook has deteriorated with the intensification of the global financial crisis in mid-September. *First*, the depreciation of the won accelerated (Figure 2.3). *Second*, credit conditions have tightened considerably. For example, the yield on three-year corporate bonds rose 160 basis points between mid-September and the end of November to 8¾ per cent, the highest since 2000 (Figure 2.4). Moreover, the stock market lost 23% over

Figure 2.3. **Exchange rate trends**[1]

2000 = 100

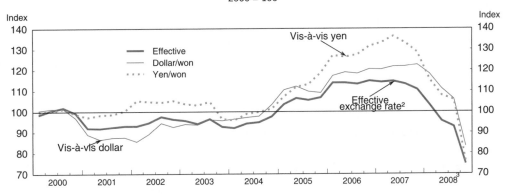

1. A rise indicates an appreciation of the won.
2. Calculated *vis-à-vis* 41 trading partners.
3. The rate shown for the fourth quarter is the average of October and November.
Source: OECD Economic Outlook Database and Bank of Korea.

StatLink ᕕᓕ http://dx.doi.org/10.1787/513373564342

Figure 2.4. **Monetary and credit conditions in Korea**[1]

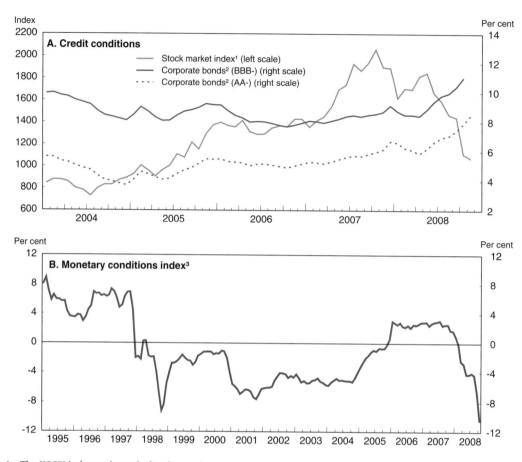

1. The KOSPI index at the end of each month.
2. Monthly average for three-year maturities.
3. An increase indicates a tightening of monetary conditions. The OECD calculates the index using a weight of 1 on the real short-term interest rate (90-day CD rate), deflated with core inflation and a weight of 0.3 on the real effective exchange rate. Levels of monetary conditions are expressed with respect to the average since 2000.

Source: OECD Economic Outlook Database and Bank of Korea.

StatLink ᵐˢ⋑ http://dx.doi.org/10.1787/513411851745

that period, on top of a similar decline between May and mid-September, driven by capital outflows. *Third*, the global financial crisis led to a sharp fall in business-sector confidence in September (Figure 1.4). In such an environment, the priority for the monetary authorities should be to support economic activity and financial-market stability. Accordingly, the Bank of Korea cut the policy rate to 4% by early November to "contribute to soothing the financial market turmoil and to avoiding a severe contraction of economic activity". With the cut in interest rates and the depreciation of the won, monetary conditions by October 2008 were judged to be more relaxed than at any time during the past 15 years (Figure 2.4, Panel B). The future direction of monetary policy should depend on the extent and duration of the economic downturn.[4]

The government has attempted to contain inflation by monitoring the prices of 52 daily necessities since March 2008. However, this policy is ineffective and may even be counterproductive, as it may raise inflation expectations by focusing on the prices that are rising most rapidly. In addition, the government is drawing up price stabilisation measures for items that have recently recorded large price hikes. It is important that such measures do not result in price controls, which were used unsuccessfully in the 1970s and 1980s to try and control inflation.

Exchange rate policy

The authorities intervened in the foreign exchange market in July to stabilise the won and arranged a $30 billion currency swap with the US Federal Reserve in October. Between June and October 2008, Korea's foreign exchange reserves fell by $46 billion, to $212 billion (Figure 2.5). The won continued to depreciate, falling by 26% in trade-weighted terms between early July and the end of November, by which time it was down 36% from the beginning of the year.

Figure 2.5. **Foreign exchange reserves and short-term foreign debt**

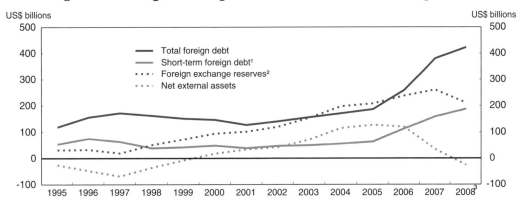

1. Maturity of less than one year.
2. Useable reserves only, i.e. excludes illiquid deposits at offshore Korean banks.
3. For 2008, end of October for foreign exchange reserves and end of September for other data. End of December for preceding years.

Source: Bank of Korea and Ministry of Strategy and Finance.

StatLink ᕱᕱᕱ http://dx.doi.org/10.1787/513437473568

Won depreciation was driven by the deficits in the current account (around 1½% of GDP) and the capital account (1%) in the first three quarters of 2008.[5] The latter is partly a result of the net outflow of FDI.[6] However, capital outflows also reflect global financial turbulence and the funding needs of foreign investors. First, there has been a large outflow from the equity market, amounting to $36 billion in the first three quarters of 2008, on top of more than $50 billion in the second half of 2007 (Figure 2.6). The withdrawal of foreign funds was a key reason for the decline in equity prices in Korea noted above. Second, there has been a marked slowdown in overseas borrowing by domestic banks (included in the other category in Figure 2.6) in the context of a global credit squeeze that has intensified since mid-September. Korean banks are particularly vulnerable, given that overseas borrowing accounts for about 12% of their total funding.[7] The increase in the stock of overseas borrowing by Korean banks, from $83 billion at the end of 2005 to $222 billion in September 2008, was a key factor driving up Korea's foreign debt, making it a net debtor country (Figure 2.5). Much of the debt, though, appears to have relatively low risk.[8]

International credit rating agencies have changed their evaluation of Korean banks,[9] despite their strong fundamentals. Indeed, in June 2008, the non-performing loan ratio was 0.7% and the capital adequacy ratio 11.6%, while the return on assets was 0.9% in the first

Figure 2.6. **The capital account**

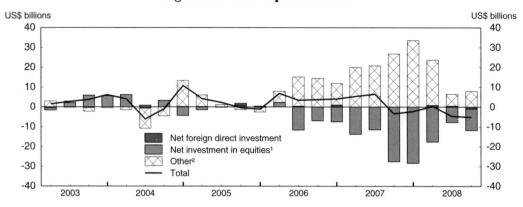

1. A component of portfolio investment.
2. All other capital transfers and flows including the "debt securities" component of portfolio investment, net other investment and net financial derivatives.

Source: Bank of Korea.

StatLink ⬛⬛ *http://dx.doi.org/10.1787/513468648127*

half of the year. To counter the impact of the global financial crisis, Korea announced a four-point programme on 19 October 2008:

- The government will guarantee $100 billion of banks' foreign overseas borrowing to help them overcome difficulties in obtaining offshore loans and reduce their funding costs. Around $80 billion of external borrowing by Korean banks will reach maturity by mid-2009. Similar guarantees have been introduced in the United States, Australia and some European countries.

- An additional $30 billion of dollar liquidity is to be provided from foreign exchange reserves.

- Tax incentives will be provided to long-term investors in order to help stabilise the stock market.

- The government will inject 1 trillion won ($680 million) into a public bank, which could boost lending to SMEs by 12 trillion won.

There are no plans at present to re-capitalise banks or expand deposit guarantees.

Korea still holds a large stock of foreign exchange reserves – the sixth largest in the world – despite recent declines. With the rise in overseas borrowing and the fall in reserves, short-term foreign debt has increased from 31% of foreign exchange reserves at the end of 2005 to 79% in September 2008.[10] The government announced in October 2008 that it would issue $5 billion in foreign currency-denominated bonds in 2009 in order to secure more foreign reserves. Given the global forces putting downward pressure on the won, intervention is likely to be costly and ineffective. It is essential not to repeat the 1997 mistake of using up foreign exchange reserves in the midst of a liquidity crisis. In this context, a commitment to stabilise the won would be worrisome.[11]

Fiscal policy

Maintaining a sound fiscal position in Korea is a priority given future spending pressures, including those stemming from population ageing and the potential cost of intensified economic co-operation with North Korea. Government spending is the third lowest in the OECD area, while public debt is the sixth lowest, with Korea one of nine OECD countries in which government financial assets exceed liabilities. Nevertheless, the pace of spending growth – 9% per annum, excluding financial-sector restructuring costs since 2002 – has significantly boosted the share of the public sector in the economy and kept the consolidated central government deficit, excluding the social security surplus,[12] in deficit through 2006 (Table 2.1). However, a surplus of 0.4% of GDP was recorded in 2007, thanks to a record-high overshooting of revenue by 2% of GDP.

Table 2.1. **Consolidated central government budget**[1]

	2005	2006		2007		2008	2008
	Outcome	Initial budget[2]	Outcome[3]	Initial budget[2]	Outcome[3]	Initial budget[2]	Estimated outcome
A. Total							
Revenue	191.5	208.1	209.6	225.1	243.6	247.2	247.2
Growth (per cent)	7.1	4.2	9.5	8.2	16.3	9.8	9.8
Per cent of GDP	23.6	24.5	24.7	24.9	27.0	25.5	25.5
Expenditures	187.9	209.0	205.9	211.7	209.8	230.2	235.1
Growth (per cent)	8.3	7.7	9.6	1.3	1.9	8.7	11.1
Per cent of GDP	23.2	24.6	24.3	23.4	23.3	23.8	24.3
Balance	3.5	–0.9	3.6	13.4	33.8	17.0	12.1
Per cent of GDP	0.4	–0.1	0.4	1.5	3.8	1.8	1.3
of which:							
Social security balance	23.6	26.0	26.4	27.0	30.2	28.0	28.1
Per cent of GDP	2.9	3.1	3.1	3.0	3.4	2.9	2.9
Privatisation revenues	0.1	2.0	0.7	0.0	0.0	0.0	1.0
Per cent of GDP	0.0	0.2	0.1	0.0	0.0	0.0	0.1
Financial-sector restructuring costs	12.0	12.0	12.0	0.0	0.0	0.0	0.0
Per cent of GDP	1.5	1.4	1.4	0.0	0.0	0.0	0.0
B. Alternative measures of the balance							
Excluding social security	–20.1	–26.8	–22.8	–13.6	3.6	–11.0	–15.9
Per cent of GDP	–2.5	–3.2	–2.7	–1.5	0.4	–1.1	–1.6
Excluding social security, and financial-sector restructuring costs	–8.1	–14.8	–10.8	–13.6	3.6	–11.0	–15.9
Per cent of GDP	–1.0	–1.7	–1.3	–1.5	0.4	–1.1	–1.6
Excluding social security, privatisation and financial-sector restructuring costs	–8.2	–16.8	–11.5	–13.6	3.6	–11.0	–16.9
Per cent of GDP	–1.0	–2.0	–1.4	–1.5	0.4	–1.1	–1.7
Memorandum items							
Adjusted expenditures[4]	175.9	197.0	193.9	211.7	209.8	230.2	235.1
Growth (per cent)	8.9	8.2	10.2	7.5	8.2	8.7	11.1

1. On a GFS basis. Includes public enterprises, but excludes local government.
2. Growth rate relative to previous year's initial budget.
3. Growth rate relative to previous year's outcome.
4. Excludes financial sector restructuring costs.
Source: Ministry of Strategy and Finance.

The initial budget for 2008 envisaged a deficit of 1.1% of GDP, excluding social security. However, tax receipts were once again unexpectedly buoyant in the first half of the year, increasing 13% thanks to strong corporate profits in 2007 and continued improvements in tax compliance (see Chapter 3). This additional revenue, including the surplus stemming from higher-than-budgeted revenue in 2007, is financing a supplementary budget and tax rebates equal to almost 1% of GDP that was passed in September 2008. It includes 0.4% of GDP in income tax rebates to around 80% of taxpayers, focused on lower-income workers.[13] Additional spending, amounting to 0.5% of GDP, will be used to support energy conservation, build roads and subsidise utilities, which had minimised hikes in charges in the summer of 2008. Such subsidies distort energy prices and encourage excessive consumption. However, electricity and gas prices were raised in November 2008. Taking the supplementary budget into account, the budget in 2008 is likely to record a deficit of around 1½ per cent of GDP, excluding social security.

The government had initially planned to slow the pace of spending growth to 6.5% in 2009, which would have been the lowest since 2004. However, revenue growth will also be damped by rate cuts on personal and corporate income taxes,[14] which the authorities estimate will reduce revenue by 2% of GDP by 2012. The government initially expected a budget deficit, excluding social security, of around 1% of GDP. It is likely to be larger than projected, given that real GDP growth is likely to be well below the 5% assumed in the budget. Moreover, the government announced a 14 trillion won (1.4% of GDP) fiscal package in November 2008, which includes 11 trillion won of additional public expenditure in 2009 (see Box 1.1). The package also provides 3 trillion won in tax reductions by extending the Temporary Investment Tax Credit until the end of 2009. The government's medium-term goal is a balanced budget by 2012. Given that it expects the tax cuts to reduce revenue by more than 2% of GDP, achieving the 2012 target would require a sharp slowdown in government spending after the economy recovers from the global financial crisis.

The government announced a plan in October 2008 to privatise 38 state-owned enterprises, including Korea Development Bank and the Industrial Bank of Korea. However, network industries, such as electricity, gas and water companies, have been excluded from the plan. Although Korea sold eight important public enterprises in the wake of the 1997 crisis, privatisation has stalled since 2002. The plan also calls for streamlining the public enterprise sector by consolidating 38 institutions into 17 and abolishing five. In addition, efficiency is to be increased by realigning the functions of 20 public institutions. Also, all public institutions will see their budgets and manpower downsized.

The National Pension Scheme

Benefits paid by the National Pension Scheme (NPS) are only 0.6% of GDP at present, reflecting the relatively young age of the population and the relatively recent launch of the NPS in 1988. However, rapid population ageing (see Chapter 1) and the maturation of the NPS will boost such spending to 7% of GDP in 2078 despite reforms to lower the replacement rate from 70% initially to 40%. There remain concerns about the coverage of the NPS, as the number of contributors has levelled off at one-third of the working-age population (Figure 2.7). In contrast, mandatory public pension systems cover around two-thirds of the working-age population on average in OECD countries. Moreover, the average contribution period of beneficiaries in Korea – projected by the NPS at 17.3 years in 2030 – suggests that many elderly will receive small pension benefits. In addition, there is a large gap in the level of contributions between employees (whose average income was around 2 million won in June 2008) and individually-insured persons (around 1 million won), who tend to be self-employed. In sum, the low level of coverage, short average contribution period and the small payments by the self-employed raise the risk that the NPS will not be sufficient to reduce the relative poverty rate for households with elderly persons, which was already estimated to be 39% in 2000.

The introduction of a means-tested benefit in 2008 that will be available to about 60% of the elderly is thus a step in the right direction, although the benefit will be relatively small at less than 5% of the average wage. Given the difficulty in broadening the coverage of the NPS and raising the level of contributions among the self-employed, increasing the

Figure 2.7. **The coverage of the National Pension Scheme**
Number of contributors

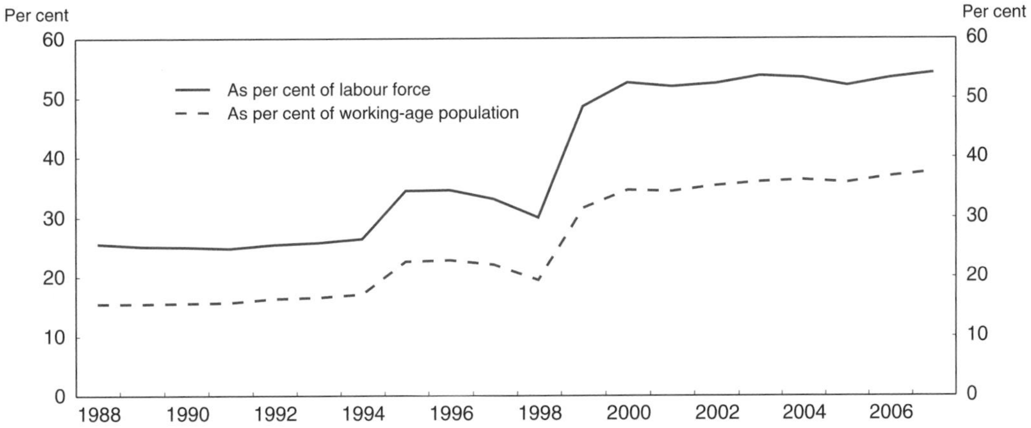

Source: National Pension Service and the Korea National Statistical Office.

StatLink ⬛⬛ http://dx.doi.org/10.1787/513470310374

means-tested benefit over time toward the minimum cost of living (20% of the average wage) and widening its coverage would help reduce poverty among those over 65. As such an expansion of the basic benefit would significantly increase the tax burden, it should be accompanied by a scaling back of NPS benefits to limit the overall cost of providing for the elderly. Another option, currently also under consideration in Korea, would be to increase means-tested benefits while narrowing the coverage for elderly persons who are poor. In the meantime, it is essential that the means-tested social assistance programme be adequate to lower the relatively high incidence of poverty among the elderly. Finally, the public occupational pension schemes for the civil service, military and private-school teachers, which cover 6% of the population, should be reformed to reduce their reliance on government subsidies and to allow portability with the NPS, and thereby encourage labour mobility. The plan announced in September 2008 to raise the contribution rate and cut the replacement rate for the civil service pension is an important reform.

Economic co-operation with North Korea

The South's efforts to increase contact with the North have led to closer economic ties. Indeed, trade rose by more than 2.5 times between 2004 and 2007 (Figure 2.8), as the South overtook China as the top destination for North Korean exports. Although political tensions led to a suspension of the inter-governmental dialogue in March 2008, trade expanded further by 23% (year-on-year) during the first half of 2008. Commercial trade now accounts for 94% of inter-Korean trade, as economic rather than political factors increasingly drive North-South exchanges.[15] However, North-South trade is only 0.2% as large as the South's international trade.

The Gaeseong Industrial Complex, which was established in 2004 as an industrial site for South Korean small and medium-sized enterprises (SMEs), accounts for about a quarter of inter-Korean trade. Infrastructure, including rail and road links, electricity and communications, is provided by the South Korean government and the firms involved, while a public financial institution provides low-interest loans and insurance. Low production costs make the complex attractive to SMEs. Indeed, North Korean workers employed in Gaeseong are paid an average of $70 per month, less than 3% of the average

Figure 2.8. **Inter-Korean economic relations**

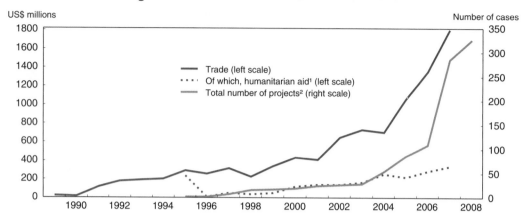

1. Includes both public and private assistance, primarily for food.
2. The number of approved private economic co-operation projects. The 2008 number is through June.
Source: Ministry of Unification.

StatLink http://dx.doi.org/10.1787/513630345317

manufacturing wage in South Korea. The complex contained 72 factories employing about 30 000 North Korean workers and 1 300 South Koreans as of July 2008. About 80% of the output is sold in the South, with the remainder exported to other countries. Although the North expelled some South Korean officials from the complex in 2008, Gaeseong-related trade increased by 88% in the first half of 2008. However, the Mt. Geumgang project was suspended after a South Korean tourist was killed in July. The project, which began in 1998, had been supported by government subsidies. In addition to these government-initiated ventures, private-sector economic co-operation is deepening, as the number of approved projects has risen to more than 300 (Figure 2.8). The creation of new projects will be facilitated by Seoul's decision in May 2008 to ease red tape on doing business in the North. As a result, individuals no longer need specific approval to cross the border or to engage in joint ventures with the North.

Following modest output growth from 1999 to 2005, the North Korean economy is estimated to have contracted in both 2006 and 2007, further widening the gap with the South. One factor was the floods in 2007, which reduced agricultural output, resulting in the largest food shortfall in a decade. The South Korean economy is now about 36 times larger than the North's and 16 times larger on a per capita basis (Table 2.2), and the widening gap will boost the eventual cost of economic integration. The expansion of trade driven by private-sector firms in the South, in line with the new government's strategy of limiting co-operation to projects that are economically viable and that do not overburden taxpayers in the South, provides the best hope for limiting the gap.

Conclusion

The priority for macroeconomic policy is to cushion the downturn in output and support financial-market stability as the world economy copes with the global financial crisis. Fiscal policy has a role to play in providing such support. However, foreign exchange intervention is likely to be costly and ineffective and should hence be limited to smoothing. The appropriate course of monetary policy depends on the duration and the extent of the growth slowdown, which will be determined to a large degree by world economic developments. Specific recommendations are summarised in Box 2.1.

Table 2.2. **Comparison of North and South Korea in 2007**

	(A)	(B)	(A/B)
	North Korea	South Korea	Comparison (%)
Population (millions)	23.2	48.5	47.9
GDP (billion US$)	26.6	969.9	2.7
GDP per capita (US$)	1 148.4	20 015.2	5.7
GDP growth (in volume, in per cent)	−2.4	5.0	...
Total trade (billion US$)	2.9	728.3	0.4
Exports	0.9	371.5	0.2
Imports	2.0	356.9	0.6
Inter-Korean exports (billion US$)	0.8	1.0	74.1
Commercial exports[1]	0.8	0.7	114.8
Non-commercial exports[2]	0	0.4	...
Industrial statistics			
Power generation (billion kWh)	237.0	4 031.0	5.9
Steel production (million tonnes)	1.2	51.5	2.4
Cement (million tonnes)	6.1	52.2	11.7
Agricultural statistics			
Grains (million tonnes)	4.0	5.0	79.7
Fertiliser (million tonnes)	0.4	3.4	11.8

1. Processing-on-commission trade accounts for about half of commercial trade.
2. Mostly includes humanitarian aid in the form of commodities such as rice and fertiliser.
Source: Bank of Korea and Ministry of Unification.

Box 2.1. **Summary of recommendations for macroeconomic policy**

- In the near term, the monetary authorities should put a greater-than-usual weight on supporting economic activity and financial-market stability.

- Given that exchange market intervention is likely to be costly and ineffective, limit intervention to smoothing operations, thus helping maintain foreign exchange reserves above the rising short-term external debt.

- Use fiscal policy to cushion the downturn by implementing the income tax rebates in the supplementary budgets and the tax cuts planned for 2009 and allowing the automatic stabilisers to operate.

- Once the economy recovers, slow the pace of government spending to achieve the goal of a balanced budget for the consolidated central government (excluding the social security surplus) by 2012.

- Follow through on the plan to privatise 28 public institutions and to consolidate or abolish another 34.

- Given the difficulty in expanding the coverage of the National Pension Scheme, increase the means-tested benefit from 5% of the average wage to reduce poverty among the elderly.

Notes

1. The target was changed in 2007 from core to headline CPI inflation for 2007 to 2009.

2. The Bank of Korea made this survey public for the first time in September 2007 (on a quarterly basis), but it is now released monthly. The September 2008 survey showed that one-third of households expect inflation to be between 4.5% and 5.5% over the next 12 months.

3. Import prices in September 2008 were up 42.6% year-on-year.

4. The economic downturn is projected to bring inflation back to the target zone in 2009. In contrast, the oil shocks in the 1970s led to extended periods of high inflation. Inflation was 11% per annum between 1968 and 1973, before increasing to around 25% in 1974-75. It did not slow to 10% until 1977. Inflation climbed to 18% following the second oil shock and did not return to single digits until 1982.

5. Statistical tests indicate that the basic balance drives changes in the exchange rate. Granger causality runs one-way from the basic balance to the exchange rate, based on quarterly data from 1981 to 2008. In October 2008 the current account recorded a surplus of $4.9 billion and the government projects a surplus of $9 billion in the fourth quarter of 2008.

6. However, foreign purchases of Korean bonds, which jumped from only $2 billion in 2006 to $36 billion in 2007, remained an important source of capital inflows in the first half of 2008.

7. Wholesale funding accounts for about 44% of banks' funding, reflecting the low ratio of deposits to loans.

8. Of Korea's total external debt of $421 billion in June 2008, $152 billion had lower risk: i) $94 billion was banks' foreign exchange borrowing to cover foreign exchange forward sales; ii) $51 billion was advance receipts from export contracts in the shipbuilding industry; and iii) $7 billion was foreign investors' loans to Korean companies. In addition, 22% of total external debt belonged to local branches of foreign banks.

9. Moody's lowered the outlook for the financial strength of four Korean banks from stable to negative in October 2008.

10. With the decline in reserves to $212 billion in October 2008, the ratio would be 89%.

11. The Vice Minister of Strategy and Finance recently stated that "We are determined to stabilise the foreign currency market" (*Korea Herald*, 3 October 2008).

12. The government's preferred fiscal measure excludes the social security surplus as this is intended to cover the future liability of public pensions, as well as the cost of financial-sector restructuring between 2002 and 2006. Korea uses the GFS measure of the government budget. General government on a SNA93 basis is available through 2006, when it reported a surplus of 3.6% of GDP, compared to 0.4% for the consolidated government budget, including the social security surplus and the cost of financial-sector restructuring (Table 2.1). The difference reflects the fact that GFS does not include local government, but does include net lending items, some of which are financial in nature.

13. The rebates will be given to wage earners in November and to the self-employed in December. Given that only 50% of the labour force pays income taxes, this actually benefits the upper half of workers.

14. The four rates in the personal income tax are to be cut from a range of 8% to 35% to 6% to 33% by 2010. The corporate income tax rate (national and local) is to be reduced from 27.5% to 22%.

15. The remainder is primarily humanitarian food aid. Its share has fallen from 35% in 2005.

ISBN 978-92-64-05425-7
OECD Economic Surveys: Korea
© OECD 2008

Chapter 3

Reforming the tax system to promote economic growth and cope with rapid population ageing

Korea has one of the lowest tax burdens in the OECD area, reflecting its small public sector. However, rapid population ageing will put upward pressure on government spending. The challenge is to meet the long-run need for greater expenditures and tax revenue while sustaining strong economic growth. A pro-growth tax reform implies relying primarily on consumption taxes for additional revenue. There is also scope for raising personal income tax revenue from its current low level by broadening the base by reducing the exemptions for personal income. The planned cuts in the corporate tax rate should be financed at least in part by reductions in tax expenditures. The broadening of direct tax bases would also help finance an expansion of the earned income tax credit to address widening income inequality. In addition, the local tax system should be simplified and reformed to enhance the autonomy of local governments.

Korea's tax burden is the second lowest in the OECD area and well below the average of 37% (Figure 3.1). However, it is likely to continue rising with rapid population ageing and the development of a social safety net. Korea should take advantage of its sound fiscal position to implement a revenue-neutral tax reform to reduce existing distortions, which will become more harmful as tax pressure mounts in the future. A fundamental overhaul of the tax system should address the challenges discussed in Chapter 1:

- Supporting economic growth in the context of rapid population ageing and globalisation.

- Generating sufficient revenue to cope with the upward pressure on spending from population ageing and the maturation of the social insurance systems (Figure 1.9).

- Reversing the rising trend in income inequality and relative poverty (Figure 1.10 and Table 1.6).

- Improving the complicated local tax system while enhancing the autonomy of local governments.

This chapter begins by comparing the Korean tax system with other OECD countries and then analyses how each of the major taxes can be reformed to meet these four objectives. The chapter concludes with recommendations for a comprehensive tax reform, which are summarised in Table 3.9.

The Korean tax system in an international perspective

The central government tax system consists of; i) ten "internal taxes";[1] ii) three earmarked taxes (education, local development and transport-energy-environment);[2] and iii) customs duties. The central government transfers 19.2% of internal tax revenues to

Figure 3.1. **The tax burden in Korea is rising toward the OECD average**
In per cent of GDP

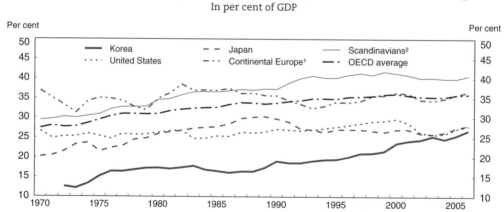

1. France, Germany and Italy.
2. Denmark, Norway and Sweden.

Source: OECD (2008b), *Revenue Statistics 1965-2007*, OECD, Paris (http://dx.doi.org/10.1787/366725334503).

StatLink http://dx.doi.org/10.1787/513647126122

local governments as general grants known as the "Local Share Tax", based on a formula aimed at reducing inequality in regional income. Another 19.4% is transferred to the education special account.

In terms of the tax mix, Korea is unique in a number of respects (Table 3.1):

- *Direct taxes on households* are exceptionally low, accounting for only 15.2% of total tax revenue in 2006, the fifth-lowest share in the OECD area. Only one-half of wage earners pay personal income tax (PIT) due to a number of deductions and, consequently, only one-half of wage income is subject to tax. PIT revenue is further reduced by preferential tax treatment of income from a number of sources, including retirement benefits and agriculture.[3] Capital gains from financial assets are largely untaxed.

- *Corporate income tax (CIT)* revenue accounted for 14.3% of tax revenue in 2006, well above the OECD average of 10.7%. The standard rate of 27.5% and the amount of revenue, at 3.8% of GDP, are in line with OECD averages.

Table 3.1. **The tax mix in OECD countries**

A. Tax revenue as a per cent of GDP

	2000		2006			Change 2000 to 2006	
	Korea	OECD	Korea	Rank	OECD	Korea	OECD
Direct taxes on households	3.4	9.7	4.1	27	9.2	0.7	−0.5
Direct taxes on firms	3.3	3.6	3.8	10	3.9	0.5	0.3
Social security and payroll	3.9	9.3	5.7	22	9.4	1.8	0.1
Goods and services	9.0	11.2	8.7	26	11.1	−0.3	−0.1
Value-added tax	4.0	6.6	4.5	24	6.8	0.5	0.2
Taxes on specific goods and services	4.0	4.4	3.4	22	4.1	−0.6	−0.3
Customs and import duties	1.0	0.2	0.8	2	0.2	−0.2	0.0
Property	2.9	1.9	3.5	3	2.0	0.6	0.1
Recurrent taxes	0.6	0.9	0.8	12	1.0	0.2	0.1
Taxes on property transactions	2.0	0.7	2.4	1	0.7	0.4	0.0
Estate, inheritance and gift taxes	0.3	0.3	0.3	7	0.2	0.1	−0.1
Other	0.9	0.3	0.9	4	0.3	0.0	0.0
Total	23.4	36.0	26.7	26	35.9	3.3	−0.1

B. Tax revenue as a per cent of total tax revenue

	2000		2006			Change 2000 to 2006	
	Korea	OECD	Korea	Rank	OECD	Korea	OECD
Direct taxes on households	14.6	26.1	15.2	26	24.8	0.6	−1.3
Direct taxes on firms	14.1	10.1	14.3	5	10.7	0.2	0.6
Social security and payroll	16.9	25.5	21.2	21	26.2	4.3	0.7
Goods and services	38.3	31.6	32.6	12	31.5	−5.6	0.0
Value-added tax	17.0	18.5	16.8	21	19.3	−0.2	0.7
Taxes on specific goods and services	16.9	12.4	12.7	8	11.6	−4.2	−0.7
Customs and import duties	4.3	0.6	3.1	3	0.6	−1.2	0.0
Property	12.4	5.5	13.2	1	5.7	0.8	0.2
Recurrent taxes	2.5	2.6	3.1	9	3.0	0.6	0.3
Taxes on property transactions	8.5	2.0	9.1	1	2.1	0.6	0.1
Estate, inheritance and gift taxes	1.4	0.9	1.1	3	0.6	−0.3	−0.2
Other	3.7	1.2	3.5	3	1.1	−0.2	−0.1
Total	100.0	100.0	100.0		100.0	0.0	0.0

Source: OECD (2008b), *Revenue Statistics 1965-2007*, OECD, Paris (http://dx.doi.org/10.1787/366725334503).

- *Social security contributions* have become the largest single source of government revenue. However, the share of contributions in GDP, at 5.7%, is well below the OECD average due to relatively low contribution rates and weak compliance with the public pension system.

- *Taxes on goods and services* account for about one-third of government revenue, as in the OECD area. The VAT accounts for half of this amount, although the rate, at 10%, is the fourth lowest in the OECD. The other half is derived from a wide range of excises on specific products. Customs and import duties provide 3.1% of tax revenue, one of the highest shares in the OECD area.

- The *property tax* accounted for 13.2% of tax revenue in 2006, well above the OECD average of 5.7%. This is due to transaction taxes on property, such as the registration and acquisition taxes. Taxes assessed on property itself (recurrent taxes) are much lower than the OECD average. Estate, inheritance and gift taxes in Korea accounted for 1.1% of tax revenue, the third highest in the OECD area.

- Another unusual aspect of Korea's tax system is the important role of so-called *quasi-taxes*, which include a wide range of fees, charges and contributions that are not imposed by the tax laws. Most are levied on firms in a discretionary and non-transparent manner for financing off-budget spending. There were some 100 such quasi-taxes in 2006, generating income of 1.4% of GDP.

Local government taxes account for about one-fifth of total tax receipts and cover about one-third of local government spending. There are basically two levels of local government in Korea. The upper-level local government consists of nine provinces, six metropolitan cities and Seoul special city, while lower-level local government includes cities, counties and wards (*OECD Economic Surveys: Korea*, 2005). Authority for education is located in the "local education governments", which are independent of local general government and rely primarily on the central government for revenue. The 16 local taxes generated an estimated 4.2% of GDP in 2007. Nine key taxes accounted for 93% of local tax revenue in 2007. The remaining taxes, each generating less than 2% of local tax revenue, reflects the reliance on earmarked taxes, which in total account for 21% of local government tax revenue.[4] One of the five earmarked taxes, the Local Education Tax, is a major revenue source. It was introduced in 2001 as a surcharge on five local taxes, but is transferred directly to local education governments and thus does not enhance the autonomy of local general governments (Kim, 2005). Property taxes account for about half of local tax revenue (Figure 3.2), with levies on transactions accounting for about four-fifths of that amount. However, local property taxes were reduced with the introduction of a national Comprehensive Property Tax (CPT) in 2005. In contrast, local taxes on consumption, business and personal income, as well as local social security and payroll taxes, are relatively insignificant compared to other OECD countries.

Korea has made some progress in implementing the tax reform recommendations in the 2000 *OECD Economic Surveys: Korea* (Annex 3.A1). In September 2008, the government announced a tax reform package aimed at boosting private consumption and business and housing investment:

- PIT rates will be cut by two percentage points by 2010, lowering the range from 8% to 35% to 6% to 33%. Inheritance tax rates, currently 10% to 50%, will be brought in line with the PIT. In addition, the personal income tax deduction will be hiked from 1 million won to 1.5 million won.

Figure 3.2. **Composition of sub-national government tax revenues**
2006

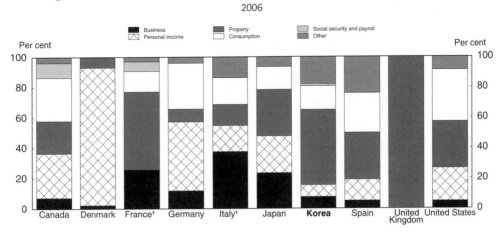

1. Including other taxes paid solely by business (*taxe professionnelle* in France and IRAP in Italy).

Source: OECD (2008b), *Revenue Statistics 1965-2007*, OECD, Paris (*http://dx.doi.org/10.1787/366725334503*).

StatLink ⓘ *http://dx.doi.org/10.1787/513664244307*

- The CIT rate (central government) will be cut from 25% to 22% in 2009 and 20% in 2010. The rate for small and medium-sized enterprises (SMEs) was reduced from 13% to 11% in 2008 and will be lowered further to 10% in 2010 and the threshold for this lower rate will be doubled to 200 million won. As a result, 90% of firms will pay the SME rate.

- The threshold for paying capital gains tax for those owning only one house will be raised from 600 million won ($409 000) to 900 million won ($613 000). The special deduction for long-term ownership will be expanded from 4% to 8% per year (up to a maximum of 80%). The tax rates on capital gains, which are one percentage point higher than the PIT for each bracket, and the thresholds will be brought into alignment with the PIT in 2009.

- The CPT will be significantly revised. *First*, the rates will be cut from a range of 1% to 3% to 0.5% to 1%. *Second*, the threshold for paying the tax will be raised from 600 million won to 900 million won. *Third*, the "application ratio" used to calculate the tax base will be kept constant rather than increased as originally planned. *Fourth*, tax rates on land will also be reduced.

While there are a number of positive elements in this plan, it does not fully address the four challenges noted above, which require a more comprehensive tax reform. The following sections examine the CIT, PIT, consumption taxes (including environmentally-related taxes) and property taxes.

Corporate taxation

Overview of the corporate income tax

Corporate tax receipts have increased in recent years, rising from 3.3% of GDP in 2000 to match the OECD average of 3.8% by 2006 (Table 3.1). One factor is the 66% rise in the number of corporations, as restructuring in the wake of the crisis prompted newly-unemployed persons to create enterprises and firms to spin off unprofitable divisions.[5] In addition, taxable profits have risen markedly, in part due to deleveraging in the corporate sector since the financial crisis; the debt-equity ratio in the manufacturing sector fell from nearly 400% in 1997 to less than 100% by 2005, thereby reducing deductions for corporate interest payments. In addition, with loss carryovers limited to five years, the large losses recorded in the wake of the crisis can no longer be used to offset profits.

Table 3.2. **Tax expenditures in Korea**

	2000	2002	2004	2006	Number[1]
Personal income tax (trillion won)	5.2	5.6	7.4	9.1	96
Per cent of revenue	25.9	26.1	28.3	26.2	
Per cent of all tax expenditures	38.9	37.7	40.5	42.7	
Per cent of GDP	0.9	0.8	0.9	1.1	
Corporate income tax (trillion won)	4.3	4.6	5.7	6.1	84
Per cent of revenue	22.5	21.6	20.8	18.9	
Per cent of all tax expenditures	32.6	31.2	31.1	28.5	
Per cent of GDP	0.7	0.7	0.7	0.7	
Value-added tax (trillion won)	2.6	3.0	3.2	3.8	25
Per cent of revenue	11.4	9.6	9.2	10.0	
Per cent of all tax expenditures	19.9	20.6	17.4	17.8	
Per cent of GDP	0.5	0.4	0.4	0.4	
Other indirect taxes (trillion won)	0.9	1.3	1.8	2.1	60
Per cent of revenue	1.6	1.8	2.1	2.2	
Per cent of all tax expenditures	7.0	8.6	9.6	9.6	
Per cent of GDP	0.2	0.2	0.2	0.2	
Property taxes (trillion won)	0.2	0.3	0.3	0.3	3
Per cent of revenue	1.2	1.3	1.2	1.0	
Per cent of all tax expenditures	1.6	1.9	1.4	1.4	
Per cent of GDP	0.0	0.0	0.0	0.0	
Total tax expenditures (trillion won)	13.3	14.7	18.3	21.3	219
Per cent of revenue	9.7	8.8	9.5	9.4	
Per cent of GDP	2.3	2.2	2.3	2.5	

1. The number of individual tax expenditures in 2006. The total number is less than the components as some tax expenditures apply to more than one tax.
Source: Ministry of Strategy and Finance.

The corporate tax system accounted for 84 of the 219 tax expenditures in 2006 and 28.5% of the total amount of tax expenditures (Table 3.2). Since 2000, they have remained steady at around one-fifth of corporate tax revenue. This is relatively high compared with other OECD countries, notably Japan, where they amounted to 7% of corporate tax revenue in 2006. Incentives for investment promotion, R&D and SMEs accounted for 80% of the total (Table 3.3). Tax expenditures for investment promotion include measures to attract foreign

Table 3.3. **Tax expenditures in the corporate tax system**
Per cent of corporate tax revenue

	2000	2002	2004	2006
Investment promotion	4.8	4.3	8.1	8.0
R&D promotion	5.0	4.4	4.5	4.0
Promotion of SMEs	2.0	3.3	3.6	3.0
Social security payments	4.1	4.2	1.7	1.7
Promotion of agriculture and fishing	0.3	0.4	0.1	1.0
Rural development	0.7	1.3	1.2	0.4
Restructuring of financial industry	3.5	1.7	1.1	0.3
Education and culture	0.8	1.0	0.3	0.2
Other	1.3	1.0	0.3	0.1
Total tax expenditures	**22.5**	**21.6**	**20.8**	**18.9**

Source: Ministry of Strategy and Finance.

direct investment (FDI) inflows by cutting or eliminating taxes on foreign companies for up to seven years. In addition, the rate of tax subsidy for R&D expenditures in Korea is relatively generous, ranking in the upper half of OECD countries (Figure 3.3). As for SMEs, in addition to tax expenditures, Korea is one of ten OECD countries that levy a reduced CIT rate on small firms.

Figure 3.3. **Tax treatment of R&D in Korea is relatively generous**

Rate of tax subsidy for one unit of R&D in 2008[1]

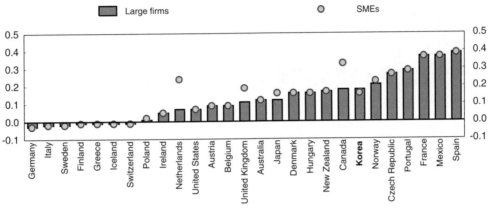

1. For example, the score of 0.18 for large firms in Korea means that 100 won of R&D spending resulted in 18 won of tax relief for them.

Source: OECD (2008c), *Science, Technology and Industry Scoreboard*, OECD, Paris.

StatLink 🔗 http://dx.doi.org/10.1787/513664773833

Promoting economic growth

Statutory corporate tax rates have fallen in the OECD area (Figure 3.4), reflecting a growing recognition that taxes on corporate income distort saving and investment decisions, reducing economic growth. In addition, there has been active competition to lower rates to attract FDI in a world of increasingly mobile capital. Evidence suggests that differences in corporate tax rates affect international flows of capital and profits and the location decisions of firms. For example, an OECD study found that a one percentage-point increase in the effective corporate tax rate reduces the stock of FDI by between 1% and 2% (Hajkova et al., 2006). Another study reported that a one percentage-point cut in the rate can raise the stock of FDI by about 3.3% (de Mooij and Ederveen, 2003). In addition, globalisation has increased opportunities for tax avoidance. International differences in corporate tax rates create incentives for more aggressive use of transfer pricing by multinationals, which shift profits to subsidiaries in countries that have lower tax rates and costs to countries with higher tax rates.[6]

The statutory corporate tax rate in Korea fell from 30.8% (including the local government tax[7]) in 2000 to 27.5% in 2005, a rate close to the OECD average, which itself has declined over time (Figure 3.4). As noted above, the rate is to be cut from 27.5% to 22% by 2010, which would be the third lowest in the OECD. The government's concern is to compete with other Asian countries. For example, the rate is 25% in both China and Taiwan, China, 18% in Singapore and 16.5% in Hong Kong, China.

A further cut in the corporate tax rate may help end the downward trend in business investment – from 26% of GDP in 1996 before the crisis to 19% in 2006. The business sector

Figure 3.4. **International comparison of statutory corporate income tax rates**

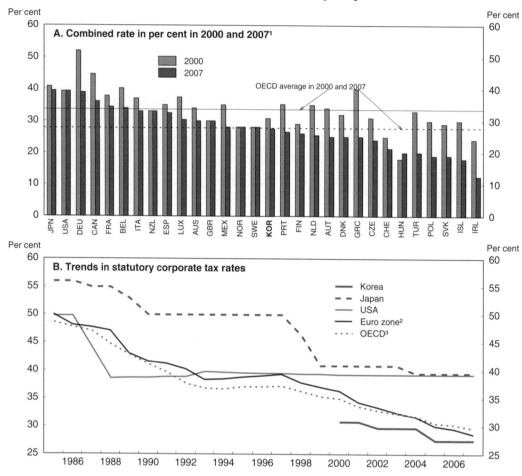

1. Basic combined central and sub-central (statutory) CIT rate. Averages are unweighted.
2. Unweighted mean, excluding Luxembourg.
3. Unweighted mean of 22 OECD countries. It thus differs from the OECD averages shown in Panel A, which include all 30 OECD countries.

Source: OECD (2008d), *Tax Database*, OECD, Paris (*www.oecd.org/ctp/taxdatabase*).

StatLink 🖳 http://dx.doi.org/10.1787/513685232074

argues that, in addition to lower tax rates, their tax burden should be lightened by expanding deductions and credits, depreciation allowances and loss carryovers. However, such an approach would risk complicating the tax code, thereby raising both compliance costs and incentives for tax evasion. Therefore, the reduction in the corporate tax burden should be achieved by cutting the tax rate rather than narrowing the base.

In addition to lowering tax rates, the tax burden on corporations should be cut by phasing out quasi-taxes. The 2001 law on quasi-taxes required that both the authority responsible for the collection of quasi-taxes and the purpose of the revenue be clearly identified and placed restrictions on the creation of new quasi-taxes. While this reform helped keep the number of quasi-taxes constant at around 100, their total amount rose from 1.1% of GDP in 2001 to 1.4% in 2006.[8] Given that quasi-taxes reduce transparency and predictability, they should be phased out.

Ensuring adequate revenue

The CIT should not be considered as a source of additional revenue to meet the spending demands related to population ageing, given that cuts in the tax rate to boost growth may reduce revenue. The government expects the cut in the CIT rate to reduce revenues. Indeed, following the 2005 cut from 29.7% to 27.5%, corporate tax revenue fell by 0.3 percentage point of GDP in 2006.[9] The longer-term impact of the planned CIT cut on total revenue is not clear-cut, however. Its impact is likely to be partially mitigated by positive supply-side effects, as the lower rates crowd in previously unprofitable projects. Indeed, the amount of taxable corporate income tends to be higher in countries with low CIT rates (Figure 3.5) and, consequently, there is almost no correlation between the statutory CIT tax rate and corporate tax receipts as a share of GDP (Panel B). In any case, tax rate cuts should be accompanied by base broadening to limit any revenue loss. Base broadening would also reduce distortions and improve the allocation of capital. Achieving

Figure 3.5. **International comparison of corporate tax rates and tax bases**
Average 2001-07

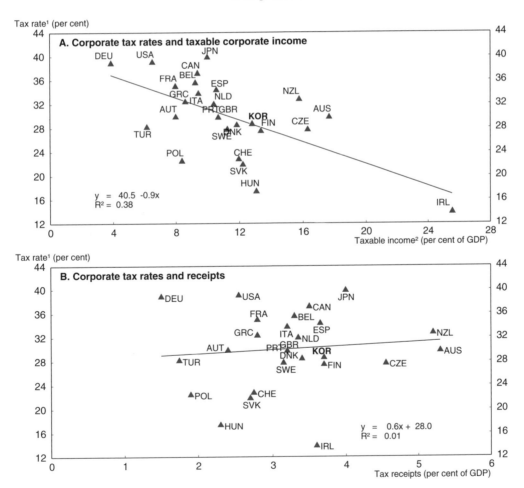

1. Combined central and sub-central statutory CIT rate.
2. Calculated by grossing up corporate tax revenue and dividing by the tax rate.

Source: OECD (2008b), *Revenue Statistics 1965-2007*, OECD, Paris (*http://dx.doi.org/10.1787/366725334503*) and OECD (2008d), *Tax Database*, OECD, Paris (*www.oecd.org/ctp/taxdatabase*).

StatLink ⟶ http://dx.doi.org/10.1787/513685831045

the positive impact of tax cuts on growth depends in part on the efficient allocation of the higher level of investment.

With tax expenditures amounting to one-fifth of corporate tax revenue (Table 3.3), reducing their number and scope would add significantly to the revenue base. The amount of foregone revenue from measures to promote FDI has doubled from 200 billion won in 2002 to 400 billion won in 2006. However, FDI inflows have been on a declining trend since 2004 (on a notification basis), suggesting that tax incentives are not the most important factor in attracting foreign firms. Tax expenditures to promote R&D have been justified on the grounds that without them, investment in R&D would fall short of the socially optimal level, due to spillover effects. However, some countries such as Finland and Sweden, which are front-runners in innovation, do not provide any tax relief for R&D. While tax incentives tend to provide a stronger stimulus for R&D than direct subsidies, their overall impact on innovation appears to be small (Jaumotte and Pain, 2005). Korea should ensure that the benefits of additional R&D spending resulting from tax expenditures outweigh their costs. As for SMEs, they face a CIT rate of only 11%. However, it is uncertain whether the lower tax rate is the best way of addressing the problems facing SMEs. Small firms are less influenced by the corporate tax rate as they tend to have low profitability (Johansson et al., 2008). Moreover, a low tax rate encourages small firms to remain small in order to benefit from the lower tax rate. Compared to preferential rates for SMEs, a lower general corporate tax rate would have a larger impact on productivity. In sum, the special tax rate for SMEs should be phased out.

It is also important to effectively implement recent reforms to control tax expenditures. In particular, strictly applying the sunset clause in the 1998 Special Tax Treatment Law and implementing the 2007 National Fiscal Act would help limit tax expenditures. First, a "PAYGO" principle is applied to requests for additional tax expenditures. This requires that the expected revenue effect of any new tax expenditure be offset by the reduction or elimination of existing tax expenditures. Second, the amount of tax expenditures, as a share of total revenue plus tax expenditures, is not allowed to rise by more than 0.5% from its average over the preceding three years. Third, a tax expenditure budget, containing expenditures for the preceding year and estimates for the current and following year, is to be adopted in 2010. Fourth, the "Tax Expenditure Evaluation Committee", established in 2007, should focus on quantitative assessments of the effectiveness of tax expenditures. In sum, broadening the tax base by reducing tax expenditures would limit the revenue losses from cutting tax rates and make the tax system more efficient and less complicated, thereby promoting growth.

Improving the local tax system

At present, the local CIT is set at 10% of the rate imposed by the central government, currently 25%. With a rate of 2.5%, the local CIT accounts for only 8% of local tax revenue. Given its high volatility in revenue and the large gap in tax bases between jurisdictions, the CIT is not an appropriate source of local government revenue.

Personal income taxation

Overview of the personal income tax

The PIT in Korea is exceptionally low, accounting for only 4.1% of GDP in 2006 (Table 3.1), the fourth lowest in the OECD area. The top rate was cut from 40% in 1999 to 35% in 2005 compared to the OECD average of 43% (Figure 3.6). Moreover, as the top rate only

Figure 3.6. **Top marginal rates and corresponding income threshold**
In 2006

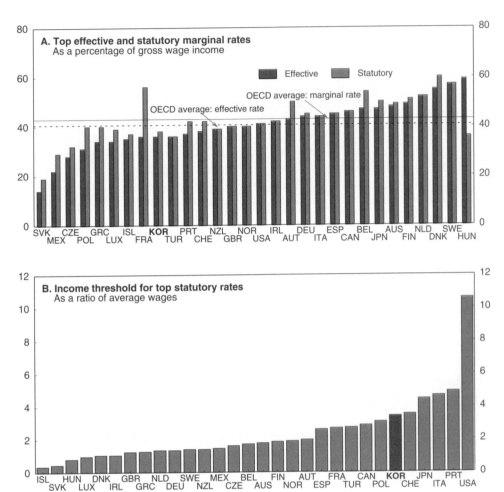

Source: OECD (2008d), *Tax Database*, OECD, Paris (*www.oecd.org/ctp/taxdatabase*).

StatLink 🔗 *http://dx.doi.org/10.1787/513702316402*

applies to incomes exceeding 3.5 times the average wage (Panel B), most taxpayers face much lower rates. In addition, only half of workers pay income tax due to a number of deductions in the PIT system, which accounts for 42.7% of total tax expenditures in Korea (Table 3.2). Most important is the deduction on earned income,[10] which alone accounts for more than half of tax expenditures in the PIT. As a result of the deductions, only half of wage income is subject to tax, the third lowest OECD-wide and well below the average of 84% (Figure 3.7).

Such deductions are intended to create a level playing field between employees and the self-employed, who face a lighter effective tax burden for several reasons. *First*, they are able to split household income among family members, thus circumventing the progressivity of the PIT. *Second*, they can deduct some consumption spending as business expenses, while benefiting from some tax incentives given to corporations. *Third*, the simplified VAT system for small businesses exempts them from keeping detailed books. *Fourth*, weaknesses in enforcement make outright evasion a problem. Comparing national

Figure 3.7. **International comparison of wage income subject to personal income tax**

At the central government level in 2007

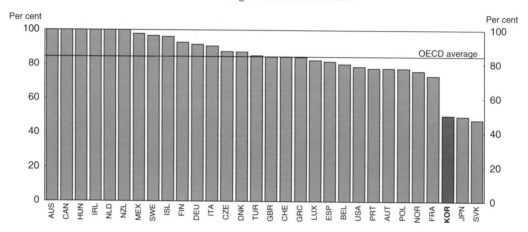

Source: OECD (2007c), *Taxing Wages 2006-2007*, OECD, Paris.

StatLink ᴍᴵᔆᴸ http://dx.doi.org/10.1787/513703585064

income with data from the National Tax Service (NTS) indicates that only about half of self-employed income is reported, compared to more than 80% for wage income (Table 3.4). However, considering that non-taxable incomes are included in national income, reported income of the self-employed is estimated at 60% to 70% of their total taxable income (Sung and Park, 2008). While taxing the self-employed on an equal basis with wage earners is a concern in most OECD countries, the problem is more severe in Korea given that the proportion of self-employed is the fourth highest in the OECD area.

Table 3.4. **Capture ratio of employee and self-employed income**

Trillion won

	2005	2006	Increase rates (%)
National accounts (A)			
Compensation of employees	365.0	384.8	5.4
Self-employed income	79.7	82.5	3.5
Income reported to tax authorities[1](B)			
Employee income	279.4	317.9	13.8
Self-employed and rental income	38.1	42.7	12.0
Income capture ratio (B/A) in per cent			
Employee income[2]	76.5	82.6	6.1
Self-employed and rental income[2]	47.8	51.7	3.9

1. From the National Tax Service's *Annual Report on National Taxes*.
2. The increase shown is in percentage points.
Source: Bank of Korea and National Tax Service.

Given the extensive deductions, the PIT burden for a single individual at average earnings in Korea is less than 5% of gross earnings, the second lowest in the OECD and well below the average of 16% (Figure 3.8). The overall tax wedge, including social security contributions, was only 16% in 2006, again the second lowest among OECD countries (Panel B).[11] Another pro-growth aspect of the PIT system is that it does not discourage second-earner participation in the labour force to any significant degree, as the tax unit is the

Figure 3.8. **Korea has a relatively low tax wedge on labour**

For a single person with no children

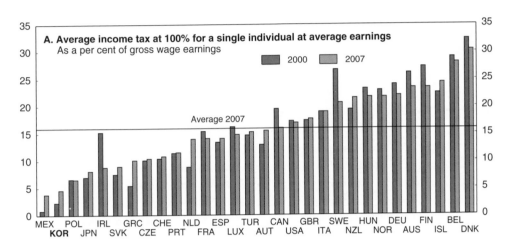

A. Average income tax at 100% for a single individual at average earnings
As a per cent of gross wage earnings

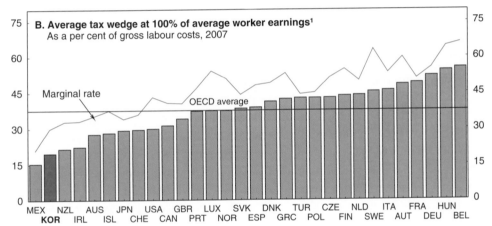

B. Average tax wedge at 100% of average worker earnings[1]
As a per cent of gross labour costs, 2007

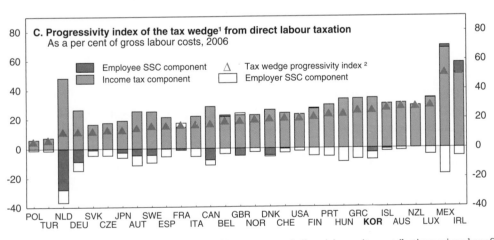

C. Progressivity index of the tax wedge[1] from direct labour taxation
As a per cent of gross labour costs, 2006

1. The average tax wedge is defined as the share of income tax and all social security contributions minus benefits in gross labour costs. Marginal rates are defined as the increase in income tax and all social security contributions minus benefits as a share of the related increase in gross labour costs.
2. The progressivity index of the tax wedge is calculated as (TW167 – TW67)/ TW167, where TW167 and TW67 are the tax wedges for workers at 167% and 67% of the average wage, respectively.

Source: OECD (2008d), Tax Database, OECD, Paris (www.oecd.org/ctp/taxdatabase).

StatLink http://dx.doi.org/10.1787/513760352415

individual rather than the household. In many OECD countries, family taxation tends to discourage the employment of second-earners, typically married women, due to effectively heavier taxation (Jaumotte, 2003). Moreover, the spouse allowance in Korea is relatively low and does not favour non-working spouses. Hence, the low labour force participation rate for women – the fourth lowest in the OECD area (see Chapter 5) – cannot be blamed on the tax system.

In 2008, Korea introduced an earned income tax credit (EITC), an in-work tax credit used in a number of OECD countries, including the United States, the United Kingdom, Denmark, the Netherlands and Sweden. Korea's EITC is initially limited to salaried workers with two or more children, who do not own a home and have assets of less than 100 million won ($68 000). The income ceiling is 17 million won, 70% of the average gross household income and 20% higher than the minimum cost of living for a family of four. The EITC provides 10% of earnings up to 8 million won and is phased out beginning at 12 million won. The government expects that 0.3 million households (1.8% of the total) will receive the EITC in 2009, with total payments of 150 billion won (less than 0.1% of government spending). The main targets are daily workers[12] (2.2 million, 9% of the labour force) and temporary workers (5.2 million, 21%).

Promoting economic growth

Cross-country research by the OECD suggests that taxes on labour, such as the PIT and social security contributions,[13] tend to reduce labour supply and demand, saving and capital investment, thereby reducing potential output growth. According to one study, a 10 percentage-point reduction in the tax wedge on labour (including social security contributions) would boost the employment rate by 3.7 percentage points (OECD, 2006a).[14] Another OECD study found that a one percentage-point increase in the tax wedge on labour income would lower overall employment by 0.25% (Bassanini and Duval, 2006). Taxes on labour can also reduce hours worked, especially for women (Causa, 2008). Korea's low marginal tax rate thus boosts working hours and may help explain the low incidence of part-time work by women at 12.5%, about half of the OECD average. Korea should try to maintain a low tax wedge on labour income, thereby helping to sustain labour input, which is currently the highest in the OECD area in terms of hours worked relative to the population.

The planned reduction in income tax rates, even if PIT revenue were boosted through base broadening, would be positive for economic growth by enhancing entrepreneurship and incentives for FDI and education.[15] An OECD study shows that a five percentage-point decrease in the marginal tax rate leads to a 0.3 percentage-point rise in the graduation rate from tertiary education, thereby boosting economic growth (Oliveira Martins et al., 2007). Another study found that the impact of labour taxes on FDI inflows is substantially larger than that of corporate tax rates (Hajkova et al., 2006). As for entrepreneurship, reductions in top PIT rates have been found to raise productivity in industries with high rates of enterprise creation (Johansson et al., 2008). Finally, a further cut in the top personal rate from the planned 33% in 2010 may help ensure the integrity of the tax system once the national corporate rate falls to 20%, because the wider gap between the two rates may encourage high-income individuals to shelter their income within corporations.

Like many OECD countries, Korea has adopted dual taxation of labour and capital income, with a low uniform rate of 14% on dividend and interest income, an approach that has a number of advantages: i) it reduces any disincentives to save; ii) it helps offset the fact that capital income taxes are applied to the nominal rather than the real return on savings; *iii)* it reduces the incentive for capital owners to move their savings offshore; and *iv)* it reduces the scope for arbitrage between different sources of capital income. However, since 2001, interest and dividend income in excess of 40 million won ($27 000) is subject to "global taxation", *i.e.* it is taxed at the same rate as labour income. The number of affected taxpayers rose from 14 000 in 2001 to 36 000 in 2006 and their tax payments from 0.5% of GDP to 0.8%. The rationale for this threshold is uncertain and leaving it at this level would mean that a growing share of the population will be subject to global taxation.

Changing the favourable tax treatment of the "retirement allowance", which is taxed over a number of years at low rates, would encourage the employment of older workers. Firms are required by law to pay a lump sum of at least one month of wages for each year worked to departing employees. In practice, many firms pay about double that amount. Given that the lump sum is based on an employee's final wage, which rises sharply with seniority, there is a disincentive to keeping older workers. Most firms therefore set a mandatory retirement age that is well below the age of 60 recommended by the government. Indeed, average tenure peaks around 50, much earlier than in other OECD countries. Making more effective use of older workers is important in an ageing economy (see Chapter 5). The retirement allowance, which is actually a separation allowance paid each time a worker changes jobs, also discourages labour mobility, given that it is based on seniority and wages. The reduction in mobility has negative consequences for productivity. In 2005, the government introduced a company pension system, which allows firms to transform the lump-sum retirement allowance into a pension, based on agreement between labour and management. However, by September 2008, less than 9% of firms had adopted a pension system. The government should remove the tax preferences for retirement allowances to promote the employment of older workers, labour mobility and the shift to company pensions.

Ensuring adequate revenue

Boosting PIT revenue from its current low level to offset declines in the CIT resulting from rate cuts would be positive for growth. The key is to further improve tax compliance among the self-employed. The upward trend in the share of PIT revenue in GDP reflects the rise in the proportion of self-employed paying income tax from less than 40% in 1998 to 63% in 2006 (Figure 3.9), as a result of measures to increase transparency about their income. *First*, the scope for special treatment of small businesses under the VAT was scaled back (see below), increasing their bookkeeping obligations. *Second*, the government introduced policies in 2000 to encourage the use of credit cards: 20% of credit card purchases exceeding 20% of wages are deductible up to a maximum of 20% of income. In addition, a lottery using credit card receipts was introduced. Between 1999 and 2002, the number of credit cards jumped from 39 million to 104.8 million (three cards per adult), while the amount of purchases increased by more than six times, accounting for 70.3% of private consumption by 2002 (Table 3.5). Accordingly, the share of sales captured in the VAT net expanded sharply, increasing transparency about the income of small businesses.[16]

Policies to further boost the tax compliance of the self-employed remain a priority. Although there is no simple way to accomplish this task, a package of measures may be effective. *First*, more intensive use of information technology would free up resources to improve enforcement. *Second*, the number of audits should be increased from its relatively low level and the threshold for investigating suspicious transactions should be lowered.

Figure 3.9. **Share of workers paying personal income tax**

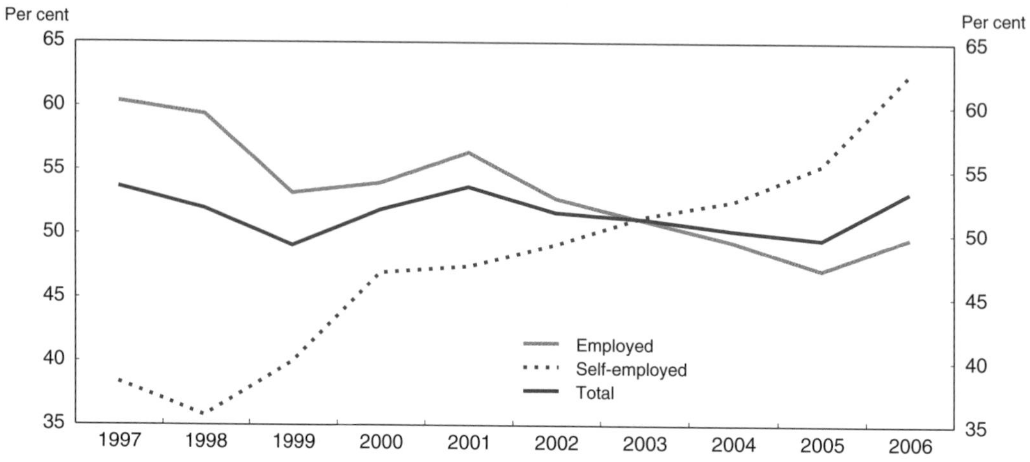

Source: Ministry of Strategy and Finance.

StatLink ⚙ http://dx.doi.org/10.1787/513801611348

Third, penalties for tax evasion should be strengthened. *Fourth*, the self-employed should be required to separate their business accounts from their personal accounts.

In contrast to the self-employed, the share of employees paying PIT declined from 60% in 1997 to 50% in 2006, reflecting the large deductions for wage income, keeping the overall proportion of taxpayers at 53% of workers (Figure 3.9). Given the increasing tax compliance of the self-employed, there is scope to further boost revenues from the PIT by reversing the fall in the share of employees paying taxes. This requires reducing deductions, notably for wage income, which alone amounts to 15% of PIT revenue. Such a decline is appropriate given that the amount of deductions for wage income needed to level the playing field with the self-employed is declining.[17] It should be done by cutting the fixed-amount deduction for each tax bracket so as to not raise marginal tax rates.[18] Raising the share of wages subject to income tax to the OECD average of 84% would boost PIT receipts from employees from 1.5% of GDP to more than 2.5%. Such additional revenue could offset the possible decline in corporate tax revenue in the context of falling CIT rates, as well as the planned cut in the PIT rates. However, using base broadening to finance a cut in the PIT rates would have negative implications for equity.

Table 3.5. **The use of credit cards**[1]

In trillion won

	1998	1999	2000	2002	2004	2005	2006	2007
Number issued (in millions)	42.0	39.0	57.9	104.8	83.4	86.0	90.9	89.6
Amount of sales using credit cards	30.8	42.5	79.9	268.0	229.9	258.2	278.9	312.0
Per cent of private consumption	12.9	15.5	25.6	70.3	57.3	61.2	62.7	63.6

1. Includes only non-bank credit card companies.
Source: Financial Supervisory Service.

Coping with income inequality

Korea's PIT system is relatively progressive: the ratio of the tax wedge for a high-income relative to a low-income worker is high (Figure 3.8, Panel C). However, the narrow income tax base and the small share of PIT receipts in GDP limit its redistributive impact, especially given that tax allowances tend to benefit high-income groups as low-income people are already exempted from income tax. Taxes and social benefits reduce Korea's relative poverty rate by 3 percentage points, compared to an OECD average of 16 points, leaving relative poverty at a high level of 15% (Figure 1.10). Concerns about inequality and poverty led to the introduction of the EITC, which can "make work pay" for low-skilled persons. It can thus help meet distributional objectives without the negative impact on output growth that may result from raising marginal tax rates on high-income earners.

In practice, the effect of an EITC on employment depends on the potentially offsetting income and substitution effects and the increase in marginal tax rates as the subsidy fades out. The impact in terms of increasing total labour supply and decreasing unemployment is greater in countries with a wide earnings distribution, low tax rates on labour and low benefits for the non-employed, such as the United States and the United Kingdom (Bassanini et al., 1999). This suggests that the EITC will also be effective in Korea, as it is similar in many respects (Figure 3.8). Indeed, strict eligibility conditions and the short duration of unemployment benefits reduce the proportion of unemployed receiving benefits to 34%, compared with an OECD average of 92%. Other government transfers are quite limited in Korea. The main social welfare programme, the National Basic Livelihood Security Programme, is limited to just 3% of the population. In sum, the EITC is likely to have a positive effect on aggregate employment and poverty in Korea.[19]

The EITC is starting on a small scale, with initial coverage of 0.3 million households, a small fraction of the 7.4 million daily and temporary workers targeted by the scheme. An expansion of the EITC could be financed by broadening the PIT base, as discussed above. The major challenge to successfully implementing and expanding the EITC is the lack of transparency about the income of daily and temporary workers, who are generally below the threshold for the income tax. The NTS began to require employers to report the income of such workers only in 2006. Given the lack of transparency and the scope for fraud, the introduction of the EITC on a limited basis is appropriate. The authorities will consider in 2014 whether to extend the eligibility of EITC benefits to the self-employed, where the lack of transparency is even more severe. Given that Korea seems well-suited to an EITC, the objective should be to increase transparency about the income of daily and temporary workers and the self-employed so that the EITC can be available to a larger share of the 15% of the population living in relative poverty.

Another way to improve income distribution would be to increases taxes on fringe benefits. At present, many benefits, such as subsidies for employees buying houses or using lodging or cars owned by their employer, are deductible for firms and not taxable for employees. Fringe benefits are a thus a means to avoid taxes. Given that most non-regular workers do not receive fringe benefits, their tax-free treatment tends to worsen income distribution. Taxing such benefits as individual income, giving priority to those that are most important to high-income earners, would thus increase fairness.

Improving the local tax system

A local income tax on individuals is one option for increasing local government autonomy. At present, the local income tax, which is levied at a rate of 10% of the PIT and a fixed per capita payment for individuals (the resident tax), accounts for 7% of local government tax revenue. This share could be increased, either by boosting the per capita levy (collected by the local government), although this would raise inequality, or by hiking the rate on income (collected by the central government). Although local governments are allowed to set the rate between 5% and 15%, it remains at 10% throughout Korea, reflecting their reluctance to diverge from norms set by the central government. Achieving greater revenue autonomy for local governments would require transferring greater spending responsibilities to them, given that many jurisdictions in the capital region are already largely self-sufficient, even though they do not receive the Local Share Tax. Decentralisation would improve the quality of public services in line with local needs. Enhanced local autonomy should be accompanied by increased transfers that are not earmarked to avoid widening regional differences in fiscal capacity.

Consumption taxes

Overview of consumption taxes

The VAT accounted for 16.8% of total tax revenue in 2006, while a number of excises on specific goods and services provided another 15.8% (Table 3.1). The VAT rate has been fixed at 10% since its introduction in 1977 and is well below the OECD average of 18%. The relatively low rate is offset by a broad base, as reflected in the VAT Revenue Ratio (VRR) of 72% in 2005, the fifth highest in the OECD area (Figure 3.10). The combination of a low rate and a broad base is not unusual as a cross-country comparison indicates a negative correlation between the standard VAT rate and the broadness of the base.[20] The scaling back of the preferences for small businesses with annual turnover of less than 150 million won ($102 000) has helped broaden the base. In 1998, nearly 60% of the 2.9 million businesses paying the VAT were granted "special" or "simplified" treatment, allowing them to pay between 2%

Figure 3.10. **Value-added taxes in OECD countries**

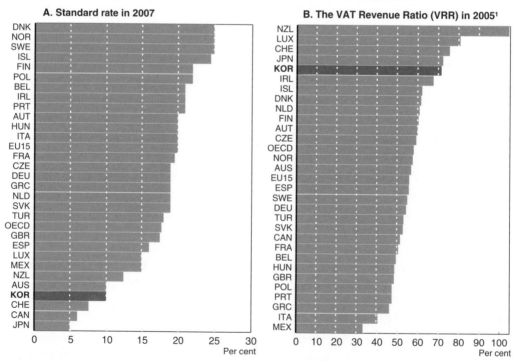

1. VAT Revenue Ratio = (VAT revenue) / [(consumption expenditures – VAT revenue) * standard VAT rate]. The most recent year for which complete data are available is 2005.

Source: OECD (2008a), *Consumption Tax Trends*, OECD, Paris.

StatLink ᠊᠊᠊᠊ http://dx.doi.org/10.1787/513808504238

and 4% of turnover. With the abolition of the special treatment in 2000 and the cut in the ceiling for the simplified scheme to 48 million won, the share of businesses receiving preferential treatment fell to 49% in 2001. It declined further to 38% in 2006,[21] reflecting the increased transparency resulting from greater use of credit cards as well as the unchanged ceiling of 48 million won, which has fallen by a fifth in real terms.

Excises on specific goods and services are relatively large in Korea. Although the number of "individual consumption taxes" was reduced from 27 to 20 in 2004, their revenue remains around 0.6% of GDP. Excises were placed on goods considered to be luxury items[22] in order to offset the regressive impact of the introduction of the VAT on income distribution. Excises are also imposed on six energy products.

Promoting economic growth

A revenue-neutral reform that raised the share of indirect taxes in total tax revenue is likely to boost the level of per capita income, as noted above. Although consumption taxes lower the real after-tax wage and thereby have a negative effect on labour supply, the extent of the distortion is less than for income taxes.[23] Korea's broad base for the VAT is appropriate as it reduces the need for a higher rate. Another advantage is that the VAT is simple and relatively difficult to avoid or evade in Korea.

Ensuring adequate revenue

Consumption taxes should be the primary revenue source to finance increased spending in the future. Given the already broad base, generating additional revenue implies hiking the VAT rate from its relatively low level. In addition, there is still room to generate more revenue by broadening the base,[24] in particular by scaling back the scope of exemptions and limiting the use of the simplified scheme for small businesses. While the scheme alleviates the administrative burden, it distorts competition between firms of different sizes and facilitates tax evasion through a number of channels. First, firms using the special scheme can easily disguise their true turnover as there is no bookkeeping obligation. Second, the absence of bookkeeping also facilitates tax evasion by larger firms that have transactions with businesses using the simplified scheme. The problem extends beyond the VAT as under-reporting of turnover makes it easier for the self-employed to under-report personal income as well. The objective of the simplified scheme should be to reduce administrative burdens on small firms rather than grant them favourable treatment. This requires bringing the value-added ratios used in place of bookkeeping into line with actual value-added. Using new technology to reduce the compliance cost of the standard VAT would reduce the need for a specialised scheme for small businesses.

Coping with income inequality

A shift in the tax structure from income to consumption taxes would reduce the tax system's already low redistributive impact, with negative implications for income equality. The need to eventually boost the VAT rate raises the issue of whether to introduce multiple rates in order to limit the regressive impact of the VAT by exempting or imposing lower rates on food and other necessities. Such an approach is used in some European countries, which have standard VAT rates as high as 25%. However, differentiating VAT rates is not an efficient way to provide assistance to those who need it. High-income households tend to benefit most from lower rates on some items because their level of consumption is higher (OECD, 2008a). In addition, introducing multiple VAT rates has a number of drawbacks.

First, it would entail higher administrative and compliance costs. *Second*, it would provide opportunities for fraud through the misclassification of items. *Third*, it would have to be compensated by a higher standard rate. *Fourth*, it would reduce the neutrality of the VAT, thus distorting consumption decisions and decreasing welfare. In sum, it is important to maintain a single rate (and limit the number of zero-rate products), while addressing income distribution through better-targeted policy tools, such as the EITC.

Consumption taxation should be further improved by simplifying the unnecessarily complex structure of excises. The wide variation in excise rates distorts consumption choices. In particular, the excises on 20 items in the individual consumption tax do not have much impact on the progressivity of the tax system, as some items such as perfume can hardly be considered as luxuries anymore. In any case, using a complicated system of excises is not the most efficient means of achieving equity objectives. Instead, excises should be focused on addressing externalities rather than on raising revenue. This suggests limiting excises to products such as tobacco and liquor for health reasons and to energy for environmental reasons, with the rate based on the size of the externality (Box 3.1), while eliminating the other excises.

Simplifying the system of excises should be accompanied by a phasing-out of earmarked taxes, which accounted for 14% of total tax revenue in 2007. The education tax, for example, is financed by surcharges on tobacco, liquor and the individual consumption tax. Earmarking is used in some countries as a political tool to foster public support for tax increases to cover specific expenditures. It can allow a closer link between those who pay the tax and those who benefit, although the connection between taxpayers and beneficiaries is quite weak in Korea.[25] However, earmarking has a number of disadvantages. *First*, it reduces the flexibility of policymakers to adjust spending as expenditure needs change over time. *Second*, when earmarked revenues exceed the expenditures for which they are targeted, it can be difficult to reallocate the additional funds to other more productive purposes, encouraging excessive spending in the targeted area. *Third*, earmarked taxes significantly increase the complexity of the tax system. *Fourth*, earmarking nurtures vested interests within and outside the government. In sum, reducing earmarking would promote the efficient management of public finances. Given the negative aspects of earmarking, the government has announced a plan to eliminate the three national earmarked taxes (education, local development and transport-energy-environment) in 2010 and integrate them into other taxes.

Improving the local tax system

One proposal to increase local government tax revenue is to create a local VAT with a 2% rate, with an offsetting cut in the national rate to 8%, leaving the overall rate at 10%. The central government would collect the tax and allocate it to local governments based on consumption patterns. Although a local VAT would transfer more revenue to local governments, it would not increase their autonomy. The need for more local government revenue is not pressing at the moment. Indeed, the hike in the Local Share Tax from 15% of national internal taxes to 19.2% has increased local government revenue and reduced their borrowing. If the additional revenue from a local VAT were offset by a reduction in the Local Share Tax, which is allocated so as to reduce regional inequality, it would have adverse implications for equity.

Box 3.1. **Environmentally-related taxes**

Environmentally-related taxes are another way to broaden the tax base, while avoiding the distortions inherent in income taxes and improving welfare. Environmental taxes in Korea have risen to almost 3% of GDP, slightly above the OECD average (Figure 3.11), reflecting a tripling of the tax on diesel between 2001 and 2007. In addition, the proportion of the revenue from the transportation-energy-environment tax that is earmarked for transport infrastructure, primarily roads, was reduced from 86% to 80% in 2007, and 15% was earmarked for environmental improvement.

Figure 3.11. **International comparison of environmentally-related taxes**
Revenue as a per cent of GDP

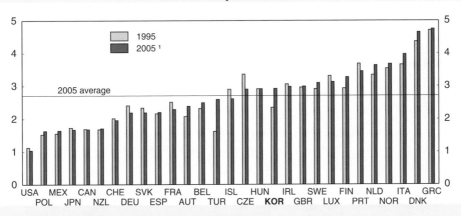

1. 2005 data not available in the case of France and Iceland (2004 data used) and Korea (2003 data).

Source: OECD (2008b), *Revenue Statistics 1965-2007*, OECD, Paris (*http://dx.doi.org/10.1787/366725334503*).

StatLink http://dx.doi.org/10.1787/513854487201

Higher energy taxes have helped slow the growth of energy consumption and reduce air pollution. A comprehensive air quality plan in 2005 for the Seoul metropolitan area targets a further 41% to 47% cut in pollutant emissions by 2014 through several measures. First, for stationary sources, the cut in emissions is to be achieved through a total pollution load management and emission trading ("cap and trade") system introduced in the capital region in 2007 for SOx, NOx and TSP. It was initially applied to large sources and will be extended to mid-sized sources in 2009. Second, a wide range of measures are being implemented to reduce emissions and energy consumption by on-road mobile sources, the major emission source in Seoul. These measures include tighter emission standards, inspections, stronger fuel standards and the use of low-emission vehicles in the public sector.

Greater use of economic instruments to address the externalities of pollution and congestion would allow a liberalisation of the regulations currently used to limit the concentration of population in the Seoul metropolitan region. The construction of large-scale facilities, including factories and universities, is still prohibited or controlled by regulations dating back to the 1960s. Their effectiveness is reduced by a number of exceptions that have been introduced, such as those for SMEs, venture businesses, FDI and advanced-technology firms. Despite the regulations, the capital region's share of the population has risen from 18% in the 1980s to nearly half. Moreover, the regulatory approach to limit concentration has a number of negative side effects. First, the policies are holding back Seoul's international competitiveness. In an increasingly globalised economy, firms that are not allowed to invest in the Seoul region may invest instead in other countries. Second, addressing negative externalities by imposing restrictions on the location of certain economic activities is a costly approach as enterprises that would benefit the most from locating in the capital region are often excluded, while the possibility of obtaining exemptions to restrictions prompts lobbying.

Box 3.1. **Environmentally-related taxes** (cont.)

The taxation of energy should be improved. First, the earmarking of the transportation-energy-environment tax, which is subject to a 2009 sunset clause, should be ended. Allocating 80% of the revenue from energy taxes to the transport sector undermines the effectiveness of those taxes. Second, the tax should be converted to a tax on energy consumption, phasing out exemptions and reductions for energy-intensive sectors and activities. There is considerable scope to increase fuel efficiency. Indeed, the energy-to-GDP ratio in Korea is the sixth highest in the OECD area. However, one concern in Korea is that boosting taxes on energy consumption will reduce the international competitiveness of energy-intensive sectors. Third, the government should not reduce energy taxes to offset the impact of higher oil prices, as it did in March 2008 when the gasoline tax was cut by 10% (the government promised more cuts if the price of oil were to reach $170 per barrel). A 10 trillion won (1% of GDP) package announced in June 2008 included fuel subsidies for truckers, farmers and fishermen. Only by allowing the right price signals to affect demand and supply can better balance be established in these markets. Concern about the living standards of low-income households is better addressed through taxes and social transfers. The June 2008 package is to provide such assistance through income tax rebates, although more than one-half of workers are eligible for rebates.

Another challenge is to reduce the level of greenhouse gas emissions. Korea, which was classified as a developing country in the 1997 Kyoto Protocol and thus exempted from mandatory cuts, is the world's tenth-largest source of greenhouse gas emissions, as its emissions almost doubled between 1990 and 2005. The Environment Ministry announced in March 2008 that it would seek to cap emissions at the 2005 level by 2012 by encouraging the use of environment-friendly vehicles and fuels, and staging nationwide energy-saving campaigns. The official reduction target, though, has not yet been set. To cut emissions, the government is considering the introduction of tax benefits for investment in emission reduction and a carbon tax, which taxes the combustion of fossil fuels according to their carbon content. A number of OECD countries, including the United Kingdom and the Netherlands, have introduced instruments that have elements of a carbon tax. Higher taxes on greenhouse gas-emitting activities would also provide scope for reducing more distortive taxes on income.[*]

[*] Carbon taxes may need to be accompanied by permit trading. Both approaches have their pros and cons. A permit system gives certainty about emissions at the price of uncertainty about the costs, whereas a tax has the opposite effect. Taxes may entail smaller administrative costs and could be technically easier to implement in developing countries, but tradable permits build up a stronger political constituency (permit holders) with an interest in enforcing the policy in the future.

Property taxes

Overview of property taxes

Property-related taxes are high in Korea, at 3.5% of GDP in 2006 compared with an OECD average of 2.0%. However, their prominent role is primarily due to taxes on transactions – 2.4% of GDP, the highest in the OECD area – which hamper mobility by creating lock-in effects. The government reduced property transaction taxes by cutting the rate on acquisitions from 2.2% in 2004 to 1.1% in 2007 and the rate on registrations from 3.6% to 1.2%.[26] As for capital gains, single homeowners are not taxed on the sale of houses owned at least three years and valued at less than 600 million won ($409 000). As a result, less than 2% of households are subject to capital gains taxes. The thresholds are similar to those of the PIT while the tax rates are one percentage point higher. However, a uniform rate of 40% is applied to property held between one and two years, and 50% for that held less than one year (Table 3.6). In recent years, the government has strengthened

Table 3.6. **Recent changes in the capital gains tax on property**

Situation	Tax rates through end-2006	Tax rates from 2007	Tax rates from 2010
Normal tax rates[1]	9% to 36% depending on the size of the gain	No change	6% to 33% depending on the size of the gain
Owned less than 1 year	50%	No change	No change
Owned 1 to 2 years	40%	No change	No change
Unregistered property	70%	No change	No change
Households owning 3 or more houses[2]	60%	No change	No change
Households owning 2 houses[2]	Normal tax rate (9-36%)	50%	No change
Land held for non-business purposes	Normal tax rate (9-36%)	60%	No change

1. Applies to households with one house with a selling price of more than 600 million won (about $409 000), which accounts for 2-3% of total houses in Korea. The threshold is to be raised to 900 million won in 2010. The taxable gain is calculated as: [(S − 600 million)/S] *(S − P), where S is the selling price and P is the purchase price. Thus, if the selling price were 1.8 billion won and the purchase price were 1 billion won, the taxable gain would be 0.53 billion won.
2. In addition, the special deduction in the capital gains tax for long-term ownership, which can go as high as 30%, was eliminated for multiple homeowners in 2007.

Source: Ministry of Strategy and Finance.

capital gains taxes as part of its effort to stabilise housing prices and increase income redistribution. *First*, actual sales prices are used to calculate capital gains,[27] rather than the value assessed by the National Tax Service, which is 50% to 70% of the market value. *Second*, the government has focused higher capital gains taxes on persons who own more than one dwelling. A rate of 50% was imposed in 2007 on persons with two houses and a rate of 60% on those owning three or more.[28]

In contrast to transaction taxes, taxes on property holding were much lower at 0.5% of GDP in 2005. However, there was a major overhaul of property taxes that year. The local taxes on structures (six rates between 0.3% and 7%) and on land (nine rates between 0.2% and 5%) were combined. The new local tax on property has three rates, ranging from 0.15% to 0.5% (Table 3.7). In addition, the evaluation of real estate values for tax purposes was brought closer into line with market values. The evaluation was raised from 36% (the so-called "application ratio") of the value of the house as assessed by the Ministry of

Table 3.7. **Property holding taxes in Korea**

	Local property tax			National Comprehensive Property Tax[1]		
	Housing	Land for business	Land for non-business	Housing	Land for business	Land for non-business
Asset value threshold (won)	0	0	0	600 million (900 million)	4 billion (8 billion)	300 million (500 million)
Calculation of tax base	Per property	Cumulative value per person	Cumulative value per person	Nationwide cumulative value per household	Nationwide cumulative value per person	Nationwide cumulative value per household
Tax rates[2]	0.15-0.5%	0.2-0.4%	0.2-0.5%	1-3% (0.5-1.0%)	0.6-1.6% (0.5-0.7%)	1-4% (0.75-2%)
Ceiling on increase in tax payment[3]	105 to 150%	150%	150%	300% (150%)	150%	300% (150%)
Application ratio[4]	50%	60%	60%	80%	60%	80%

1. Changes announced in September 2008 are shown in parentheses.
2. There are three tax rates for each category except the Comprehensive Property Tax on housing, which has four.
3. Relative to the preceding year.
4. The proportion of the value assessed by the Ministry of Construction and Transport that is used as the tax base.

Source: Ministry of Strategy and Finance.

Construction and Transportation (MCT) to 50%. Given that the MCT's assessed value is about 80-90% of the market price, the tax base has risen from about 29-32% of the market value to 40-45%.

The changes in the local property tax were accompanied by the introduction in 2005 of the CPT, a national tax applied to households and firms owning housing with a combined assessed value exceeding 900 million won. The threshold was subsequently reduced to 600 million won. In 2006, 1.3% of households were subject to this tax, whose revenues are transferred to local governments to reduce regional inequalities, based on a formula that gives an 80% weight to their fiscal needs. The CPT is very progressive with rates from 1% to 3%. Its top rate is thus 20 times higher than the lowest rate of local property tax on households, which is set at 0.15%. Thus, the burden on CPT-payers is very heavy, even though the overall burden of property-holding tax is rather low in Korea. In contrast, most OECD countries impose a flat rate, or moderately progressive rates, on property holding.

Promoting economic growth

A tax on property holding is more favourable for growth than other taxes as it has less impact on decisions to supply labour, produce, invest and innovate (Johansson *et al.*, 2008). Increasing the share of property tax in the overall tax mix would reduce the need for other more distorting taxes, in addition to promoting the efficient use of land. However, the introduction of the CPT proved problematic for a number of reasons (see below). Higher holding taxes should be accompanied by a reduction in transaction taxes. The planned reform of the capital gains tax in 2010 – by raising the threshold for single homeowners to 900 million won ($613 000) and bringing the rates into line with the PIT – is a positive step in this regard as it will reduce the lock-in effect that blocks the supply of houses (Kim, 2005). Indeed, the low level of property transactions during the past year appears to be partly related to the increased taxation of capital gains introduced in 2006-07.

Ensuring adequate revenue

Following the changes in the valuation of real estate for the local property tax and the introduction of the CPT, the total tax on holding property rose to 0.8% of GDP in 2006. It is still well below the OECD (weighted) average of almost 2% (Figure 3.12), indicating scope to further increase property taxes toward the levels in the most advanced countries in order to meet future revenue needs. A higher effective rate should be achieved by gradually raising the overall holding tax, rather than through the CPT, which led to a sudden increase on a small group of taxpayers. Moreover, the CPT was aimed at controlling short-term fluctuations in housing prices and redistributing income (*OECD Economic Surveys: Korea*, 2007). Property taxes should instead be based on a long-term perspective of efficiency considerations and government revenue needs. Given that housing prices are determined by many factors, including macroeconomic conditions and regulations, using tax policy to influence house prices in the short run is unlikely to be successful and will result in a sub-optimal tax policy.

The government's plan to revise the CPT by reducing the rates to 0.5% to 1%, raising the threshold for paying the tax to 900 million won and freezing the "application ratio" is thus appropriate[29] and should allow an increase in property-holding taxes in the medium term. As with the highly progressive rate structure of local property taxes in the past, the CPT makes it difficult to raise the average tax on holding property from its relatively low

Figure 3.12. **International comparison of taxes on immovable property**

As a per cent of GDP in 2006

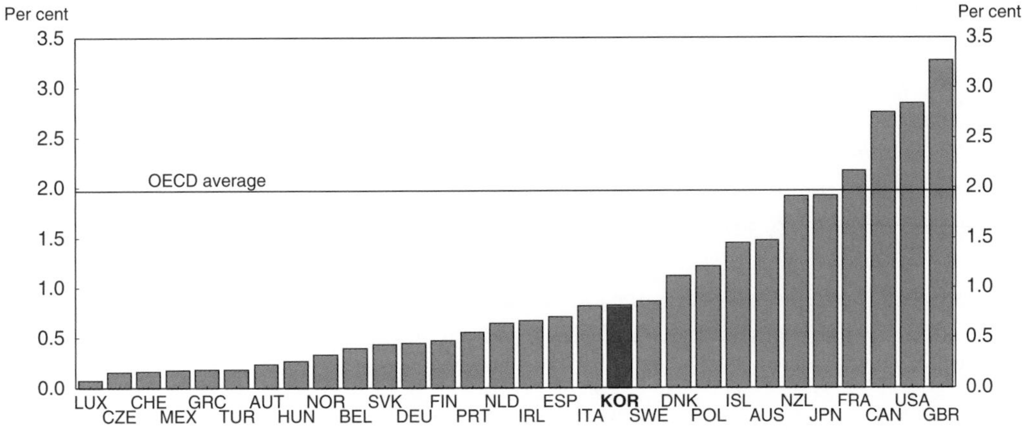

Source: OECD (2008b), *Revenue Statistics 1965-2007*, OECD, Paris (*http://dx.doi.org/10.1787/366725334503*).

StatLink ⟶ *http://dx.doi.org/10.1787/513857080702*

level. Moreover, given that income redistribution is not the role of local governments, they avoided relying on the highly progressive local property tax as a revenue source, limiting it to only 8% of their revenue. The introduction of the CPT in 2005 continues to limit the scope for local authorities to raise the local property tax.

Coping with income inequality

Although recent changes in property taxation are aimed at improving income equality, they raise several problems. Regarding capital gains, the wide variation in tax rates applied to gains of similar size creates equity issues. For example, the owner of five or more dwellings can be treated as a rental business and subject to tax rates ranging from 9% to 36%, while the owner of three or four dwellings pays 60%. The tax should be based on the size of the capital gain rather than on the number of houses owned (Kim, 2007). As for property holding taxes, the emphasis on redistribution conflicts with the benefit principle, which states that local taxes should reflect the use of local public services rather than the ability to pay. Moreover, relying on real estate taxes for redistribution is inappropriate as it does not include other forms of wealth. Consequently, persons holding real estate are taxed more heavily than those who invested in other assets. While housing ownership in Korea does increase with income, the relationship between household income and housing wealth is not strong, thus reducing the effectiveness of property tax in reducing income inequality (Sung and Kim, 2008 and Ro, 2007).

Improving the local tax system

Providing local governments with sufficient revenue-raising autonomy to make them accountable to local citizens and encourage fiscal discipline is important to improve efficiency and welfare. As noted above, there are drawbacks to using direct taxes and consumption taxes to finance local governments in Korea. In contrast, a tax on property holding has a number of desirable properties: it is visible, imposes discipline on local authorities and is relatively resistant to tax-base flight. In most OECD countries, property tax is a purely local tax, reflecting its advantages as a source of finance for local governments. However, the use of a national property holding tax in Korea limits the scope for using local property taxes and increasing the autonomy of local governments. Moreover, imposing both national and local taxes on property holding is a possible source of confusion. The government's planned revision of the CPT should be a first step toward phasing it out over the medium term and thereby allowing a larger role for local property taxes.

One rationale for introducing a national property tax was the tendency of some revenue-rich local governments to cut their local property tax rates, thereby undermining the central government's objective of raising the effective tax rate on property. Such an outcome reflects the increasing revenue of local governments in the capital region, which has half of the country's population, and their lack of spending responsibilities. Indeed, major services such as education and police services are funded primarily by the central government. The objective of raising the effective rate of property tax is thus linked to the issue of fiscal decentralisation and the need for a greater local government role in providing public services.

Improving the administration of the tax and social insurance systems

Upgrading the management of tax and social insurance contributions is important to expand the coverage of the social safety net and reduce the cost of compliance. Korea's social security system has developed gradually with the introduction of insurance for industrial accidents (1964), medical care (1977), pensions (1988), employment (1995) and long-term care (2008). Each insurance system has evolved independently, with a lack of close co-ordination with the other systems, especially in terms of collecting contributions. The collection processes differed in terms of the definition of the wage base, the payment intervals, end-year adjustments, employer ID codes and other features.[30] Separate collection has been administratively costly for the government, while differences in the base and timing have prevented the sharing of information and cross-checks between the different systems.

These problems have contributed to low insurance coverage, particularly for non-regular workers and employees at small firms. While three-quarters of regular workers were covered by pension and medical insurance at their workplace in 2005 and two-thirds by employment insurance, the share was only around 40% for non-regular workers (Table 3.8). At small firms, only a quarter of regular workers and less than 10% of non-regular workers were covered. With existing manpower, the social insurance systems and the NTS do not have the capacity to enforce compliance by non-regular workers and small firms. Low levels of compliance hinder the capacity of the social insurance schemes to achieve their intended goals. For example, the gaps in the coverage of employment insurance help to explain why only one-third of unemployed persons receive benefits. Moreover, lower social insurance contributions encourage firms to hire non-regular workers, who now account for more than one-third of employment (see Chapter 5).

A number of reforms were introduced in 2005. *First*, the wage bases of all contribution schemes were aligned on taxable income, which firms are required to report to the tax authorities each year, thus reducing the cost of verifying income. *Second*, contributions are based on the previous year's income and the contribution amount is calculated by the insurers. *Third*, a common system of ID codes for workplaces was developed. In addition, the NTS now requires firms to report the payroll of temporarily employed and contingent employees. Legislation to create a single agency in 2009 for the collection of social insurance payments, under the direction of the NTS, failed to pass the National Assembly,

Table 3.8. **Coverage of the social insurance systems by type of worker**[1]

	2003	2004	2005	2006	2007
Regular workers (per cent of total)					
National pension	70.8	72.5	75.7	76.1	76.3
National health insurance	72.5	73.8	75.9	76.1	76.7
Employment insurance	59.7	61.5	63.8	64.7	64.3
Non-regular workers (per cent of total)					
National pension	30.5	37.5	36.6	38.2	40.0
National health insurance	32.6	40.1	37.7	40.0	42.5
Employment insurance	29.2	36.1	34.5	36.3	39.2

1. This survey-based data does not match the records of the social insurance systems. For example, while the number of workers covered by the EIS based on the survey is around 8 million, the Ministry of Labour reported that more than 9 million were covered in 2007.

Source: Korea National Statistics Office, "Supplementary Survey on Economically Active Population".

in part due to opposition from SMEs who feared that it would substantially increase their payments. The creation of a unified collection agency is a necessary condition to significantly expand the coverage of social insurance.

This would also ease compliance costs for firms. According to a study by the World Bank, complying with labour taxes, including social security contributions, requires 120 hours a year for firms in Korea, more than triple the OECD average (Figure 3.13). The time needed for corporate income taxes is also about three times higher than the OECD average. Although the time necessary to comply with the VAT is relatively low, the total for the three taxes sums to 270 hours per year, almost double the OECD average. Simplifying the tax system is thus an important objective on efficiency grounds. In addition, it would weaken the incentive for tax planning, which imposes deadweight losses.

Figure 3.13. **Simplicity of tax systems**

Hours required to comply with tax obligations, 2006

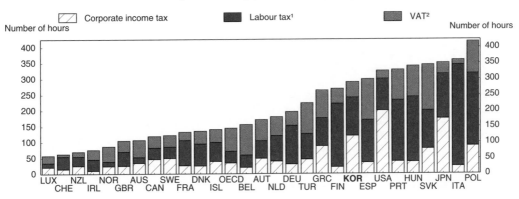

1. Including social security contributions.
2. Including consumption taxes.

Source: The World Bank (2008), *Paying Taxes 2008*.

StatLink http://dx.doi.org/10.1787/514002462373

Directions for tax reform

Korea's immediate challenge is to improve its tax system and tax administration to sustain economic growth while achieving distributional objectives and increasing the gains from decentralisation. Such reforms will make it easier to meet the second challenge of upward pressure on public spending in the context of rapid population ageing. Specific recommendations are reported in Table 3.9. From a political economy perspective, fundamental tax reform is never easy. In Korea, there has been stiff resistance to higher tax and contribution rates. For example, to ensure the financial sustainability of the National Pension Scheme, the government proposed in 2003 to raise the contribution rate from 9% to 15.9% by 2030, while cutting the replacement rate from 60% to 50%. However, this reform was rejected in favour of leaving the contribution rate at 9% and cutting the replacement rate to 40%. This reform did not ensure long-run financial sustainability, which would require a contribution rate of 12.9%, or an even larger cut in the replacement rate.

Among the reforms proposed in this chapter, the recommendation to lower the corporate tax rate while broadening the PIT base may be unpopular. It is important to note that the CIT is borne not only by shareholders, but also by workers through reduced wages and lower employment, suggesting that a cut in the corporate rate would boost household income. Indeed, a study of the United Kingdom found that workers bear about half of the corporate tax burden in the short run and all of it in the long run (Arulampalam *et al.*, 2007).

Table 3.9. **Summary of recommendations for tax reform**

	Promoting growth	Raising revenue	Reducing inequality	Improving the local government tax system
Corporate income tax	• Lower the statutory tax rate on firms to promote Korea's international competitiveness. • Reduce the share of corporate taxes in total direct taxes. • Phase out quasi-taxes.	• Broaden the tax base by reducing tax expenditures.		• Avoid reliance of local governments on corporate taxes given their volatility and the large gap between jurisdictions.
Personal income tax	• Increase the share of personal income tax in total direct taxes. • Reduce the preferential treatment of retirement allowances. • Cut tax rates to promote FDI, entrepreneurship and education .	• Broaden the personal income tax base. • Further increase compliance of the self-employed by improving enforcement and hiking penalties for tax evasion.	• Expand the earned income tax credit introduced in 2008 • Increase the taxation of fringe benefits.	• Encourage local governments to use their existing authority to change local income tax rates to increase local government revenue and autonomy.
Value-added tax and other consumption taxes	• Rely on the VAT for increased revenue and reduce the share from more distortive taxes. • Maintain a unified VAT rate and a broad base to limit distortions. • Phase out individual consumption taxes unless they are justified by health or environmental concerns. • Phase out earmarked taxes.	• Raise the VAT rate. • Further broaden the base by reducing special treatment of SMEs. • Strengthen environmentally-related taxes.	• Avoid lower VAT rates on daily necessities as these tend to benefit higher-income persons.	• Avoid a local VAT as it would widen the gap in fiscal capacity between regions while failing to enhance local government autonomy.
Property taxes	• Increase local property holding taxes, thereby reducing reliance on more distortive taxes and promoting efficient land use. • Further reduce taxes on transactions to promote mobility and reduce lock-in effects.	• Increase local taxes on property holding, thus offsetting declining revenue from transaction taxes.	• Base the capital gains tax on the size of the gain rather than the number of houses owned.	• Increase the scope for local property holding taxes by phasing out the CPT over the medium term.

Implementing a comprehensive tax reform requires clear communication of the plan and its objectives, based on transparent and well-articulated principles, so that taxpayers understand what the government is trying to achieve. This should include the following points:

● The authorities should demonstrate their commitment to improving the efficiency of spending before asking the public to pay higher taxes. The plan to privatise some state-owned enterprises and increase the efficiency of public organisations (see Chapter 2) is useful in this regard.

● It is important to recognise that the tax burden in Korea is one of the lowest in the OECD area due to its relatively low level of income per capita and young population. As Korea's income level converges to the OECD average and as rapid population ageing makes it one of the oldest countries in the OECD, it will be difficult to maintain such a low share of taxes in GDP.

● The reform must be fair to the extent possible across different segments of the population. In particular, it is essential that the broadening of the tax base also includes the self-employed, thus avoiding an unfair burden on salaried workers.

● Nearly all OECD countries have launched substantial tax reforms in recent years, driven by the need to provide a fiscal environment that is more conducive to investment, risk-taking and work incentives (OECD, 2004). While Korea's tax system has many pro-growth features, it is important to avoid falling behind in an increasingly integrated and competitive world economy.

● The proposed tax reform should address emerging concerns about inequality primarily by expanding the EITC. Such an approach would avoid increasing the rates of the personal income tax, which tends to discourage human capital formation and labour supply.

Notes

1. The ten internal taxes include the income tax, corporation tax, inheritance tax, gift tax, Comprehensive Property Tax, VAT, individual consumption tax, liquor tax, stamp tax and securities transaction tax.

2. These earmarked taxes accounted for 12% of central government tax revenue in 2007. The education tax, a surtax on four other taxes, provides revenue for the education special account. The special tax for local development, a surcharge on a number of national and local taxes, funds programmes to enhance the competitiveness of agriculture and fishing. The transportation-energy-environment tax, an excise on gasoline and diesel, is earmarked to transport infrastructure (80%), the environment (15%), energy (3%) and regional development (2%).

3. Agriculture income is taxed only at the local government level and at very low effective rates. In the FY 2007 budget, such revenue was expected to be zero.

4. Excluding the local education tax, which in practice is controlled by the central government, would reduce the share of earmarked taxes to 9% (and raise the share for the central government to 15%).

5. The proportion of firms paying corporate taxes has remained steady at around two-thirds since 2000.

6. Such transfers are facilitated by the increasing proportion of intangible assets, such as patents, in corporate assets. Indeed, intangible assets account for 75% of the total net assets of Fortune 500 companies, making it easier to relocate activities and tax bases around the world.

7. The local government tax is set at 10% of the central government rate. Thus, the overall rate of 30.8% in 2000 was the sum of the 28% central government rate and a 2.8% local government rate. At present, the rates are 25% and 2.5%, respectively.

8. Other estimates of quasi-taxes are higher. An economist at the Korea Economic Research Institute (affiliated with the Federation of Korea Industries) estimated quasi-taxes at 2.6% of GDP in 2005 (Kim, 2007). An economist at the Korea Institute of Public Finance (affiliated with the government) estimated them at between 2.3% and 3.2% of GDP in 2003, well above the government estimate of 1.4%.

9. According to one international study, the revenue-maximising corporate tax rate is around 28% (Mintz, 2007).

10. All wage income up to 5 million won (23% of the average wage) is exempted. For wages from:
    - 5 to 15 million won: the deduction is 5 million won plus half of wages exceeding 5 million won.
    - 15 to 30 million won: the deduction is 10 million won plus 15% of wages exceeding 15 million won.
    - 30 to 45 million won: the deduction is 12.25 million won, plus 10% of wages exceeding 30 million won.
    - Beyond 45 million won, the deduction is 13.75 million won plus 5% of wages exceeding 45 million won.

11. The OECD Tax/Benefits model indicates that the average effective tax rate for a transition to full-time work in Korea for persons receiving no unemployment benefits is 10% to enter work at average earnings. This is the lowest in the OECD area, where the average is 35%.

12. Daily workers are those with contracts of less than one month. About 70% are construction workers.

13. It has been argued that social security contributions have a smaller impact on labour supply than taxes because they are linked to the social benefits that workers receive later. In Korea, there is only a loose relationship between the contributions paid and the amount of benefits that will be received. First, the pension benefit depends equally on the average wage in the economy and the individual's wage. Second, frequent changes in the pension system have weakened the link between contributions and benefits.

14. The tax wedge measures the difference between total labour compensation paid by the employer and the net take-home pay of employees, as a per cent of total labour compensation.

15. Base broadening, primarily through reducing the deduction for wage income, would primarily impact the 50% of employees who do not pay income tax.

16. However, the expanded use of credit cards led to an epidemic of credit delinquency in the household sector and financial-sector problems (see the 2004 OECD Economic Surveys: Korea).

17. There is some debate about what constitutes a level playing field. While some argue that the self-employed should face a lower tax burden as they face greater risks, a higher tax burden would encourage the shift toward formal employment and would compensate employees for job-related costs.

18. At a minimum, it should be frozen in nominal terms.

19. There is a growing body of evidence in OECD countries suggesting that an EITC has a positive effect on aggregate employment (OECD, 2004b). However, there are potential negative effects as well,

such as the decline in working hours resulting from the withdrawal of the credit as income rises and the weakened incentives for human capital formation.

20. The negative correlation may reflect several factors. *First*, countries with a high standard VAT rate tend to narrow the base by applying a reduced rate to many products, owing to equity concerns. *Second*, high VAT rates encourage tax evasion.

21. These proportions exclude businesses with less than 24 million won, which are exempted from the VAT.

22. At present, the individual consumption tax covers perfume, jewellery, precious metals, luxury cameras, watches, fur, carpets and furniture, cars of more than 1 000 cc, slot machines, casinos, racetracks, hunting guns, deer antlers, royal jellies, bars and golf club memberships.

23. Consumption taxes are less efficient than property taxes. However, property taxes are better suited to local authorities. In addition, as they are particularly unpopular, few countries manage to raise substantial revenues from property taxes (Johansson *et al.*, 2008).

24. Broadening the tax base is the best way to generate more VAT revenue as this approach increases efficiency, while raising the rate tends to encourage tax avoidance and the growth of the shadow economy.

25. For example, the link between taxes on tobacco and liquor and education spending is not obvious.

26. The combined rate has thus fallen from 5.8% to 2.3% for transactions between individuals. For other transactions, the combined rate is 4.6% (2.2% for the acquisition tax and 2.4% for the registration tax).

27. The use of the actual sales price was introduced for houses valued at more than 600 million won in 1999, households owning three or more houses in 2004 and households owning two or more houses in 2006.

28. The 50% rate was introduced in 2007 and the 60% rate in 2005. A normal tax rate of 8% to 35% is applied to those who rent five or more houses if: i) they are all located in the same city or county; ii) they have been rented at least ten years; iii) the size of each rented house is 85 square metres or less; and iv) the value of each rented house does not exceed 300 million won (as assessed by the government) at the time of sale.

29. In addition, the Supreme Court ruled in November 2008 that some aspects of the CPT are unconstitutional.

30. The Ministry of Health and Welfare administers health, long-term care and pension insurance, while the Ministry of Labour manages the industrial accident insurance and the Employment Insurance System. The medical insurance contribution is based on the "standard monthly income", the pension contribution on the "standard monthly wage" and industrial accident and employment insurance contributions on total wages.

Bibliography

Arulampalam, W., M. Devereux and G. Maffini (2007), "The Incidence of Corporate Income Tax on Wages", *Oxford University Centre for Business Taxation Working Paper*, No. 07/07, Oxford.

Bassanini, A. and R. Duval (2006), "The Determinants of Unemployment Across OECD Countries: Reassessing the Role of Policies and Institutions", *OECD Economic Studies*, No. 42, OECD, Paris.

Bassanini, A., J. Rasmussen and S. Scarpetta (1999), "*The Economic Effects of Employment-Conditional Income Support Schemes for the Low-Paid: An Illustration from a CGE Model Applied to Four OECD Countries*", *OECD Economics Department Working Paper*, No. 224, OECD, Paris.

Bassanini, A. and S. Scarpetta (2001), "The Driving Forces of Economic Growth: Panel Data Evidence for the OECD Countries", *OECD Economic Studies*, No. 33, OECD, Paris.

Causa, O. (2008), "Explaining Differences in Hours Worked Among OECD Countries: An Empirical Analysis", *OECD Economics Department Working Paper*, No. 596, OECD, Paris.

De Mooij, R. and S. Ederveen (2003), "Taxation and Foreign Direct Investment: A Synthesis of Empirical Research", *International Tax and Public Finance*, No. 10.

European Commission (2006), *Structures of the Taxation Systems in the European Union*, Brussels.

Hajkova, D., G. Nicoletti, L. Vartia and K. Yoo (2006), "Taxation, Business Environment and FDI Location in OECD Countries", *OECD Economics Department Working Paper*, No. 502, OECD, Paris.

Jaumotte, F. (2003), "Labour Force Participation of Women: Empirical Evidence on the Role of Policy and Other Determinants in OECD Countries", *OECD Economic Studies*, No. 37, OECD, Paris.

Jaumotte, F. and N. Pain (2005), "Innovation in the Business Sector", *OECD Economics Department Working Paper*, No. 459, OECD, Paris.

Johansson, Å., C. Heady, J. Arnold, B. Brys and L. Vartia (2008), "Tax end Economic Growth", *OECD Economics Department Working Paper*, No. 620, OECD, Paris.

Kim, Junghun (2005), "Tax Reform Issues in Korea", *Journal of Asian Economics*, Vol. 16.

Kim, Kyung Hwan (2007), "On Reforming the Taxation of Housing in Korea", *Research on Expert Assessment*, Vol. 17, No. 2, Korea Real Estate Research Institute, Seoul (in Korean).

KRILA (Korea Research Institute for Local Administration) (2007), *Local Government in Korea*, Seoul.

Mintz, J. (2007), *2007 Tax Competitiveness Report*, C.D. Howe Institute, Toronto, Canada.

OECD (2003), *OECD Employment Outlook*, OECD, Paris.

OECD (2004), "Recent Tax Policy Trends and Reforms in OECD Countries", *OECD Tax Policy Studies*, No. 9, OECD, Paris.

OECD (2005a), *OECD Economic Surveys: Korea*, OECD, Paris.

OECD (2005b), *OECD Territorial Reviews: Busan, Korea*, OECD, Paris.

OECD (2006a), *OECD Employment Outlook*, OECD, Paris.

OECD (2006b), *OECD Environmental Performance Reviews: Korea*, OECD, Paris.

OECD (2006c), "Fundamental Reform of Personal Income Tax", *OECD Tax Policy Studies*, No. 13, OECD, Paris.

OECD (2007a), *OECD Economic Surveys: Korea*, OECD, Paris.

OECD (2007b), *OECD Employment Outlook*, OECD, Paris.

OECD (2007c), *Taxing Wages 2006/2007*, OECD, Paris.

OECD (2008a), *Consumption Tax Trends*, OECD, Paris.

OECD (2008b), *Revenue Statistics*, OECD, Paris (*http://dx.doi.org/10.1787/366725334503*).

OECD (2008c), *Science, Technology and Industry Scoreboard*, OECD, Paris.

OECD (2008d), *Tax Database*, OECD, Paris (*www.oecd.org/ctp/taxdatabase*).

Oliveira Martins, J., R. Boarini, H. Strauss, C. de la Maisonneuve and C. Saadi (2007), "The Policy Determinants of Investment in Tertiary Education", *OECD Economics Department Working Paper*, No. 576, OECD, Paris.

Ro, Younghoon (2007), *The Real Estate Market and Real Estate Tax Policy*, Korea Institute of Public Finance, Seoul (in Korean).

Sung, Myung Jae and Hyunsook Kim (2008), "Estimation of Joint Distribution of Income and Real Assets and Related Tax Burdens" (in Korean).

Sung, Myung Jae and Ki Baek Park (2008), "Redistributive Effects of Taxes and Transfers Including Consumption Taxes and In-kind Benefits", *Research on Fiscal Studies*, Vol. 56, February (in Korean).

World Bank (2008), *Paying Taxes 2008; The Global Picture*, Washington, D.C.

Yeo, Y., M. Kim, T. Kim, S. Yang and H. Choi (2005), *An Analysis of Trends and Contributing Factors for Poverty and Inequality*, Korea Institute of Health and Social Affairs, Seoul.

ANNEX 3.A1

Recent progress in tax reform in Korea:
A follow-up of the 2000 OECD Economic Surveys: Korea

The 2000 *OECD Economic Surveys: Korea* focused on taxation, pointing out a number of problems in the tax system and calling for comprehensive reform. Despite some progress since then, many of the problems identified in 2000 remain unresolved. The major recommendations in the 2000 *Survey* included:

i) *The PIT base should be broadened by reducing allowances and credits as well as improving the taxation of fringe benefits.* Tax expenditures in the PIT system rose from 0.9% of GDP in 2000 to 1.1% in 2006, reflecting increased income deductions for the elderly and childcare. However, better coverage of the self-employed boosted the proportion paying income tax, lifting the share of direct taxes on households from 3.4% of GDP in 2000 to 4.1% in 2006. Meanwhile, there has been little progress on taxing fringe benefits.

ii) *Taxation of the self-employed should be improved.* Korea has introduced a number of measures: i) incentives to use credit cards implemented in 2000 increased transparency about self-employed income; ii) the ceiling for using the "simplified" scheme for VAT was lowered from 150 million won of sales to 48 million won, thus strengthening bookkeeping obligations; iii) a cash receipt income deduction system was introduced in 2005; and iv) tax audits of high-income self-employed were increased. These measures helped raise the proportion of the self-employed paying income tax from 38% in 2000 to 63% in 2006.

iii) *Personal capital income should be taxed more evenly across sources.* Dividend and interest income below 40 million won ($27 000) is taxed separately at a 14% rate. Above that threshold, it is subject to "global taxation" at the same rate as earned income. Meanwhile, the scope for tax-exempt and tax-deductible saving instruments has been narrowed somewhat. Taxation of capital gains on real estate has been increased, while capital gains on small shareholders' stock in listed companies are still tax-exempt.

iv) *The corporate tax base should be broadened by reducing and streamlining the incentives given to small and medium-sized enterprises (SMEs), R&D and overall investment.* Tax expenditures for the CIT have remained around 0.7% of GDP and 20% of CIT revenue since 2000.

v) *The VAT base should be broadened, in part by including agricultural products and reducing the special treatment granted to small businesses.* Korea has made progress in broadening the VAT base, as reflected in the rise in its VAT Revenue Ratio from 61% in 2000 to 72% in 2005. Perhaps most important were the measures to expand the use of credit cards and to scale back the special treatment granted to small companies. However, agricultural products remain exempt from the VAT.

vi) *The consumption tax structure should be simplified.* The telephone tax was abolished in 2001. In addition, the number of items included in the individual consumption tax was reduced from 27 in 2000 to 20 in 2004.

vii) *The taxation of pensions should be strengthened, in part by shifting from a "TEE" system to "EET" (i.e. making employees' contributions tax deductible while taxing pension benefits) and taxing all pension income as ordinary income.* Korea moved to an EET system in 2002 and this system was applied to the company pension system introduced in 2006. Pensions are taxed as ordinary income.

viii) *Earmarked taxes and quasi-taxes should be abolished.* While there have been some changes in earmarked taxes, they continue to play an important role, accounting for 14% of government revenue in 2007. According to the September 2008 tax reform package, the three national earmarked taxes (education, local development and transport-energy-environment) will be abolished and integrated into underlying taxes in 2010. As for quasi-taxes, they rose from 1.1% of GDP in 2000 to 1.4% in 2006.

ix) *Local autonomy in the area of taxation should be strengthened.* There has been little change to the local tax system. The Local Share Tax, a general grant from the central government, was raised from 15% of national internal taxes in 2000 to 19.2% in 2006, while the role of earmarked grants was reduced.

x) *Property taxation should be reformed by raising the tax on holdings while reducing transaction taxes and the capital gains tax in order to promote the efficient use of land.* The tax on property holdings was increased by the Comprehensive Property Tax in 2005, while the registration and acquisition taxes on purchases have been reduced. In contrast, the capital gains tax has been increased for those owning more than one home.

xi) *Compliance should be strengthened by increasing the number of audits and enhancing co-operation between the National Tax Service (NTS) and other government bodies, including the social security system.* Although the number of tax audits has been on a downward trend, they have been more focused on high-income self-employed persons. The number of tax evaders that were prosecuted increased from 119 in 2001 to 369 in 2006. The NTS has required firms to report the payroll of non-regular workers since 2006. However, the legislation to consolidate the collection of the four social insurance contributions (pensions, health, employment and industrial accident) in one agency was rejected by the National Assembly.

ISBN 978-92-64-05425-7
OECD Economic Surveys: Korea
© OECD 2008

Chapter 4

Boosting productivity in Korea's service sector

Labour productivity growth in the service sector has been low relative to manufacturing. This is explained in part by weak competition in services resulting from strict product market regulation and the low level of import penetration and inflows of foreign direct investment (FDI). Increasing productivity growth in the service sector, which accounts for 67% of employment and 58% of value added in Korea, is essential to sustain high potential growth. The priority is to strengthen competition by eliminating domestic entry barriers, accelerating regulatory reform, upgrading competition policy and reducing barriers to trade and inflows of FDI. Another challenge is to enhance the performance and accelerate the restructuring of small and medium-sized enterprises, which account for over 90% of service-sector employment. Furthermore, it is essential to boost productivity in service industries with high growth potential, such as telecommunications and financial and business services.

Although the share of the service sector increased from 50% of GDP in 1990 to 58% in 2007, it is still far below the OECD average of 70%. The upward trend in the share of the service sector in GDP and total employment[1] in Korea is expected to continue in the context of rapid population ageing and intense competition with low-cost manufacturers in Asia. Moreover, the competitiveness of manufacturing increasingly depends on the performance of the service sector, given growing outsourcing. The expansion of the service sector and its impact on other parts of the economy make it a key determinant of economic growth. However, productivity in the service sector has consistently lagged behind that in manufacturing, thus weighing down economy-wide labour productivity, which was only 34% of the US level per hour worked in 2006 (Figure 1.6). There is thus significant scope to boost productivity in the service sector, and to thereby sustain Korea's long-term growth potential.

This chapter addresses the challenges of fostering a more dynamic and competitive environment conducive to higher productivity in services. It begins by discussing the main reasons for low productivity and the problems of small and medium-sized enterprises (SMEs) in the service sector. The following sections analyse policies to improve the overall productivity of the service sector as well as the major issues in key service industries. The chapter concludes with recommendations, summarised in Box 4.2.

Reasons for low productivity in the service sector

Labour productivity growth in services decelerated from an annual rate of 2.6% during the 1980s to 1.2% between 1997 and 2007, in contrast to nearly 9% growth in manufacturing since 1990 (Table 1.7). To some extent, low service-sector productivity is the legacy of an export-led growth strategy that attracted the most productive resources into manufacturing. In recent years, the government has removed some policies favouring manufacturing in the areas of taxation, mandatory charges (quasi-taxes) and energy prices.[2] However, considerable discrimination remains. For example, the manufacturing sector is exempted from the Comprehensive Property Tax (see Chapter 3) and mandatory charges for site development and the environment that are imposed on services, which also face higher energy charges.

Insufficient competition in services also explains its productivity gap with manufacturing, which widened from 24% in 1997 to 40% in 2005. In manufacturing, efficiency gains have been driven by intensified competition as Korea became more integrated in the world economy. Low mark-ups in manufacturing in Korea, which at 12% are only a third of those in non-manufacturing, indicate that competition is stronger in manufacturing (Figure 4.1).[3] Services are more sheltered from international competition and subject to numerous domestic regulations deterring potential competitors. Of the 543 service business lines, almost a third impose entry barriers (on top of registration and declaration), and the proportion is more than half in financial intermediation, communications, education and transport and storage, according to a central bank study

Figure 4.1. **Mark-ups in manufacturing and non-manufacturing and economy-wide product market regulation**

Regulation in 0-6 scale from most to least favourable to competition

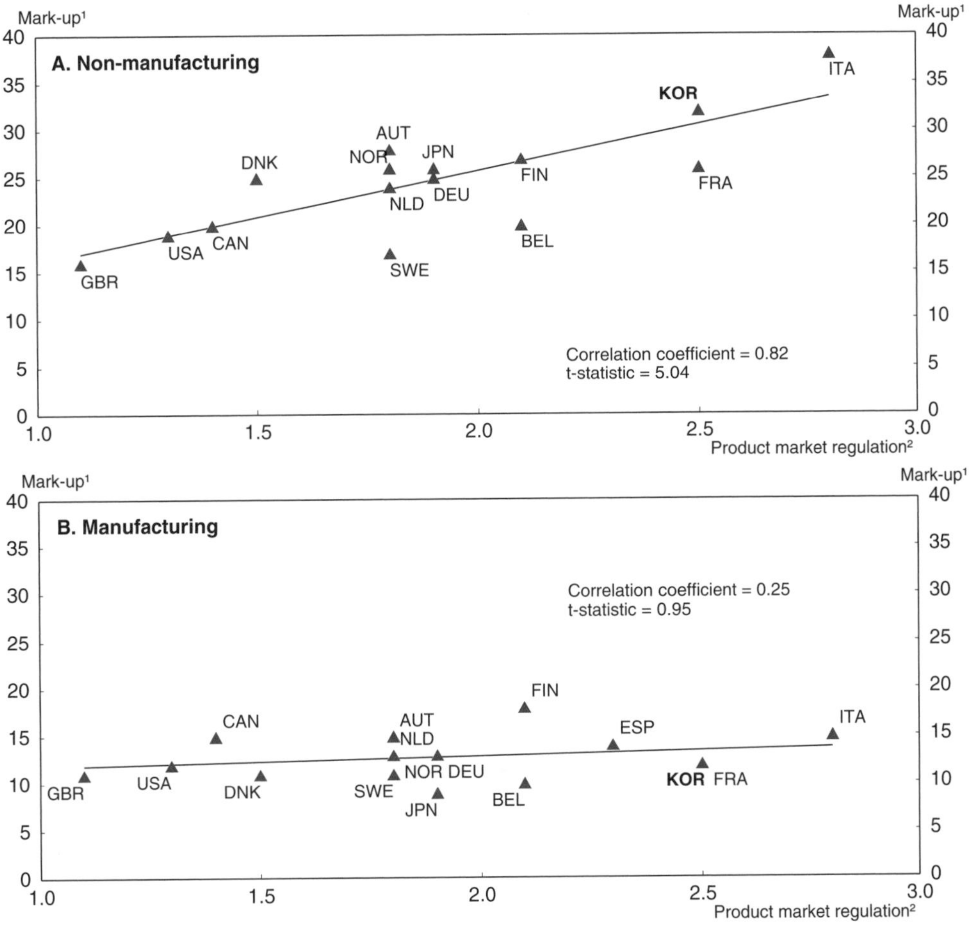

1. Mark-ups are calculated for individual two-digit ISIC sectors and aggregated using country-specific final sales as weights.
2. Product market regulation is the overall indicator for 1998.

Source: Høj *et al.* (2007).

StatLink http://dx.doi.org/10.1787/514008682746

(Table 4.1). Regulations limiting entrepreneurship are especially harmful for productivity growth in sectors where firms are dynamic and better placed to adopt new technology.

International comparisons suggest that Korea's services are heavily regulated: the OECD's indicator of product market regulation for the non-manufacturing sector ranked Korea as the fifth-most restrictive country in the OECD area in 2003 (Conway and Nicoletti, 2006 and Conway *et al.*, 2006). For the economy as a whole, however, Korea was close to the OECD average,[4] suggesting that the stringency of regulation in manufacturing is low by comparison. Market-unfriendly regulations in product markets disproportionately damage entrepreneurship in services (Nicoletti, 2001). Moreover, stringent product market regulations are positively correlated with high mark-ups in the non-manufacturing sector, indicating weak competition (Figure 4.1, Panel A). The mark-ups in Korea were the second highest among OECD countries. The correlation is much weaker in manufacturing,

Table 4.1. **Legal entry barriers in the service sector**

Number in June 2007

Service industry	Number of business lines	Government monopoly	Author-isation	Approval	License	Permission	Subtotal	Percent of total business lines	Registration and declaration	Total
Wholesale and retail trade	162	–	2	21	2	–	25	15.4	42	67
Restaurants and hotels	22	–	–	4	–	–	4	18.2	18	22
Transport and storage	48	2	1	7	13	1	24	50.0	18	42
Communications	9	1	–	4	–	–	5	55.6	4	9
Financial intermediation	34	4	3	15	–	5	27	79.4	7	34
Real estate and leasing	21	–	–	1	3	–	4	19.0	10	14
Business services	70	–	–	4	7	–	11	15.7	26	37
Education	23	–	–	–	–	12	12	52.2	11	23
Health and social work	22	1	–	7	–	1	9	40.9	13	22
Recreational and cultural activities	55	–	2	6	–	3	11	20.0	30	41
Other public and personal services	49	1	–	10	2	–	13	26.5	15	28
Other[1]	28	27	–	–	–	–	27	96.4	–	27
Total	543	36	8	79	27	22	172	31.7	194	366

1. House-keeping services, public administration and social security and international and foreign organisations.
Source: Lee *et al.* (2007).

StatLink 🔗

suggesting that product market regulation is more critical to competition in non-manufacturing. Moreover, according to a study by the World Bank, starting a business in Korea is relatively complicated, costly and time-consuming: Korea ranks 26th in the OECD area and 126th among 178 economies in the world (Table 4.2). The number of procedures, as well as their time and cost, and the minimum capital requirement, were all significantly above the OECD average.

Another factor explaining low productivity in services is R&D and ICT investment. In Korea, manufacturing accounted for 90% of R&D, as against only 7% in services. In contrast, the service sector's share averaged 25% in the OECD area and 43% in the United States. Moreover, over 90% of R&D in the service sector in Korea is concentrated in telecommunications and business services, including computer-related services. A number of studies have found that increased investment in ICT boosts labour productivity growth (Nicoletti and Scarpetta, 2005). For example, a large share of the increase in US labour productivity achieved since the mid-1990s originated in services that use ICT intensively. In Korea, though, the contribution of ICT-using services to labour productivity has diminished since the early 1990s (Figure 4.2, Panel A), partly because the level of ICT investment over the period 1995-2003 lagged behind top OECD performers (Panel B). Finally, there is a large inflow of older workers, with lower-than-average human capital, from manufacturing into services, given the early age of retirement from firms (see Chapter 5). Lacking other alternatives, two-fifths of workers over the age of 55 are self-employed in the service sector. Moreover, one-third of workers in services are either self-employed or family workers compared with an average of around one-fifth in the OECD area.

Table 4.2. **Time and cost of starting a new business**

Countries shown by their rank from least to most restrictive

Countries	Rank in the world	Number of procedures	Time (days)	Cost (% of income per capita)	Minimum capital (% of income per capita)
New Zealand	1	1	1	0.4	0.0
Canada	2	1	5	0.5	0.0
Australia	3	2	2	0.8	0.0
Ireland	5	4	13	0.3	0.0
United States	6	6	6	0.7	0.0
United Kingdom	8	6	13	0.8	0.0
France	14	5	7	1.0	0.0
Denmark	16	4	6	0.0	40.1
Iceland	17	5	5	2.6	13.6
Finland	18	3	14	1.0	7.4
Belgium	20	3	4	5.2	19.9
Hungary	27	4	5	8.4	10.8
Sweden	30	3	15	0.6	30.3
Norway	33	6	10	2.1	21.0
Portugal	34	6	6	2.9	34.3
Turkey	43	6	6	14.9	10.9
Slovak Republic	48	6	16	3.3	30.4
Netherlands	51	6	10	5.9	51.7
Switzerland	52	6	20	2.1	27.6
Italy	53	6	10	18.5	9.7
Japan	64	8	23	7.5	0.0
Luxembourg	69	6	26	6.5	21.3
Czech Republic	86	8	15	9.6	31.8
Germany	102	9	18	5.6	42.2
Austria	104	8	28	5.1	52.8
Mexico	115	9	28	12.5	11.0
Korea	**126**	**10**	**17**	**16.9**	**53.8**
Greece	133	15	19	10.2	19.6
Spain	140	10	47	14.9	13.1
Poland	145	10	31	18.8	168.8
Average		6.1	14.2	6.0	24.1

Source: World Bank (2008), *Doing Business 2009.*

Encouraging investment in R&D and ICT in services requires an efficient reporting system for intellectual and intangible assets and a better intellectual property rights system that balances incentives to innovate with adequate access to and sharing of knowledge. In business services in particular, investment in intangibles, such as training, customer relationship management, brand image, internal organisation and software plays a key role (OECD, 2007a). Reliable information about the intangible assets of firms reduces uncertainty and can thereby increase their valuation in financial markets, thus facilitating outside funding and the creation of such firms. This promotes efficient resource allocation and helps encourage innovation.

Figure 4.2. **The role of ICT-using services in labour productivity growth**

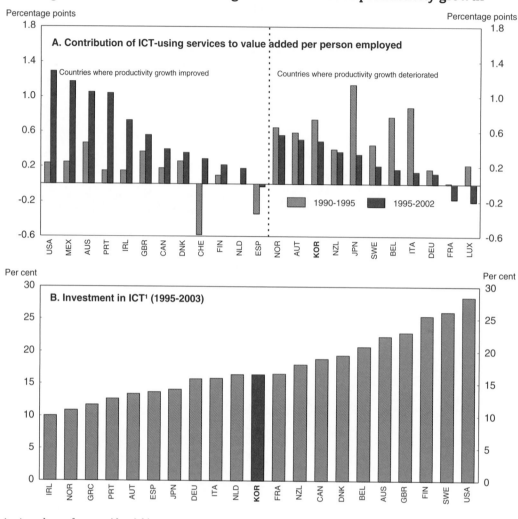

1. As a share of non-residential investment.
Source: OECD Productivity Database and Pilat (2007).

StatLink ⬛ http://dx.doi.org/10.1787/514104700326

The link between low productivity in services and problems in small and medium-sized enterprises

SMEs play a dominant role in services, accounting for 79% of output and 91% of employment, with particularly high shares in such areas as hotels and restaurants (97%), wholesale and retail trade (95%) and personal services (95%).[5] However, the performance of SMEs has consistently lagged behind large corporations in terms of profitability (Table 4.3). In addition, the SMEs, which were less indebted than the large companies at the time of the 1997 crisis, are now significantly more so. Lagging SME performance has widened the gap with large companies. By 2005, productivity per employee at SMEs in services was only 45.2% of that in large companies (Table 1.8). Given the overlap between the service sector and SMEs, the factors noted above as a cause of low productivity in services – the export-led development strategy, weak competition, the inflow of older workers and weak investment in ICT and R&D – also explain low productivity in SMEs.

Table 4.3. **Comparison of large corporations and SMEs**

Per cent

		1997	1999	2001	2003	2005	2006	2007
Operating profits/sales	Large firms	9.7	7.4	6.0	8.2	7.2	6.0	6.7
	SMEs	5.0	5.2	4.5	4.6	4.4	4.3	4.5
Salary/sales	Large firms	–	8.7	8.4	8.9	8.3	8.3	8.2
	SMEs	–	11.7	12.9	12.7	12.6	12.5	12.5
Borrowing-to-asset ratio	Large firms	56.5	44.5	42.0	25.9	19.1	18.1	18.0
	SMEs	46.8	37.8	34.6	33.5	30.8	30.9	32.0
Average borrowing rate[1]	Large firms	10.3	11.9	9.9	7.0	5.8	6.1	6.1
	SMEs	11.8	10.2	8.1	6.6	6.2	6.5	6.7
R&D/sales	Large firms	–	1.8	1.5	2.0	2.1	2.3	2.2
	SMEs	–	0.5	1.0	0.8	1.0	1.1	1.1

1. Interest expenses divided by total borrowings.
Source: Bank of Korea.

However, perhaps the most important factor explaining weak SME performance is extensive government assistance, which has damped competitive pressure and slowed restructuring. In the wake of the 1997 crisis and widespread restructuring of the big business groups, the authorities increased support to SMEs to prevent widespread bankruptcies. Indeed, SMEs were supported by 163 subsidy programmes in 2007, with total spending of 0.7% of GDP (Table 4.4). Although this is less than the 216 programmes and 0.9% of GDP in 2001, it remains high. In addition, SMEs pay a corporate income tax rate that is only half that levied on larger firms (see Chapter 3).[6] Furthermore, the government funnels considerable support to SMEs through financial markets:[7]

● *Policy loans*: the Small Business Corporation provides loans at below-market interest rates to SMEs. The amount of loans is around 0.5% of GDP per year, with the total stock amounting to 1.5%. Loan size and the share of firms receiving loans rise with the age of the firm.

● *Credit guarantees*: public financial institutions[8] guarantee loans to SMEs, helping them reduce their financing costs close to the level of large firms (Table 4.5). The guarantee is between 50% and 85% of the loan depending on its maturity and the firm's credit rating. The proportion of firms receiving guarantees is highest among young SMEs. The stock of guarantees doubled after the 1997 crisis, but has since levelled off. In 2007, they amounted to 5% of GDP and covered almost 12% of total loans outstanding to SMEs, down from 23% in 2001.

● *Venture capital investment*: The public sector accounts for 42% of investment in this sector. However, the proportion of SMEs that attract venture capital investment is quite low.

Of the three types of financial assistance, credit guarantees have had the least positive effect on firm performance, suggesting that they are used, in part, to rescue unviable firms. Venture capital investment had the most positive effect, reflecting the role of the private sector in selecting firms with greater potential. The role of policy loans was more neutral (Kang, 2007). The use of public financial assistance for SMEs is at most a second-best approach that distorts the price mechanism, thus reducing the efficiency of resource allocation. Indeed, the average effective borrowing rate for SMEs has been close to that for large companies (Table 4.3), despite the higher risk, suggesting that some companies receive more credit at lower cost than they should based on their creditworthiness and debt service capacity. In addition, the performance of companies with credit guarantees deteriorates over time in terms of profitability and debt ratios and their performance has been significantly worse than companies without guarantees (Kang, 2007).

Table 4.4. **Programmes to assist small and medium-sized enterprises**

Billion won

Ministry	2007 Outlays	2007 Number of programmes	Selected programmes
Small and Medium Business Administration	4 074	65	● Restructuring and start-up support ● Stable operation support ● Regional SME support ● Technology development support ● Venture company support
Ministry of Commerce, Industry and Energy	1 485	44	● Industrial technology development ● Modernisation of distribution networks ● Activation of industrial complexes ● Energy-saving support
Ministry of Labour	815	22	● Workplace accident prevention ● Workplace environment improvement ● Vocational training support
Ministry of Information and Communication	236	4	● ICT equipment investment support ● Technology development support ● Multi-media industry support ● Software development support
Ministry of Environment	131	5	● Anti-pollution facility support ● Environmental technology development support ● Recycling industry support
Intellectual Property Office	63	4	● Technology evaluation support
Ministry of Agriculture and Forestry	45	5	● Rice processing factory support ● Agricultural product processing ● Agricultural machine product support
Ministry of Maritime Affairs and Fisheries	44	5	● Marine product distribution support ● Fishing net support
Ministry of Health and Welfare	15	1	● New drug development support
Ministry of Culture and Tourism	14	3	● Film promotion fund support ● Sporting goods development support
Defence Acquisition Program Administration	5	2	● Defence industry R&D support
Ministry of Construction and Transportation	5	2	● Construction technology innovation support
Ministry of Science and Technology	1	1	● Technology development support
Total	6 933	163	

Source: Presidential Commission on SMEs (2007).

The decision to limit the eligibility for credit guarantees to eight to ten years, while focusing on newer firms is a positive step. In addition, the new administration has introduced important reforms in SME policies, in particular by streamlining 22 loan programmes into six and establishing a single window for providing support to SMEs. The

Table 4.5. **Credit guarantees for small and medium-sized enterprises**

Trillion won

	(1) Balance of guarantees	(2) Defaults	(2)/(1) Default rate (in per cent)	Net loss
1997	17.1	3.0	17.5	1.8
1999	31.4	1.0	3.2	1.8
2001	38.5	1.9	4.8	1.7
2003	45.1	3.4	7.5	2.4
2005	44.0	3.0	6.8	2.6
2007	44.3	1.8	4.1	1.3

Source: Small and Medium Business Administration.

authorities are concerned that the extensive programmes to help SMEs tend to encourage some firms to remain small in order to receive such benefits. To prevent this, the government plans to revise the definition of SMEs. In addition, it announced plans to introduce a graduation system to remove SMEs that are relatively large and capable of surviving on their own from government programmes and to exclude the affiliates of large companies. The government expects that these changes will reduce the number of SMEs by around 2 000, thus increasing the number of large companies (*i.e.* those not qualifying as SMEs) by almost 50% from its current level of about 4 300. Finally, the authorities intend to shift the policy focus to market failures by providing support for entrepreneurship and R&D by SMEs.

However, the government is also planning new initiatives to ease the financial distress of SMEs in the wake of the global financial crisis and economic slowdown. The government will:

- Provide 1.3 trillion won to state-owned banks, such as the Korea Development Bank, to expand financial assistance to SMEs.
- Expand credit guarantees to SMEs by 6 trillion won (0.7% of GDP), with an additional 1.5 trillion won provided by the Regional Credit Guarantee Fund.
- Increase financial aid through the Korea Exim Bank (from 7.5 trillion won in 2008 to 8.5 trillion won in 2009) and expand export and foreign exchange insurance by 3.5 trillion won.
- Support small businesses through financial aid, education, consulting support and business start-up services.
- Encourage banks to roll over loans to viable SMEs by signing MOUs, as a follow-up measure for the government guarantee on banks' external debt.

Public assistance to SMEs, including subsidies, financial assistance and tax incentives, weakens small companies by sheltering them from competition and should thus be scaled back in the longer run. Korea should instead focus on policies to strengthen competition and encourage more FDI, while avoiding preferential measures that cause distortions. Programmes to support SMEs should thus shift from financial support to management consulting and training. In particular, it is important to reduce the use of guarantees, which are among the highest in the world, along with Japan, and well above the 0.2% of GDP in the United States and 0.6% in France (IMF, 2006). Credit guarantees should focus on new start-ups rather than on existing firms. In addition, the share of loans that is guaranteed should be lowered to reduce moral hazard problems, while the price of guarantees should be raised to reflect credit losses. Directly addressing the deterrents to SME financing would be a better approach. The recent creation of a specialised credit bureau to increase the availability of information about SMEs is a step in the right direction. In addition, measures to facilitate the use of intangible assets as collateral would promote private-sector lending to SMEs. Scaling back public support would reduce the disincentive for SMEs to grow and thereby lose access to the wide range of assistance available to them.

Policies to promote higher productivity in the service sector

OECD research shows that strengthening competition through regulatory reform, upgrading competition policy and lowering barriers to trade and FDI can increase the level and rate of productivity growth by stimulating business investment and promoting innovation (Nicoletti and Scarpetta, 2005 and Conway *et al.*, 2006). It also suggests that overly strict product market regulation and non-trade barriers are associated with low R&D intensity (Nicoletti *et al.*, 2001; Bassanini and Ernst, 2002; and Jaumotte and Pain, 2005).[9] Pro-competitive reforms promote capital deepening in key non-manufacturing industries (Alesina *et al.*, 2005) and increase multifactor productivity, partly by allowing faster catch-up to the technological leader (Nicoletti and Scarpetta, 2003). Another OECD study (Conway *et al.*, 2006) found that competition has a positive impact on investment in ICT and labour productivity growth. In sum, competition, both domestic and international, is key to boosting productivity in the service sector.

In April 2008, the government announced a roadmap for the service sector (Box 4.1) that is motivated by: i) the deficit in services in the balance of payments, which has averaged around ½ per cent of GDP in recent years; ii) concern that low productivity in services is undermining the competitiveness of manufacturing; and iii) the impending opening of the service market in the context of free trade agreements with the United States and the European Union. Given the diversity of service activities, this sector is affected by a wide range of policies. This section will focus on the key priorities of regulatory reform, competition policy and international competition, while labour market flexibility, which is also essential to productivity and restructuring in the service sector, is discussed in Chapter 5.[10]

Box 4.1. **The government roadmap for the service sector**

The government announced "Service PROGRESS-I" in April 2008 to improve Korea's service account balance, focusing on deficit areas such as tourism, medical care, overseas language training and knowledge-based services. This was followed in September 2008 by PROGRESS-II, which aimed at streamlining regulations in services. These two initiatives are summarised below. PROGRESS-III, which is to be announced in December 2008, is intended to make the service sector a main growth engine alongside manufacturing. The word "Progress" stands for productivity growth, regulatory reform, openness to know-how from abroad, global standards, rivalry, environmental improvement, specialisation and scale economy to raise efficiency.

Service PROGRESS-1

Tourism

The government will increase financial support and ease regulations on the tourism industry in an effort to build the necessary infrastructure and facilitate co-operation by the private sector and local authorities to create new projects. Local tourism boards will be formed and their projects will receive financial and promotional support from the government. In addition, Jeju Island will be exempted from three tourism-related laws to help it develop into an international tourist destination. The government also plans to: i) increase financial assistance to attract well-known budget hotel chains; ii) include more foreign languages on road signs; iii) revise the Tourism Promotion Act to offer one-stop services to tourism resort developers; and iv) expand the coverage of zero value-added taxes for tourists.

Medical service

The rules covering medical services will be reformed to attract more foreign patients. *First*, the visa-issuing process will be streamlined. *Second*, specialised medical tourism products, such as plastic surgery, will be developed to attract foreign patients. *Third*, regulations on medical institutions will be eased to bring more diversity to medical services. *Fourth*, the legal framework will be reformed to facilitate M&As in the medical sector. *Fifth*, Korean hospitals will be encouraged to seek international accreditation to improve their credibility among foreign patients.

Box 4.1. **The government roadmap for the service sector** *(cont.)*

English-language education

In response to rapidly growing spending on English-language education abroad, the government is developing measures to help Korean students meet their educational needs locally. Rules on the establishment of foreign educational institutions will be eased to allow students to attend high-quality language programmes in Korea. In addition, the ceiling on the share of Korean students in international foreign schools in Korea will be increased from 10% to 30%. The quality of English classes in local schools is to be raised by increasing the number of teachers who are native speakers. Finally, the plan to build an English-only city on Jeju Island will be implemented as scheduled.

Knowledge-based services

The government will promote the creation of a high value-added business service market by extending export assistance, including guarantees, which has thus far been limited mainly to manufacturing. It will also encourage outsourcing to boost demand for knowledge-based services. For example, SMEs will receive subsidies for management consulting services. In addition, "Partnership Taxation", which includes only personal income tax rather than both personal and corporate income taxes, will be applied to qualified law and accounting firms to encourage knowledge-based companies to expand. Finally, the share of government R&D in industrial technology that goes to the service sector is to be doubled from 3.1% in 2008 to 6.2% in 2012.

Service PROGRESS-II

Broadcasting and telecommunications*

Restrictions on the ownership of broadcasting facilities by large businesses and newspaper publishers will be relaxed. For example, ceilings on the ownership of satellite broadcasting, including digital multimedia broadcasting (DMB), will be abolished and shareholding of up to 49% will be permitted in the case of land-based DMB. The ownership ceilings for cable and satellite broadcasting facilities by daily newspaper publishers and for foreign ownership of satellite broadcasting facilities will be raised from 33% to 49%. In addition, regulations on broadcasting will be streamlined. For example, prior approval of cable TV subscription fees will be converted to a reporting requirement. Entry regulations will be relaxed for key telecommunication operators. Licensing standards will be simplified to help them integrate segmented "facilities-based" telecommunications businesses and deliver a wider range of services. In addition, key telecommunication operators will find it easier to gain approval for side businesses.

IT services, software and contents

Regulations restricting the location of software workstations to the neighbourhoods of their customers will be eased. Data centres will be designated as "knowledge-based service firms", and thus subject to lower electricity rates. Protection against illegal copying will be reinforced by offering users of copyrighted works "exclusive usage rights" to thwart copyright infringement by third parties. Restaurants and coffee shops will be allowed to sell music CDs.

Legal services*

Regulations on the establishment of law firms will be eased. For instance, law firms will be permitted to open branches in counties and cities, and the ceiling on a law firm's investments in other law firms will be relaxed. In addition, electronic notarisation systems will be introduced.

Box 4.1. **The government roadmap for the service sector** *(cont.)*

Employment services

Competition among private job placement services will be strengthened by easing price regulations and by allowing such firms to offer a wider range of services, including pre-employment services, job training and employee outsourcing. The market for job training services will be expanded by paying training grants directly to job seekers, who can choose appropriate training. Educational institutions will be encouraged to take part in providing job training.

Healthcare and food

An institutional and legal foundation will be established to create markets for healthcare services. Case studies of foreign countries will be conducted to explore ways to permit private insurance companies to provide healthcare insurance as a sideline business. The food service industry will receive greater support, in part by allowing it to benefit from the SME support programmes. The phasing out of the VAT deductions on purchases of agricultural products planned for the end of 2008 will be delayed by two years.

*Overhaul of the business services market**

Competition in business services has been very limited due to regulations on entry and business activities (see below). As a result, consumer dissatisfaction with the quality and prices of business services has continued to grow. Zero-based reviews of the business service sector will be aimed at strengthening competition and providing customer-oriented services. This will include studies of business service markets in other countries in order to develop reforms and lay the legal and institutional framework. Key options for upgrading the business service market include easing regulations on business boundaries and investments in other business service providers and improving disclosure of fees.

* Reforms in this sector are covered below in more detail.

Pursuing regulatory reform

Korea has made progress during the past decade in introducing policies, institutions and tools to assure high quality regulation (OECD, 2007b). The initial impetus for reform was to promote recovery from the 1997 crisis through the creation of the Regulatory Reform Committee (RRC)[11] and the Regulatory Reform Task Force (RRTF).[12] The large role of the private sector in these institutions demonstrates the government's commitment to address the issues that are most important to the business sector.[13] Finally, the creation of Free Economic Zones (FEZs) since 2003 to attract more FDI (see below) and Special Economic Zones (SEZs) since 2004 for regional development has led to the liberalisation of regulations in certain geographic areas. The 58 SEZs allow deregulation in such areas as education, healthcare, immigration and land use for both domestic and foreign firms. One risk of such an approach, as illustrated by the experience of other OECD countries, is that these zones prefer to maintain their competitive advantages, thus posing an obstacle to the implementation of nationwide reforms (*OECD Economic Surveys: Japan*, 2008). In addition, the special zone approach distorts locational decisions.

Services accounted for more than two-thirds of the 671 reforms implemented by the RRTF (Table 4.6). Table 4.7 shows the impact of reform by the size of the affected industry and the strictness of the regulations that were liberalised. By this measure, four of the seven industries most affected by reform were in services: telecommunications, financial intermediation, public services and business services. The average prices in these

Table 4.6. **Number of regulations addressed by the Regulatory Reform Task Force**

Between August 2004 and August 2007

Industry	Number of Regulations
Agriculture	5
Manufacturing	82
Construction	89
Services	464
Electricity and gas	12
Wholesale and retail trade, hotels and restaurants	98
Transport and storage	71
Telecommunications	28
Financial intermediation	43
Business services	113
Public services	57
Entertainment	42
Other (services for citizens)	31
Total	671

Source: Regulatory Reform Committee (2007), *Regulatory Reform White Book*, Seoul.

industries were estimated to have fallen between 0.8% and 1.3% during the year following the reform, while output was projected to increase by 2% to 3% over ten years, thanks to the reform.

The new government has made regulatory reform a top priority to improve the business environment. The Presidential Council on National Competitiveness (PCNC), composed of private-sector experts and high-level government officials and chaired by the president, is playing a leading role in regulatory reform. In April 2008, the government decided 30 core tasks, which have not been disclosed publicly, along with 815 deregulation objectives. The priority should be to focus on the entry barriers, as shown in Table 4.1. The RRC will continue to pursue regulatory reform, while the RRTF was abolished in 2008.

Table 4.7. **Impact of regulatory reform by industry**

Rank	Industry	Regulatory reform index[1]	Price change (%)[2]	Output change (%)[3]
1	Construction	22.0	−1.6	4.1
2	Telecommunications	13.7	−1.2	2.6
3	Financial intermediation	11.8	−1.3	2.9
4	Food and cigarette	11.3	−0.9	1.9
5	Public services	8.6	−0.8	2.9
6	Oil and chemicals	7.5	−0.6	2.8
7	Business services	6.9	−0.9	2.5
8	Electronics	6.8	−0.7	5.7
9	Transportation equipment	5.2	−0.5	2.7
10	Metals	4.7	−0.4	2.8
11	Wholesale and retail trade, hotels and restaurants	4.1	−0.7	3.0
12	Entertainment	3.9	−0.9	2.9
13	Transportation	3.7	−0.7	1.4

1. Regulations are given a weight of 1.0 for prior approval, 0.78 for input standard, 0.64 for output standard and 0.38 for information regulations. This index includes only reforms implemented by the RRTF.
2. Change in price during the four quarters following the implementation of the reform.
3. Projected increase in output during the decade following the implementation of the reform.
Source: Regulatory Reform Committee (2007), *Regulatory Reform White Book*, Seoul.

Progress in regulatory reform has fluctuated with the business cycle, with more reform momentum during downturns than during expansions. More consistent commitment to reform would lead to better results. In addition, successful regulatory reform requires correct goals, proper policies and the administrative machinery to carry them out, backed by political support at the highest level. The process of regulatory reform in Korea should be improved by:

- Enhancing the role of RIAs through training, including in local governments, and adopting an explicit rule that regulations can be introduced only if benefits outweigh costs.

- Ensuring that the reform process is comprehensive and consistently applied across policy areas. For example, important topics such as industrial policies, the tax system and regional development policies should be included in the reform process.

- Creating a permanent mechanism in the National Assembly to ensure the regulatory quality of laws initiated by members of the Assembly. The growing proportion of legislation that is initiated in the Assembly escapes detailed scrutiny by the RRC and is not subject to RIAs.[14]

- Setting a government-wide strategy on public consultation on proposed regulations, lengthening the minimum comment period from 20 days and making all comments publicly available.

- Extending reforms that are successful in FEZs and SEZs to cover the entire country and phasing out the special zone approach.

- Improving co-ordination among the many institutions currently working on regulatory reform.

- Reducing reliance on administrative guidance – recommendations by regulatory bodies that are not legally binding – by reducing the scope for discretion in the administration of regulations.

Upgrading competition policy

Competition policy is central to regulatory reform, as its principles provide a benchmark to assess the quality of regulations, and should therefore be integrated into the policy framework for regulation. Moreover, as regulatory reform stimulates structural change, vigorous enforcement of competition policy is needed to ensure that violations of competition law do not prevent the realisation of the benefits. The competition agency, the Korea Fair Trade Commission (KFTC), has played a central role in reform efforts (OECD, 2007b). The "Clean Markets" campaigns of 2001-03, which produced a surge in actions against violations, focused on the service sector.[15] In 2003, the KFTC launched "the Market Reform Roadmap" and the "Task Force for Advancing the Market Economy",[16] which led to the amendment of the Monopoly Regulation and Fair Trade Act (MRFTA) in the spring of 2007. *First*, a number of steps were taken to improve the leniency programme introduced in 1997.[17]*Second*, the merger review system was streamlined through a pre-notification system, bringing it more closely into line with other OECD countries. *Third*, the surcharge against cartels was doubled from 5% to 10% of turnover, comparable to the rate in most European countries. At the same time, the base was changed from the firms' average total turnover during the previous three years to the relevant turnover during the violation period, making the surcharge lower in effective terms than in other countries.[18]

In addition, policies toward large business groups (*chaebol*) were reformed. The KFTC strengthened *ex post* supervision while minimising *ex ante* regulation, relaxed the requirements to create holding companies, and reinforced the monitoring function of markets to counter complex shareholding structures and undue subsidisation. The shift in KFTC priorities from its historic focus on *chaebol* financial structure and governance toward core competition problems, as recommended in past *OECD Economic Surveys: Korea*, is reflected in the changing allocation of KFTC staff. In addition, the ceiling on the total amount of shareholding in other domestic companies by *chaebol* affiliates was increased from 25% to 40% of net assets and the asset threshold of groups subject to the ceiling was raised from 6 trillion won to 10 trillion won. In March 2008, the government announced that it will abolish the shareholding ceiling.

The improvement in competition law was accompanied by strengthened enforcement. The total amount of surcharges jumped from 36 billion won in 2004 to 423 billion won in 2007 (Table 4.8). In addition, 48 criminal cases were filed by the KFTC in 2007, up from 22 in 2004.[19] Increased enforcement partly reflects greater resources: the KFTC's budget doubled between 2000 and 2007 while the number of staff rose from 402 to 503. Vigorous enforcement contributes to Korea's high ranking in the OECD's indicator of competition policies (Høj, 2007).

Table 4.8. **Enforcement activity by the KFTC**

		1996	1998	2000	2002	2004	2005	2006	2007
Warning, etc.		606	649	520	2 013	2 388	2 421	2 514	2 124
Recommendation for correction		179	57	35	110	100	163	178	124
Corrective order		250	538	441	497	478	754	644	927
Total		1 035	1 244	996	2 620	2 966	3 338	3 336	3 175
Surcharges	Number of cases	22	69	49	91	91	274	157	325
	Billion won	16	136	226	88	36	259	175	423

Source: Korea Fair Trade Commission (2008).

While significant progress has been achieved, further challenges remain. *First,* although financial penalties have risen, their deterrent effect is still weaker than in most other OECD countries, indicating a need for further increases. Criminal penalties, which are rarely applied, should be more credible. No one has ever spent any time in jail for violating the competition law,[20] although the KFTC treats horizontal cartels as illegal *per se*. *Second,* the KFTC's investigative powers, originally designed for voluntary processes, need to be strengthened. The administrative fine for non-compliance with an investigation is so low that some firms prefer to pay the fine rather than provide sensitive information. The KFTC cannot conduct a "dawn raid" to enter premises and take possession of evidence, a right that is granted to other administrative enforcement bodies that deal with labour, tariffs, environment and taxes. The KFTC needs such compulsory investigative powers to be more effective.[21] *Third,* special protection for SMEs should be further scaled back. In particular, the MRFTA provision that prevents large companies from acquiring small firms in industries dominated by SMEs should be repealed.[22] The possibility of entry by large firms would encourage small firms to increase their efficiency and the prospect of acquisition by a larger firm could increase their value and improve their access to financing. *Fourth,* remaining exemptions from the MRFTA should be scaled back or eliminated.

Strengthening international competition

Strengthening links to the world economy is another means to boost productivity growth. Despite increasing openness, Korea's level of integration with the world economy is still very low in terms of import penetration, the share of foreign workers and the stock of inward FDI (*OECD Economic Surveys: Korea*, 2007). Korea experienced a big surge in FDI inflows in the second half of the 1990s as a result of reductions in barriers and the restructuring of the economy in the wake of the 1997 crisis (Figure 4.3).[23] Nevertheless, the stock of inward FDI in Korea in 2006 was the third lowest in the OECD area, at 8% of GDP. Moreover, inflows have slowed since 2004 despite policies aimed at attracting foreign investors, notably the three FEZs launched in 2003 that offer financial incentives to foreign companies, such as preferential tax treatment and exemptions from some regulatory requirements.

Figure 4.3. **The flow of inward FDI to Korea by sector**

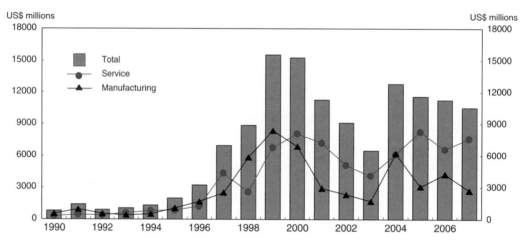

Source: Ministry of Knowledge Economy.

StatLink ⟪⟫ http://dx.doi.org/10.1787/514112832214

The globalisation of services has been driven by technological advances, such as broadband networks and digitalisation, regulatory reform and trade liberalisation. The share of the service sector in FDI inflows in Korea has increased, accounting for half of the total since 1997, primarily due to the financial sector, as banks that had been re-capitalised using public money after the financial crisis were privatised.[24] Nevertheless, the share of the service sector in the cumulative inward FDI stock was the third lowest in the OECD area, at 49% in 2006 (Figure 4.4). As a result, foreign affiliates accounted for only 8% of service sector turnover and 4% of employment in 2004 (MOCIE, 2005), compared to OECD averages of 19% and 10%, respectively (OECD, 2005c). As for trade, imports of services amounted to only 20% of Korea's total imports of goods and services in 2007, below the OECD average of 26%.

Strengthening international competition and thereby promoting faster productivity growth in services requires measures to reduce barriers to inflows of FDI and service imports. Despite a significant fall between 1998 and 2003, the OECD's indicator of barriers to trade and investment ranked Korea as the sixth highest in the OECD area in 2003. To reverse the downward trend in FDI inflows, Korea should further relax FDI restrictions, including foreign ownership ceilings in key services, and liberalise product market regulations. In addition, it is important to foster a foreign investment-friendly environment, thereby encouraging more

Figure 4.4. **Share of the service sector in the stock of inward FDI in OECD countries**

In 2006[1]

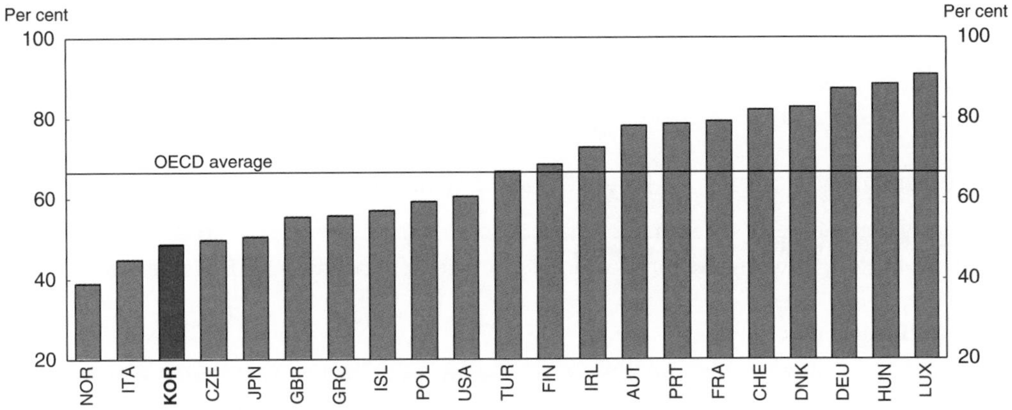

1. For France, Germany, Greece, Iceland, Italy, Luxembourg, Norway and Portugal, data are only available for 2005.
Source: OECD Economic Globalisation Indicators Database.

StatLink ⫘ http://dx.doi.org/10.1787/514150287171

cross-border M&As, enhance the transparency of tax and regulatory policies and reform the labour market (see Chapter 5). The treatment of manufacturing and services in FEZs should be more balanced. While all manufacturing industries qualify for benefits, including tax breaks and rent support, logistics, tourism, education, R&D and medical services are the only service industries eligible. Finally, the emphasis on special zones should not distract policymakers from the top priority of improving the business climate.

Measures to improve the FDI environment should be accompanied by trade liberalisation, which in turn promotes inflows of FDI. Although Korea did not belong to any FTAs prior to 2004, it has since implemented FTAs with Chile, Singapore, the European Free Trade Association and ASEAN (Table 4.9). The Korea-US FTA, which is awaiting ratification

Table 4.9. **Korea's FTA strategy**

Country	Status	Share of exports in 2007 in per cent		Share of imports in 2007 in per cent	
		Total	Agriculture	Total	Agriculture
Chile	Took effect in 2004	0.8	0.1	1.2	1.6
Singapore	Took effect in 2006	2.6	0.8	1.9	0.2
EFTA	Took effect in 2007	0.4	0.1	1.0	0.5
ASEAN	Took effect for trade in goods in 2007	9.6	9.2	9.3	15.4
United States	Negotiations were completed in 2007	14.5	10.6	10.4	18.6
India	Negotiations were completed in 2008	1.6	0.3	1.3	1.7
Canada	Negotiations are underway	1.2	0.9	0.9	2.6
Mexico	Negotiations are underway	1.3	0.2	0.3	0.3
EU	Negotiations are underway	15.4	4.4	10.3	9.7
GCC	Negotiations are underway	2.9	3.7	15.5	0.2
MERCOSUR	Joint government study completed in 2006	1.0	0.2	1.0	6.4
China	Joint study at government level is underway	21.8	12.1	17.7	20.9
New Zealand	Joint private study was completed in 2007	0.2	2.2	0.3	4.0
Australia	Joint private study was completed in 2008	1.3	2.0	3.7	8.6
Peru	Joint private study was completed in 2008	0.1	0.0	0.3	0.3
Russia	Joint study at private level is underway	2.2	6.6	2.0	3.0
Turkey	Joint study at private level is underway	1.1	0.1	0.1	0.2

Source: MOFAT, Korea International Trade Association and Korea Agricultural Trade Information.

in both countries, takes steps to open the service sector in such areas as law, accounting and finance. Negotiations with India were completed in 2008. At present, Korea is pursuing a multi-track approach in negotiating FTAs with Canada, the European Union, Mexico and the Gulf Co-operation Council,[25] which combined with existing FTAs, would cover half of Korea's trade. However, the high level of agricultural protection in Korea[26] limits the coverage of FTAs and hinders the negotiation of additional agreements.

Policies to boost productivity in key service industries

This section focuses on specific issues in some of the service industries that have high growth potential, namely telecommunications, financial services and business services.

Telecommunications

Regulatory reform helped Korea make impressive progress in developing its telecommunication service markets, resulting in better services, lower prices and rapid innovation. The telecommunication sector generated nearly 5% of GDP in 2005, well above the OECD average of 3% (Figure 4.5). In addition to the rapid diffusion of broadband penetration, Korea is a technological leader in other areas such as wireless broadband and digital multimedia broadcasting. There is a need, though, for further reform to stimulate competition, which would encourage the private sector to choose the appropriate technology and services. It is important that the objective of technological leadership in ICT manufacturing does not lead to distortions in the telecommunication services market.

Figure 4.5. **Telecommunication revenue as a percentage of GDP in OECD countries**

In 2005

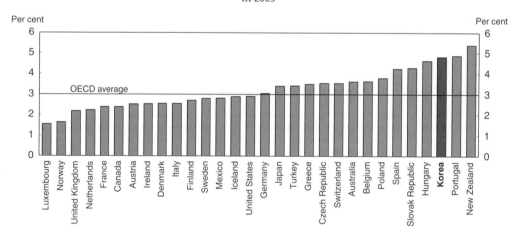

Source: OECD (2007c), *OECD Communication Outlook 2007*, OECD, Paris.

StatLink http://dx.doi.org/10.1787/514156275177

Korea's regulatory framework, based on detailed service categories, had become increasingly outdated as communication networks became integrated. Such an approach has limited competition between services by dividing the market.[27] In addition, regulations on price and bundling have slowed the development of innovative services. The government's 2007 "Roadmap for Telecommunication Policy and Regulation" aims at encouraging the development of new services through deregulation, competition and greater predictability of regulation. In addition, the Roadmap will promote the integration of service categories by; i) allowing bundling by major operators; ii) permitting number portability from PSTN to VoIP and improving the numbering policy; iii) introducing MVNO wireless services and USIM;[28] iv) relaxing price regulation; v) phasing out regulation of handset subsidies; and vi) reducing entry barriers and facilitating M&As.[29]

Another major reform was the restructuring of regulatory organisations. In February 2008, the Ministry of Information and Communication (MIC) and the Korea Broadcasting Commission (KBC) were integrated into the Korea Communications Commission (KCC), which regulates telecommunication, broadcasting and convergence sectors. The KCC should help resolve the past conflicts between the industry promotion activities in the MIC and the efforts of the former KCC, which operated in the same ministry, to foster competition. Under the new framework, industry promotion belongs to the Ministry of Knowledge Economy. The creation of the KCC is a major step towards an independent body that deals with regulatory issues, although the chairman may attend cabinet meetings.[30] In addition, the new KCC is better able to deal with the convergence of broadcasting and communications, ending the conflict between the former MIC and the KBC,[31] and should make it easier to address issues of market power and vertical integration.

Regulatory reform has also eased the conditions for market entry. Operators are classified as facility-based (requiring licenses to enter the market), special (requiring registration) and value-added (requiring notification). Previously, facility-based operators were required to get an individual license for each type of service. In 2007, services were reclassified into the categories of transmission, services that require spectrum allocation, and facility leasing, thereby easing the entry of new operators in more than one type of service.[32] Easing entry requirements is especially important in the fixed-line market, where KT's market share for local telephone calls exceeds 90%, reflecting the small number of participants[33] and the lack of effective competition. Another concern is that facility-based and special service providers are required to contribute between 0.5% and 0.75% of their annual revenue for R&D conducted by a public research institute.[34] Such charges reflect the priority given to ICT manufacturing and should be abolished.

Although operators are allowed to set service prices through notification, those that are considered to have market power in terms of business size and market share are subject to authorisation. The problem of weak competition in the mobile market should be addressed directly by providing spectrum to and licensing more market players and by requiring existing mobile operators to support MVNOs, rather than regulating prices.

Korea has used a fee-based system since 2000 for the allocation of spectrum, rather than the auction approach recommended by the OECD. The government sets a higher and lower limit for spectrum fees. The applicants that offer to pay the higher price receive more points in the "beauty contest" procedure, but this is only one criterion in choosing which firm obtains the spectrum. The winners of the contest are allowed exclusive rights for spectrum use, including the right to transfer or lease the spectrum, thus creating a type of secondary market. However, in principle, the transfer or lease is not possible until three years after the licensing, with some exceptions specified by the law, and requires approval by the KCC. An auction system, combined with a deregulated secondary market, should be implemented to achieve more efficiency in the allocation and use of spectrum.

The law on Internet Protocol Television (IPTV) in 2007 and the creation of the integrated KCC in 2008 is promoting the convergence between telecommunications and broadcasting, but there is still much scope to improve the framework. Regulation should be shifted from a vertical approach based on the type of business to a horizontal approach based on transmission and content. Another issue is the deregulation of cable TV (CATV) to create a level playing field with IPTV. At present, CATV operators are limited to regional markets, putting them at a disadvantage vis-à-vis telecommunication operators (KT and SK Broadband), which can offer nationwide IPTV services. Providing CATV operators with a nationwide franchise area would be an option. Another option is local loop unbundling, which has been little used since its introduction in 2002. According to the new law, all IPTV operators shall open their facilities to competitors, although the degree of opening is still under discussion.[35] The government decision that optical fibre cables deployed after 2004 should not be subject to unbundling requirements in order to promote investment in optical fibre may restrict competition and strengthen dominant positions in this new technology. Unbundling should thus be extended to all local loops of dominant carriers regardless of their technology or the date of implementation.

Korea limits foreign investment to 49% in the two facility-based operators (KT and SKT).[36] In addition, the authorities can prevent an investor, regardless of nationality, from becoming KT's largest shareholder, although currently the largest shareholder in KT is a foreign investor. More generally, when more than half of a company is owned by a foreigner, and the company is investing through acquisition, it is required to report to the authorities. It should be noted, however, that this is a general requirement, applying to all sectors, not just telecommunications. The government argues that such investment restrictions are justified by national security considerations. However, most countries have the capacity to protect national security and public interest through the general legal framework rather than by foreign investment restrictions. Accordingly, such ownership restrictions should be eased, particularly as new entrants are often short of capital.

Financial services

As in other countries, the financial sector in Korea is regulated to limit systemic risk and to address information asymmetries between small investors and financial institutions. The financial sector is one of the most heavily regulated areas in Korea, accounting for 16% of the 5 223 regulations registered with the RRC. Over half of them are *ex ante* regulations such as licensing, permission and registration. Korea's positive-list system, which prohibits all activities except those that are explicitly approved, increases the burden of regulation, as every new product or practice requires the approval of regulators. Regulatory reform has been slowed by the use of administrative guidance, which is not based on any explicit law or regulation, by financial supervisors. In addition, the segmentation of the financial sector between banking, securities and insurance remains strict. However, regulatory reform has advanced in recent years, making Korea more attractive to foreign financial institutions. Since 2004, the number of foreign banks in Korea has increased from 28 to 39 and their assets have nearly doubled from $28 billion to $53 billion.

The Financial Services Commission (FSC) launched a major regulatory overhaul in 2008. In the *first* stage, to be completed by the end of 2008, all regulations will be reviewed from a zero-base approach from the perspective of global standards. The *second* stage aims to integrate similar regulations in different sectors by 2010 while maintaining the distinct sectors of banking, securities and insurance. In the *third* stage of reform, the consolidation of laws across the three sectors will be reviewed as part of a possible shift to universal banking. This reform would allow financial institutions to develop a wider range of products and services. At the same time, the FSC will shift the basis of regulation from the type of business to the type of function and enhance the transparency of its monitoring activities.

Regulatory reform will be further advanced by the Capital Markets Consolidation Act (CMCA) to be implemented in early 2009, which integrates seven related laws comprising 420 provisions governing capital markets and investment services industries. The firewalls between different investment services will be lowered, allowing a single firm to provide a broader range of services. The CMCA is expected to lead to consolidation of the securities industry and the emergence of domestic investment banks. The law will also increase the scope for innovation by replacing the positive-list by a negative-list system, which allows all products and practices except those that are specifically prohibited (Cho, 2007). The implementation of the CMCA during a period of extreme turbulence in world financial markets underlines the importance of proper supervision. Given that the new law is likely to sharply boost transactions in over-the-counter markets, it is critical to ensure that enhanced supervisory capacity precedes market growth and innovation. In particular, OECD country experience suggests that the planned reform is likely to raise liquidity risk for banks by increasing their already-high reliance on wholesale funding as household savings move away from deposits.[37]

The CMCA is an essential part of Korea's Financial Hub Initiative, launched in 2003 to create a specialised financial centre based on asset management by 2010 and to become one of the top three financial hubs in Asia by 2015. The government selected four core strategic tasks as part of this initiative: i) deregulation, including further reform of the foreign exchange market; ii) fostering the asset management business, in part by the creation of the Korea Investment Corporation in 2005 to help manage the country's foreign exchange reserves; iii) encouraging the overseas expansion of domestic financial companies; and iv) improving the financial infrastructure and developing skilled professionals.

Becoming a financial hub for Asia would increase the productivity and efficiency of Korea's financial services industry by strengthening competition with foreign financial institutions. However, Korea faces severe competition from existing financial centres and other cities with ambitions to become a hub.[38] In a 2007 survey of persons working in Korea's financial sector (KDI, 2007a), 43% responded that strict regulation makes it difficult for Korea to become a hub. In addition, domestic companies need to achieve international competitiveness,[39] which is complicated by a general lack of expertise. Indeed, Korea ranked 45th in terms of financial experts, compared to 11th for Hong Kong, China and 15th for Singapore (IMD, 2008). In sum, creating a financial hub depends on modernising the regulatory structure and increasing the number of financial experts by improving business and living conditions, in part through reforms in education and healthcare, to attract more foreign investment.

As the liberalisation of Korea's financial market increases competition with global companies, domestic banks face challenges. Easing the ownership restrictions that separate banking and commerce by applying ex ante and uniform regulations on the ownership of banks by industrial capital is being considered as a way to boost efficiency and allow the emergence of strong owners that could enhance the competitiveness of banks. At present, non-financial entities can own a maximum of 4% of the shares in banks and bank holding companies (15% for local banks) while other entities can own up to 10% (15% for local banks). This regulation reflects a number of concerns about mixing industrial and financial capital.[40] First, the capital of a financial institution that is owned by an industrial firm can be used for the benefit of that firm, which could undermine the soundness of the financial institution and endanger market stability. *Second*, it is difficult for a financial institution to carry out its lending role, including the oversight of company management, when it is owned by industrial capital. *Third*, a level-playing field is not possible among industrial companies when some own financial companies. The risk of allowing industrial capital to own banks in Korea has been reduced by the improvement in market discipline and financial supervision since the 1997 crisis. Given the reduced risks and the need to increase competitiveness, the government plans to raise the limit on industrial capital's ownership of banks from 4% to 10%. The government should advance very cautiously in relaxing rules on bank ownership, given the potential risk and past experience and ensure that there are proper supervisory tools in place before any changes.[41]

Business services

The business services sector – which includes *inter alia* accounting, legal services, architecture, consulting, R&D, marketing and advertising – has risen from an average of 6.5% of GDP in the OECD area in 1993 to 8.7% in 2006, as firms outsourced to take advantage of economies of scale and scope. In contrast, its share increased from only 4% to 5% in Korea over that period. Given its importance as an input in many industries, an efficient business services sector is essential. In Korea, though, productivity growth per employee was significantly negative between 1996 and 2005 (Figure 4.6). As in other sectors, there is a negative correlation between the strictness of product market regulations and productivity growth. In 1998, the regulation index for Korea in four services – accounting, architecture, engineering and legal services (which account for the major share of the business services category) – was the third highest in the OECD. Korea has made progress since, for example by ending the fee-setting arrangements for nine professional services and reducing the minimum number of license holders needed to set up a legal entity. In addition, the number of persons allowed to pass the bar exam each year was raised from 300 in 1995 to 1 000 in 2001 and restraints on advertising were relaxed. By 2003, Korea's ranking on the regulation index was close to the OECD average, although there is scope for further progress (Panel B).

One key priority is legal services. Despite the increase in the annual quota since 2001, and some decline in the number of cases per lawyer, Korea had 5 758 persons per lawyer in 2006, the highest ratio in the OECD area and almost four times higher than the OECD average (Lee *et al.*, 2007). A law was passed in 2007 to create law schools in 2009. A total of 41 universities applied to open law schools, with a total combined annual enrolment of almost 4 000. In February 2008, however, the government decided to limit enrolment to 2 000 in 25 law schools, with an average enrolment of only 80 students, which may be too small to achieve economies of scale. It is also questionable whether the government can accurately forecast the future demand for legal services in Korea, where the number of lawsuits is rising rapidly from a low level. According to one study, an increase in the annual supply of lawyers from the current 1 000 to 3 000 would not significantly reduce the average income of lawyers in the long term (KDI, 2007b). Ensuring an adequate number of lawyers is essential to a market economy. The ceiling on the number of law students should therefore be increased or abolished, while raising and eventually eliminating the ceiling on the number of persons allowed to pass the bar exam.[42]

The government should take additional steps to strengthen competitive pressures in business services by liberalising restrictive regulations, which purportedly address market

Figure 4.6. **Product market regulation in business services**[1]

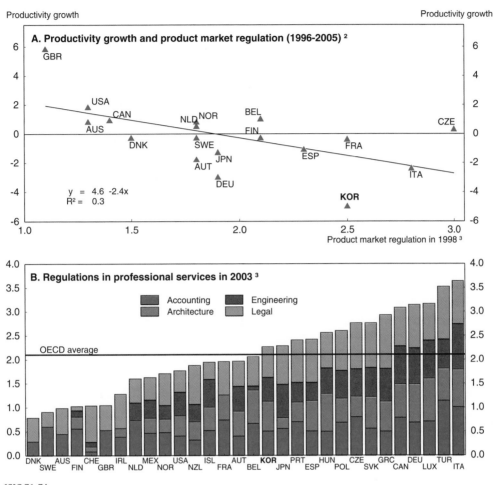

1. ISIC 71-74.
2. For Denmark, the period is 1996 to 2004.
3. Index is 0 to 6, from least to most restrictive.

Source: OECD STAN Database and Conway and Nicoletti (2006).

StatLink ⧉ http://dx.doi.org/10.1787/514214805878

failures related to information asymmetries between service providers and their clients. There is little empirical evidence that such regulations actually improve consumer welfare. Instead, they tend to boost prices and reduce innovation (Nguyen-Hong, 2000 and Patterson *et al.*, 2003) and should thus be liberalised. The fact that the stringency of regulation of professional services varies significantly across countries (Figure 4.6) suggests that entry is more restricted than necessary for client protection or market integrity. In Korea, strengthening competition in business services, which has been weak compared to other sectors, requires relaxing barriers on entry, advertising, relationships with other businesses and limits on the participation of foreign nationals. In addition, setting common industry-wide standards would increase market transparency and competition, thus enabling service providers to realise economies of scale. Reform should follow the OECD principles for regulation of business services (OECD, 2007a):

● Exclusive rights should not be granted when there are other mechanisms available to address market failure directly.

- Entrance requirements for a profession should not be disproportionate to the necessary skills.

- Regulation should focus on protecting small consumers.

- Restrictions on competition between members of a profession should be eliminated while encouraging competition between professional associations.

- Professional associations should not be granted exclusive jurisdiction and should be subject to independent scrutiny of their decisions about entrance requirements and mutual recognition.

Rapid advances in information technology and the liberalisation of trade and investment in services have expanded international competition in business services. The Korea-US FTA will help foster a competitive environment in legal services in three steps. In the *first phase* (when the agreement enters into force), US-licensed lawyers will be permitted to provide advice related to the laws of the jurisdiction in which they are allowed to practice. In addition, foreign law firms will be permitted to establish a representative office in Korea. In the *second phase* (no more than two years later), representative offices of US law firms will be allowed to enter into agreements with Korean law firms to jointly deal with cases involving domestic and foreign legal issues. In the *third phase* (no more than five years later), US law firms will be allowed to establish joint ventures with Korean law firms that can employ Korea-licensed lawyers and practice Korean law. These measures will bring high quality legal services to Korea and encourage domestic law firms to grow in size and efficiency. The FTA's provision for legal services provides a blueprint for the opening of other business services. However, even after the three phases, US legal firms will not be allowed to establish themselves in Korea. The FTA also includes a mutual recognition arrangement for engineers, architectural designers and veterinarians, which will help foreign professionals enter the Korean market.[43]

Conclusion

An efficient service sector is essential to Korea's overall economic performance and the welfare and living standards of its citizens. While reforms to enhance productivity in services have many benefits, the resulting structural changes also entail adjustment costs. However, such costs should not prevent reforms to create more open and competitive service markets. Faster productivity growth in the service sector requires strengthening competition through regulatory reform, upgrading competition policy and increasing openness to international trade and FDI inflows. A traditional industrial policy approach of targeting specific service activities for expansion should be avoided. A summary of specific recommendations to achieve these objectives is presented in Box 4.2.

Box 4.2. **Summary of recommendations to enhance productivity growth in the service sector***

Provide a favourable environment for the service sector

- Scale back government assistance to SMEs, including subsidies, financial assistance, credit guarantees and tax incentives, to make small companies less dependent on public support.

- Eliminate discrimination against the service sector by ensuring equal treatment with manufacturing.

- Establish an efficient reporting system for intellectual and intangible assets and provide adequate protection of intellectual property to encourage investment in intangible assets.

Box 4.2. **Summary of recommendations to enhance productivity growth in the service sector***
(cont.)

Accelerate regulatory reform

- Enhance the use of RIAs and public consultations, to improve the quality of regulation and adopt an explicit policy that regulations can only be adopted if the benefits justify the costs.
- Step up the pace of regulatory reform to reduce entry barriers and regulations that limit competition and expand the scope to cover additional areas, such as industrial and regional policies.
- Create a mechanism in the National Assembly to ensure the regulatory quality of proposed legislation.
- Extend successful reforms introduced in special zones on a nationwide basis and phase out the special zone approach.

Upgrade the competition framework

- Strengthen the deterrent effect of surcharges and criminal penalties, including individual sanctions.
- Provide the KFTC with compulsory investigative powers for more effective enforcement.
- Scale back remaining exemptions from the competition law and preferential measures, particularly for SMEs.

Strengthen international competition

- Promote inward FDI by eliminating restrictions on foreign ownership and improving the business climate.
- Liberalise product market regulations, which tend to discourage potential foreign investors.
- Utilise FTAs to strengthen competition in the service sector and reduce barriers that limit trade.

Remove restrictions and enhance competition in key service industries

Telecommunications

- Safeguard in practice, as spelled out in the law, the independence and transparency of the KCC's regulatory decisions.
- Relax foreign investment restrictions.
- Further liberalise entry requirements for facility-based services.
- Introduce an auction system for the allocation of spectrum, while promoting a secondary market.
- Liberalise regulations on CATV to create a level playing field with the converged services of IPTV.

Financial services

- Implement the Capital Markets Consolidation Act to promote the creation of new investment products and enhanced competition between securities firms, while upgrading supervision.
- Encourage the globalisation of Korea's financial sector by modernising the regulatory framework and improving the business and living environment to attract firms and experts from overseas.
- Be cautious in revising limits on bank ownership to limit the risk of mixing financial and industrial capital.

Business services

- Remove unnecessary constraints on entry, form of practice, advertising, and foreign participation, in line with the OECD guidelines for the regulation of business services.
- Encourage international competition by expanding recognition of certificates acquired overseas.
- Raise and eventually abolish the ceiling on the number of law students and persons passing the bar exam.

* Recommendations in each section are ranked in order of their priority.

Notes

1. The share of the service sector in total employment increased from 57.8% in 1997 to 66.7% in 2007.

2. For example, electricity charges for the logistics and tourism industries were cut to the same level as for manufacturing and the mandatory development contribution for site development was cut in half.

3. In practice, the concept of competition is difficult to measure. Given that direct indicators are lacking, they must be substituted by proxies such as mark-ups.

4. Updated indicators suggest that Korea ranks in the top third of OECD countries in terms of the restrictriveness of product market regulation for the economy as a whole (OECD, 2009).

5. Two service industries – hotels and restaurants and wholesale and retail trade – account for 36% of total SME employment, exceeding the 25% share of manufacturing.

6. SMEs also received 6% of all tax expenditures in 2006.

7. The rationale for public support is based on: i) information asymmetries between financial institutions and SMEs; ii) the SMEs' lack of tangible collateral; and iii) fixed administrative costs associated with lending, such as information gathering and credit evaluation, which discourage lending to SMEs (Kang, 2005).

8. The guarantees are provided by the Korea Credit Guarantee Fund, the Kobo Technology Fund and 16 regional Credit Guarantee Foundations (CGFs). While the guarantees of the Korea Credit Guarantee Fund and the Kobo Technology Fund have fallen in recent years, those by the regional CGFs rose from 1.0 trillion won in 2000 to 4.6 trillion won in 2007 in an effort to promote regional development.

9. On the other hand, some research suggests that the link between innovation and concentration is non-linear, with both high and low concentration levels associated with a low level of innovation (Aghion et al., 2005). Overall, though, the long-run relationship between competitive pressures and aggregate labour productivity growth is likely to be positive.

10. The 2005 OECD Ministerial (OECD, 2005b) also stressed the importance of improving education and training and upgrading innovation policies to develop the service sector.

11. The review of existing regulations by the RRC resulted in the abolition of 4 973 of the 11 125 regulations between 1998 and 2002, while 2 298 regulations were improved, in some cases by establishing a legal basis. According to one study (KIIET, 1999), the reforms reduced private-sector costs by 3.7 trillion won per year (0.7% of GDP). In addition, the RRC introduced new tools to enhance regulatory quality, such as Regulatory Impact Assessments (RIAs), which have been made mandatory.

12. The RRTF has improved the business climate by relaxing regulations on the creation of firms and the construction of factories. The on-line registration of businesses is now allowed and the time needed to establish a factory was shortened from 180 days to 100, thereby reducing the administrative cost from 150 million won to 15 million won. The time required for approval of the development of land for industrial purposes has been reduced by two to three months. The RRTF also shortened the procedure for building tourist complexes from ten steps over four years to five steps over two years.

13. In the RRC, 18 of the 25 members are from the private sector, as are 24 of the 50 members of the RRTF.

14. The share of bills initiated by members increased from 55% during the 16th National Assembly (2000-04) to 69% in the 17th National Assembly (2004-08).

15. These campaigns targeted such services as telecommunications, broadband Internet service and shopping, medical services, wedding and funeral services, media, private tutoring institutions, credit cards, non-life insurance, real estate agents, home maintenance services, job-search agencies, banking and advertising.

16. The taskforce was composed of eight subgroups involving relevant government agencies, academia, businesses and civic organisations. One focused on the policy for large business groups.

17. Violations discovered through the leniency programme accounted for 40% of the surcharges between 1997 and 2007 and 64% between 2005 and 2007. The KFTC hiked the reduction in the surcharge rate for the second applicant for leniency from 30% to 50%, while prohibiting such reductions for cartel coercers. In addition, the protection of the confidentiality of leniency applicants was strengthened.

18. In most OECD countries, financial sanctions can be as high as 10% of total firm turnover, not of the commerce affected, and there is no time limit in applying the sanctions, except in a few countries. Moreover, financial sanctions can be up to two times the gain in the United States and up to three times in New Zealand. The 2007 reform in Korea set the rate at 2% for unfair trade practices and 3% for abuse of market dominance, compared to the 10% for cartels.

19. Between 1981 and 2007, 396 cases were filed with the prosecutor's office, of which 75% resulted in indictments and 4.8% are still under investigation. There is no information on the number of convictions.

20. Since 2000, imprisonment was imposed in six competition cases, but the sentence or its service were suspended in each case. Increased use of criminal sanctions in hard-core cartel cases to make the threat of individual liability more realistic requires co-operation with the prosecutors.

21. The Ministry of Justice has opposed giving the KFTC stronger investigative powers as long as the KFTC has a monopoly on initiating prosecutions. On the other hand, the KFTC is concerned that the Ministry of Justice would pursue prosecutions of alleged competition violators purely from a criminal law perspective, without economic input, thus harming competition.

22. In addition to protecting SMEs, this rule aimed at preventing the "indiscriminate" expansion of *chaebol*.

23. *First*, the extensive restructuring in the financial and corporate sectors in the wake of the crisis created a large market for cross-border M&As. More than half of the 30 largest business groups in 1998 either went bankrupt or entered workout programmes and the number of financial institutions fell by 40% in 1998-99. Many of the rest survived thanks to links with foreign investors. *Second*, the government removed restrictions on FDI while making vigorous efforts to attract foreign investors. Of the 52 sectors previously prohibited or restricted to foreign investment, 30 have been opened completely or partially. *Third*, a significant decline in stock and land prices made investment more attractive for foreign investors.

24. The privatisation of banks re-capitalised using public funds boosted the foreign ownership share from 16% in 1997 to 64% in 2004. Foreign investors now own more than 50% of nine of the 14 commercial banks.

25. Korea's policy aims at: i) pursuing FTAs with large advanced economies and promising emerging markets; ii) achieving FTAs that have a high degree of liberalisation and are comprehensive in terms of coverage and scope; and iii) adopting a multi-track approach of simultaneous negotiations with more than one country.

26. The level of Producer Support Estimate over the period 2003-05 was 62%, double the OECD average.

27. For example, the development of IPTV (Internet Protocol TV) was delayed by the lack of agreement between the KBC, which regulated broadcasting, and the MIC, which regulated telecommunications.

28. The acronyms in this paragraph stand for PSTN (Public Switched Telephone Network), VoIP (Voice over Internet Protocol), MVNO (Mobile Virtual Network Operator), and USIM (Universal Subscriber Identity Module).

29. The implementation of some of these steps has already resulted in significant benefits. In particular, allowing bundled service, including Korea Telecom's local telephony, resulted in price discounts of up to 10% and the end of regulations on handset subsidies benefited consumers.

30. The KCC consists of five permanent commissioners, one of whom serves as chairman, a minister-level post. Two of the commissioners are appointed by the president, one of whom, designated as chairman, needs a prior hearing by the National Assembly. The current chairman was inaugurated in March 2008. The other three permanent commission members are recommended by the National Assembly, one by the president's party and two by the opposition parties.

31. In 2007, the Internet Multimedia Broadcasting Business Law, which covers IPTV service, was passed.

32. For example, facility-based services for fixed-line communication for local, long-distance and international calls, which previously required three licenses, are now treated as a single transmission service.

33. As of the end of 2007, the number of participants in the fixed-line category was three for local calls, five for long-distance calls, five for international calls, and nine for VoIP.

34. For KT, for example, such charges amounted to $64 million in 2004.

35. A study of prices for unbundled local loops would help clarify whether the limited extent of unbundling thus far is due to pricing or the existence of alternative infrastructure that reduces the need for unbundling.

36. It ought to be borne in mind that FDI restrictions should be considered together with state ownership of telecommunication operators.

37. In Japan, for example, the loss of existing customers to the capital market was a key factor in the problems in the banking sector during the 1990s (Hoshi, 2001).

38. For example, Shanghai announced its so-called "three-step strategy" in 2002 to become a regional financial centre. Sydney has also been focusing on attracting foreign companies related to asset management and venture capital business as part of its "Axis Australia" initiative. Tokyo has undertaken financial reform programmes aimed at revitalising its financial industry.

39. At the end of 2006, the share of overseas operations in total assets of domestic banks was only 2.5%, much lower than the 91% for UBS and the 56% for Citibank and HSBC.

40. Among OECD countries, 14, including France, Germany and the United Kingdom, have no direct regulations on industrial capital's ownership of banks. In seven countries, including Japan, the financial supervisor can allow industrial capital to own banks.

41. The ownership of some non-bank financial institutions, particularly the merchant banks, by industrial companies, who used them as cash cows, played a role in triggering the 1997 crisis.

42. Each year, only 1 000 of the approximately 17 500 who take the bar exam are permitted to pass.

43. This will help Korean professionals enter the US market. However, becoming a successful global supplier of business services requires a stable ICT infrastructure, a highly educated and language-proficient workforce and an efficient infrastructure, simplified administrative procedures and reasonable regulatory burdens in the domestic market (Engman, 2007).

Bibliography

Aghion, P., N. Bloom, R. Blundell, R. Griffith and P. Howitt (2005), "Competition and Innovation: An Inverted-U Relationship", *The Quarterly Journal of Economics*, Vol. 120, No. 2.

Alesina, A., S. Ardagna, G. Nicoletti and F. Schiantarelli (2005), "Regulation and Investment", *Journal of the European Economic Association*, Vol. 3, No. 4.

Bassanini, A. and E. Ernst (2002), "Labour Market Institutions, Product Market Regulation and Innovation: Cross-Country Evidence", *OECD Economics Department Working Paper*, No. 316, OECD, Paris.

Cho, Sang-hoon (2007), "Big Bang in Korea's Capital Markets: Reform Legislation and Its Impact", *Korean Economy 2007*, Korea Economic Institute of America, Washington, D.C.

Conway, P., V. Janod, and G. Nicoletti (2005), "Product Market Regulation in OECD Countries: 1998 to 2003", *OECD Economics Department Working Paper*, No. 419, OECD, Paris.

Conway, P. and G. Nicoletti (2006), "Product Market Regulation in the Non-Manufacturing Sectors of OECD Countries: Measurement and Highlights", *OECD Economics Department Working Paper*, Paper No. 530, OECD, Paris.

Conway, P., D. de Rosa, G. Nicoletti and F. Steiner (2006), "Regulation, Competition and Productivity Convergence", *OECD Economics Department Working Paper*, No. 509, OECD, Paris.

De Serres, A., S. Kobayakawa, T. Sløk and L. Vartia (2006), "Regulation of Financial Systems and Economic Growth in OECD Countries: An Empirical Analysis", *OECD Economic Studies*, No. 43, OECD, Paris.

Engman, M. (2007), "Expanding International Supply Chains: The Role of Emerging Economies in Providing it and Business Process Services", OECD, *Trade Policy Working Paper*, No. 52, OECD, Paris.

Høj, J. (2007), "Competition Law and Policy Indicators for the OECD Countries", *OECD Economics Department Working Paper*, No. 568, OECD, Paris.

Høj, J., M. Jimenez, M. Maher, G. Nicoletti and M. Wise (2007), "Product Market Competition in the OECD Countries: Taking Stock and Moving Forward", *OECD Economics Department Working Paper*, No. 575, OECD, Paris.

Hoshi, T. (2001), "What Happened to Japanese Banks", *Monetary and Economic Studies*, (February), Bank of Japan.

IMD (2008), *World Competitiveness Yearbook 2008*, International Institute for Management Development, Lausanne.

IMF (2006), *Global Financial Stability Report*, April, Washington, D.C.

Jaumotte, F. and N. Pain (2005), "Innovation in the Business Sector", *OECD Economics Department Working Paper*, No. 459, OECD, Paris.

Kang, D. (2005), "Corporate Distress and Restructuring Policies of Korean Small and Medium-sized Enterprises: Role of Credit Guarantees", mimeo, Korea Development Institute, Seoul.

Kang, D. (2007), "Empirical Evaluations on the Government Financial Assistance toward SMEs in Korea", in *Financing Innovation-Oriented Business to Promote Entrepreneurship*, edited by D. Kang, Korea Development Institute, Seoul.

Korea Development Institute (KDI) (2007a), *Survey on Financial Hub Policy*, Seoul (in Korean).

Korea Development Institute (KDI) (2007b), "Policy Issues to Advance the Service Sector", Seoul (in Korean).

Korea Fair Trade Commission (KFTC) (2007), "Recent Development in Korea's Competition Laws and Policies", Seoul.

Korea Fair Trade Commission (KFTC) (2008), *Annual Report, 2008*, Seoul (in Korean).

Korea Federation of SMEs (2008a), *Statistics of Small and Medium Enterprises*, Seoul (in Korean).

Korea Federation of SMEs (2008b), *SMEs Status Indicator*, Seoul (in Korean).

Korea Information Society Development Institute (2008), *Korea's Telecommunication Service Market Outlook, 2008*, Seoul (in Korean).

Korea Institute for Industrial Economics and Trade (KIIET) (1999), *An Analysis of the Economic Effects of Regulatory Reform*, Seoul (in Korean).

Kox, H. and H. Nordas (2007), "Service Trade and Domestic Regulation", *OECD Trade Policy Working Paper*, No. 49, OECD, Paris.

Lee, Byounghee, Byungik Cho and Youngmin Kim, (2007), "Analysis of Entry Barriers to the Service Industry", Research Paper of the Bank of Korea, August, Seoul (in Korean).

Ministry of Commerce, Industry and Energy (MOCIE) (2005), *Survey on the Management of Foreign-Invested Firms*, Seoul (in Korean).

Ministry of Science and Technology (2007), *Report on the Survey of Research and Development in Science and Technology*, Seoul (in Korean).

Nguyen-Hong, D. (2000), "Restrictions on Trade in Professional Services", Productivity Commission Staff Research Paper, AusInfo, Canberra.

Nicoletti, G. (2001), "Regulation in Services: OECD Patterns and Economic Implications", *OECD Economics Department Working Paper*, No. 287, OECD, Paris.

Nicoletti, G., A. Bassanini, E. Ernst, S. Jean, P. Santiago and P. Swaim (2001), "Product and Labour Market Interactions in OECD Countries", *OECD Economics Department Working Paper*, No. 312, OECD Paris.

Nicoletti, G. and S. Scarpetta (2003), "Regulation, Productivity and Growth: OECD Evidence", *OECD Economics Department Working Paper*, No. 347, OECD, Paris.

Nicoletti, G. and S. Scarpetta (2005), "Regulation and Economic Performance: Product Market Reforms and Productivity in the OECD", *OECD Economics Department Working Paper*, No. 460, OECD, Paris.

OECD (2000), *Competition in Professional Services*, OECD, Paris.

OECD (2005a), "The Benefits of Liberalising Product Markets and Reducing Barriers to International Trade and Investment in the OECD", *OECD Economics Department Working Paper*, No. 463, OECD, Paris.

OECD (2005b), *Growth in Services: Fostering Employment, Productivity and Innovation*, Report for the Meeting of the OECD Council at Ministerial Level, OECD, Paris.

OECD (2005c), *OECD Economic Globalisation Indicators*, OECD, Paris.

OECD (2005d), *OECD Economic Surveys: Korea*, OECD, Paris.

OECD (2007a), *Globalisation and Structural Adjustment: Summary Report of the Study on Globalisation and Innovation in the Business Services Sector*, OECD, Paris.

OECD (2007b), *Korea: Progress in Implementing Regulatory Reform*, OECD Reviews of Regulatory Reform, OECD, Paris.

OECD (2007c), *OECD Communication Outlook*, OECD, Paris.

OECD (2007d), *OECD Economic Surveys: Korea*, OECD, Paris.

OECD (2008a), *OECD Compendium of Productivity Indicators*, OECD, Paris.

OECD (2008b), *OECD Factbook*, OECD, Paris.

OECD (2009), "Product Market Regulations in OECD Countries 1998-2007: Update and Extension of the OECD Indicators", (forthcoming), OECD, Paris.

Oliveira Martins, J. and C. de la Maisonneuve (2006), "Projecting OECD Health and Long-Term Care Expenditures: What Are the Main Drivers?", *OECD Economic Studies*, No. 42, Paris, OECD.

Paterson, I., M. Fink and A. Ogus (2003), "Economic Impact of Regulation in the Field of Liberal Professions in Different Member States", Institute for Advanced Studies, Vienna.

Pilat, D. (2007), "Productivity in Business Services", in *Business Services in European Economic Growth*, edited by L. Rubalcaba and H. Kox, Edward Elgar.

Presidential Commission on SMEs (2007), *The Report on Evaluation and Prior Adjustment of Budget for SMEs in 2007*, Seoul (in Korean).

Regulatory Reform Committee (2007), *Regulatory Reform White Book*, Seoul (in Korean).

Small and Medium Business Administration (2007), *Policies for SMEs in 2008*, Seoul (in Korean).

Wölfl, A. (2005), "The Service Economy in OECD Countries", *OECD Science, Technology and Industry Working Paper*, No. 2005/3, OECD, Paris.

World Bank (2008), *Doing Business 2009*, Washington, D.C.

ISBN 978-92-64-05425-7
OECD Economic Surveys: Korea
© OECD 2008

Chapter 5

Sustaining growth by reforming the labour market and improving the education system

A well-functioning labour market is essential to sustain rapid economic growth in the face of population ageing. Priorities are to reverse the rising share of non-regular workers, which has negative implications for both growth and equity, and encourage greater employment of women and youth, who are under-represented in the labour force. Attracting more women to employment requires increasing the availability of childcare, strengthening maternity leave and creating more family-friendly workplaces. Youth employment rates should be boosted by upgrading tertiary education through stronger competition and closer links to enterprises to reduce mismatches. Educational reform should be extended to elementary and secondary schools to enhance efficiency and decrease the burden of private tutoring. The age of retirement of employees should be raised by eliminating mandatory retirement and phasing out the retirement allowance. Active labour market policies should focus on policies to expand human capital rather than wage subsidies.

Rapid employment growth, low unemployment and sustained gains in human capital have contributed substantially to Korea's economic development. However, traditional labour market institutions that had been successful in the past are no longer appropriate. Korea's integration in the world economy and technological change call for greater flexibility and increased human capital, while population ageing makes it essential to boost the relatively low participation rates of prime-age women and youth and raise the retirement age of employees. Achieving these objectives requires reforms in the labour market, social welfare policies and the education system. In sum, the framework should give firms incentives to employ regular workers, thus limiting labour market dualism, while encouraging more women and youth to accept employment and extending the working life of employees. At the same time, education should be upgraded to enhance the employability of young people and to promote human capital.

This chapter first addresses the problem of labour market dualism, which is detrimental to both growth and equity. It then analyses the low employment rates of women and youth to identify policies conducive to greater participation, including education reforms. The challenge of keeping older workers in employment is examined in the fourth section. The chapter concludes with a summary of the key recommendations shown in Box 5.2.

Reversing labour market dualism: regular *versus* non-regular workers

The trend toward greater dualism in the labour market has negative implications for human capital formation and economic growth, as it increases worker turnover and reduces firm-provided training (Chung and Lee, 2005). It also raises equity issues because non-regular workers face precarious jobs, wage discrimination and limited social protection. The share of non-regular workers rose from 27% in 2001 to 36% in 2007 (Box 5.1). Temporary workers make up the majority of non-regular workers (Table 1.9), accounting for 28% of all employees in 2007, the second-highest proportion in the OECD area (Figure 1.12), before declining somewhat to 26% in August 2008. Temporary employment in Korea is unique in several respects:

- The proportion of temporary workers who are employed part-time is only 14% compared with 30% to 50% in other OECD countries. This indicates that temporary jobs are less related to the need for working-time flexibility, particularly for women, than elsewhere.

- The incidence of temporary workers is high among all age groups in Korea, in contrast to other OECD countries, where it is concentrated among youth (Table 5.1). The high proportion for older workers is linked to the young age of mandatory retirement in many firms.

- Temporary workers in Korea are highly concentrated in the service sector, while the proportion in manufacturing and the primary sector is similar to the OECD average (Panel B).

As in other OECD countries, the incidence of temporary work is concentrated in small companies (Panel C) and among workers with low and medium levels of education (Panel D).

Box 5.1. **Definition of non-regular workers**

The definition of "non-regular" workers in Korea is broader than that of temporary workers used by the OECD. Temporary workers include employees under fixed-term contracts, seasonal workers and temporary agency jobs. Although the term non-regular worker is widely used in Korea, there is no consensus on its definition, which is generally based on; i) the term of contract (definite or indefinite) and continuity of employment; ii) working hours; and iii) the type of relationship with the firm. The Economic and Social Development Commission (formerly the Tripartite Commission, which includes the government and social partners) defines non-regular workers as:

- *Contingent workers* (22.3% of employees): those with fixed-term contracts or who expect their work arrangement to have a limited duration for involuntary reasons. This category corresponds to the OECD definition of temporary workers.

- *Part-time workers* (7.6%): those who work "fewer hours" than full-time workers.

- *Atypical workers* (13.9%): temporary agency workers (dispatched workers), individual contract workers (who work independently of the firm), home-based workers, on-call workers and other new forms of employment.

By this definition, the share of non-regular workers rose from 27% in 2001 to 36% in 2007 (accounting for overlap between the three categories). Some experts argue that the rate is as high as 57%. In any event, it is higher than the number of temporary workers under the OECD measure.

Table 5.1. **A comparison of temporary workers in Korea and the OECD**

A. By age (%)			
	15-24	25-54	55+	Total
Korea in 2005	36.1	26.2	46.1	29.4
OECD in 2005	32.7	10.4	10.4	12.8

B. By industry (normalised by distribution)[1]				
	Primary	Manufacturing	Services	Services/Manufacturing	Total
Korea in 2005	1.8	2.6	25.0	9.5	29.4
EU-15 average in 2005	1.5	3.4	9.8	2.9	14.7
OECD average in 2000	1.5	2.5	8.0	3.3	12.0

C. By firm size (normalised by distribution)[1]				
	Less than 10 persons	10-29 persons	30-99 persons	100 persons and over	Total
Korea in 2005	16.4	5.8	4.0	3.2	29.4
	Less than 20 persons	20-49 persons		50 persons and over	Total
EU-15 average in 2005	7.3	2.3		5.1	14.7
OECD average in 2000	7.4	1.6		3.0	12.0

D. By educational attainment (normalised by distribution)[1]				
	Low	Medium	High	Low/High	Total
Korea in 2005	12.1	12.4	4.9	2.4	29.4
EU-15 average in 2005	7.7	4.2	2.8	2.8	14.7
OECD average in 2000	5.5	4.6	1.9	2.9	12.0

1. The figure for each category is its contribution to the total incidence of temporary workers.
Source: Grubb *et al.* (2007).

The hourly wages of non-regular workers fell from 80% of regular workers' in 2001 to 71% in 2007. The widening gap reflects differences in job tenure and an increase in the human capital of regular workers, who have greater access to on-the-job training. However, the monthly wages of non-regular workers have remained around 63% of regular workers', reflecting a rise in working hours. Discrimination accounts for a significant portion of the wage gap according to a number of studies. For example, the Korea Employers Federation (2006) estimated that the productivity of non-regular workers is 22% below that of regular workers, while their wages are 44% less. Jeong (2003) found that non-regular workers are paid 20% to 27% less than regular workers, after adjusting for age, experience, education and other attributes. Ahn (2006) reported that 23% of the wage gap is explained by discrimination against non-regular workers.[1]

The policy response to labour market dualism

The government is concerned that labour market polarisation could undermine national competitiveness, weaken social cohesiveness and put strains on the social safety net. Therefore, it has expanded active labour market policies for non-regular workers to improve their employability[2] and taken steps to increase their coverage by the social safety net. In addition, the government has enacted a law to protect non-regular workers from "undue discrimination" and avoid their "excessive use":

● "Unjustifiable discriminatory practices" against non-regular workers are prohibited. Employees claiming discriminatory working conditions or wages can submit complaints to the Labour Relations Commission, where firms must prove that their practices are not discriminatory. This provision was implemented in companies with at least 300 employees in July 2007 and those with 100 to 299 employees in July 2008. It will be extended to smaller companies from July 2009.

● Since July 2007, workers with fixed-term contracts in all firms regardless of size are considered to be regular employees after two years of work.

The 2007 OECD Economic Surveys: Korea cautioned that prohibiting discrimination against non-regular workers may subject firms to costly and time-consuming litigation that would discourage the employment of non-regular workers and lead to higher unemployment. By February 2008, 800 cases involving 2 793 non-regular workers who had filed complaints under the new law had been settled. The Labour Relations Commission, a public mediator, imposed correction orders in two-thirds of the cases. The high proportion of correction orders is likely to encourage non-regular workers to file cases while putting pressure on firms to improve the employment conditions of non-regular workers or to terminate their contracts. While it is too early to judge, monthly employment data show that non-regular employment has had a negative impact on total employment since the law began to take effect in mid-2007 (Figure 5.1). This suggests that even smaller companies have responded to the new law by scaling back their number of non-regular workers or transforming them into regular workers.[3] The government contributed to this trend by shifting 67 000 non-regular workers in the public sector to regular status in mid-2007. In addition, some firms are outsourcing work done by non-regular workers to other firms. Labour market trends should be closely monitored as this law is implemented.

According to surveys, firms hire non-regular workers to reduce labour costs and to increase employment flexibility, given the difficulty of laying off regular workers due to the high degree of employment protection and the power of trade unions in large firms

Figure 5.1. **Contribution to employment growth by status of workers**

Year-on-year growth by month

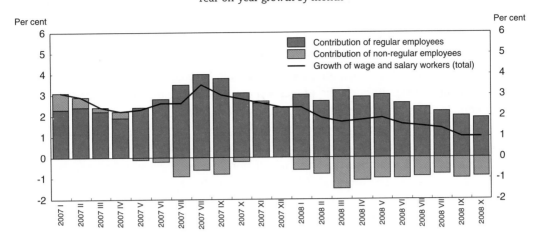

Source: Korea National Statistical Office.

StatLink ⟨⟩ http://dx.doi.org/10.1787/514226328422

(*OECD Economic Surveys: Korea*, 2007). The revision of the labour law in 1998 to allow collective dismissals for "urgent managerial reasons" has not sufficiently enhanced flexibility in practice. This reflects the attached conditions, notably that firms must exhaust "all means" to avoid dismissals, discuss proposed dismissals for at least two months (recently reduced to 50 days) with workers and notify the government. Given these constraints, firms have relied on more expensive methods to reduce employment, such as early retirement packages and incentives for voluntary departures. According to the OECD indicator, employment protection for regular workers in Korea in 2006 was slightly above China and the OECD average, and far above English-speaking OECD countries (Figure 5.2).[4] OECD studies show that countries with stricter protection for

Figure 5.2. **International comparison of employment protection legislation**

In 2006

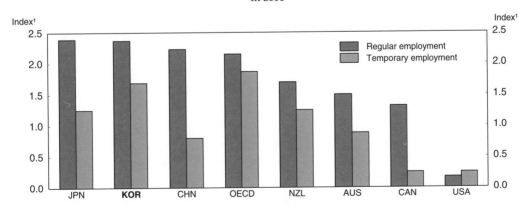

1. Index scale of 0 to 6 from least to most restrictive in 2006.

Source: OECD (2008b), *Going for Growth, 2008*, OECD, Paris.

StatLink ⟨⟩ http://dx.doi.org/10.1787/514231256720

regular workers tend to have a higher incidence of temporary employment (Grubb et al., 2007). To reduce the incentives to hire non-regular workers, past *OECD Economic Surveys: Korea* have recommended that employment protection for regular workers be relaxed. Korea's approach of raising its protection for non-regular workers, which in 2006 was slightly below the OECD average, risks reducing overall employment.

The liberalisation of employment protection should be accompanied by a strengthening of the social safety net. Although the proportion of wage and salary earners covered by the Employment Insurance System (EIS) has increased sharply since the mid-1990s to 56.8% in 2007, it still leaves a substantial portion of the labour force unprotected (Table 5.2). Gaps in coverage are concentrated among non-regular workers; the share of such workers participating in the EIS, as well as the National Pension Scheme (NPS) and the National Health Insurance (NHI), is around 40%, only one-half of the share for regular workers (Table 3.8). Part of the gap reflects differences in the law. For example, both the NPS and NHI exclude daily workers, while some part-time workers are also not covered. However, the wide gap in coverage is also due to weak compliance, particularly among workers in small firms.

Table 5.2. **Coverage of the Employment Insurance System**
Thousand employees and per cent

	1995	2000	2001	2002	2003	2004	2005	2006	2007
Wage and salary earners	12 899	13 142	13 659	14 181	14 402	14 894	15 185	15 551	15 970
Eligible for EIS	4 280	8 700	9 269	9 269	9 651	10 037	10 330	10 803	11 115
Actually insured	4 204	6 747	6 909	7 171	7 203	7 577	8 064	8 537	9 063
Eligible as a per cent of wage and salary earners	33.2	66.2	67.9	65.4	67.0	67.4	68.0	69.5	69.6
Insured as a per cent of eligible workers	98.2	77.6	74.5	77.4	74.6	75.5	78.1	79.0	81.5
Insured as a per cent of wage and salary earners	32.6	51.3	50.6	50.6	50.0	50.9	53.1	54.9	56.8
Proportion of unemployed receiving benefits			15.1	16.6	18.5	22.4	25.6	30.0	34.8

Source: Ministry of Labour.

The lower coverage of non-regular workers by the social insurance systems reduces their cost relative to regular workers, strengthening the incentive of firms to hire them. Increasing the coverage of non-regular workers would thus help narrow the gap and weaken the incentive. While the coverage of social insurance is on an upward trend, further steps are required to boost compliance, notably by integrating the collection of contributions (see Chapter 3). In sum, it is essential to relax employment protection for regular workers and broaden the social insurance coverage of non-regular workers in order to reduce labour market dualism and its negative effect on growth and equity.

Raising the female labour force participation rate

The low female participation rate for women in the 25-to-54 age group (Figure 1.13) reflects the significant proportion of women who withdraw from the labour force at the time of marriage or childbirth. Consequently, the participation rate, plotted across age cohorts, is M-shaped (Figure 5.3). Nevertheless, female participation and employment is rising, primarily due to the changing behaviour of younger women. For the 25-to-29 age group, participation has doubled from 32% for women born during the first half of the 1950s to 65% for women born during the second half of the 1970s, reflecting the trend toward later marriage. In contrast, the rate at the second peak, which occurs for the 40-to-44 age group, has remained around 63% for successive cohorts born since 1951.

Figure 5.3. **Labour force participation rate of women by age cohort**

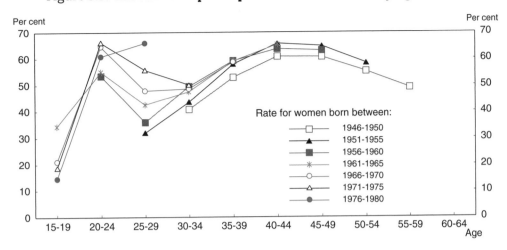

Source: Korea National Statistical Office.

StatLink ⧉ http://dx.doi.org/10.1787/514236214674

Factors limiting the labour force participation of women in Korea

The decision to return to work depends on labour market conditions. In Korea, the average wage of women is 38% below that of men, much larger than the OECD average of 18%. The large gender gap reflects a number of factors. First, a large proportion of women are non-regular workers and thus receive significantly lower salaries. While one-third of both men and women are in non-regular employment during their twenties, the rate decreases for men in their thirties and forties, while increasing to over 40% for women (Table 1.9). Even women employed as regular workers prior to interrupting their careers for child rearing are likely to end up in non-regular employment if they return to the labour force (Hwang and Chang, 2004). Second, the tradition of seniority-based wages rewards workers with long tenures (see below). As a result, women who interrupt their careers tend to be locked into low salaries regardless of performance. Third, although women make up 38% of the workforce, their share of managerial jobs is only 8%, compared with 20% to 30% in many OECD countries (OECD, 2007a). After adjusting for workers' characteristics, the gender gap in wages is estimated at about 20% for regular workers (Jeong, 2003).

In sum, unattractive employment options tend to discourage women from returning to the labour market. Indeed, Korea is one of the few OECD countries where the employment rate of female university graduates (61%) is not significantly higher than that for women with less than an upper secondary education (58%). This is explained by a high reservation wage among women with high educational attainment, making them reluctant to accept low-paying jobs. In contrast, the average employment rate for female university graduates in the OECD area, at 79%, is significantly higher than the 48% rate for women with less than an upper secondary education (Figure 5.4).

A second factor discouraging female employment is long working hours, which make it difficult to combine paid employment with family responsibilities. Despite the gradual introduction of the 40-hour work week from 2004, annual working hours were 2 261 in 2007, more than one-third higher than the OECD average,[5] reflecting in part the pro-work incentives in the tax system (Chapter 3). In 2007, 27% of Korean women worked more than 54 hours per week, while another 23% worked between 45 and 53 hours

Figure 5.4. **Employment rate of women by educational attainment in OECD countries**[1]

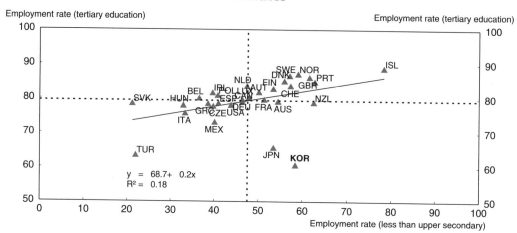

1. The OECD average is shown by the dotted lines (48% and 79%) depending on the level of education.
Source: OECD (2008a), *Education at a Glance 2008*, OECD, Paris and calculations by the Secretariat.

StatLink *http://dx.doi.org/10.1787/514305237728*

(Figure 5.5). In addition, there is substantial unpaid overtime and commuting times tend to be long. Moreover, the generally longer working hours of men – more than one-third of whom work more than 54 hours a week – tends to place family responsibilities primarily on women. Finally, opportunities for part-time employment – which is widely used in many countries to reconcile work and family responsibilities, especially when children are young – are very limited in Korea for both men and women (Table 5.3). Only 12% of Korean women in their thirties, when child-caring responsibilities are heaviest, work part-time, half of the OECD average. One disadvantage of part-time work is that it tends to be paid less, while in many countries such work is paid the same hourly wage as full-time work (OECD, 2007b).

Figure 5.5. **Distribution of weekly working hours for women in Korea in 2007**

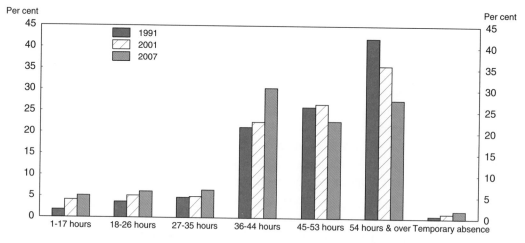

Source: Korea National Statistical Office.

StatLink *http://dx.doi.org/10.1787/514368416773*

Table 5.3. **International comparison of part-time employment**

As a per cent of total employment in 2006[1]

	15 to 24	25 to 29	30 to 34	35 to 39	40 to 44	45 to 49	50 to 54	55+	Total
Korea									
Male	14.5	3.5	3.3	2.9	4.2	4.9	5.8	14.3	6.3
Female	15.2	6.4	11.2	12.7	10.8	9.8	10.4	19.4	12.3
Total	14.9	4.9	6.1	6.6	6.8	6.9	7.6	16.4	8.8
OECD average[2]									
Male	22.4	5.6	3.8	3.4	3.6	3.7	4.6	17.4	8.1
Female	35.0	16.6	21.7	25.7	25.8	23.6	23.7	57.5	26.4
Total	28.3	10.4	11.3	12.9	13.5	12.8	13.3	34.5	16.1

1. Full-time employment based on a common definition of at least 30 hours of work per week in the worker's main job.
2. OECD average excluding Mexico for which data are not available in 2006.
Source: OECD Employment Outlook Database.

A third factor limiting female employment rates is a lack of suitable childcare. In a government survey (Ministry of Labour, 2008), more than 60% of women responded that the "burden of childcare" was the primary obstacle to joining the labour force.[6] In fact, Korea ranked 24th in the OECD in the school enrolment rates of children between the ages of three and five, at 61% in 2004 (Figure 5.6). While the share increased to 72% by 2006, it was still low by OECD standards. As for childcare, the government builds and runs public facilities, which care for 10.9% of the children enrolled in childcare (Table 5.4).

A fourth factor limiting female labour force participation is the length and coverage of maternity leave. Paid maternity leave was extended from 60 to 90 days in 2001, with 60 days paid by the employer and the additional 30 days paid by the EIS. Nevertheless, it remains much shorter than the OECD average of 4.5 months (OECD, 2007a). In 2006, the government decided that the EIS would cover 90 days for women employed at SMEs. These measures helped increase the number of women taking maternity leave by more than 50% between 2004 and 2007 to around 58 000. Nevertheless, this is equivalent to only about one-tenth of the number of births that year. The low take-up of maternity leave reflects the

Figure 5.6. **School enrolment rates of children between 3 and 5 years old in 2004**

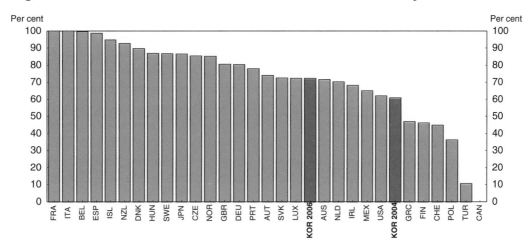

Source: OECD Family database, Ministry of Education and Human Resource Development and Ministry of Gender Equality and Family.

StatLink http://dx.doi.org/10.1787/514371588343

Table 5.4. **Childcare facilities in Korea in 2007**

	Facilities		Children (thousand)		Average size
	Number	Per cent	Number	Per cent	
Government	1 748	5.7	119.2	10.9	68.2
Private, non-profit[1]	1 460	4.7	118.3	10.8	81.0
Private sub-total	14 083	45.6	668.9	60.9	47.5
Corporation	1 002	3.2	55.9	5.1	55.8
Individual	13 081	42.4	612.2	55.7	46.8
Parents' co-operative	61	0.2	1.4	0.1	23.7
Family[2]	13 184	42.7	178.0	16.2	13.5
Workplace-based	320	1.0	15.1	1.4	47.3
Total	30 856	100.0	1 098.5	100.0	35.6

1. Social welfare corporations subsidised by the government. These facilities, as well as those of the government, must have at least ten children, while those in the private sector must have at least 20.
2. "Family" refers to childcare provided at residential houses. The number of children can range between four and 21.
Source: Ministry for Health, Welfare and Family Affairs.

StatLink

low coverage of the EIS (Table 5.2). In addition, in the 2008 survey, 58% of women replied that maternity leave, as well as parental leave, do not function properly, due in part to pressure from managers or colleagues. A system of parental leave was established in 2001 but the number of participants – 98% of whom are women – is small at only 0.2% of employees.[7]

Policies to raise the female participation rate

The government offers wage subsidies to encourage women to remain in the workforce or return to it after having children. Given the high deadweight costs associated with wage subsidies, a better approach would be to attract women back into the labour force by creating better job opportunities, in part by reversing the rising trend of non-regular workers. In addition, expanding the use of performance-based pay in place of the seniority-based system (see below) would provide better opportunities. Another important priority is to expand the availability of childcare. In 2006, the government established a target to triple the share of children in public facilities from 11% to 30% over five years (*OECD Economic Surveys: Korea*, 2007). While such an approach aims at providing a similar quality of care for each child, it would be more efficient to allow a larger role for the private sector, thereby attracting new funding and greater dynamism while limiting public outlays. Increasing the role of private firms would require removing or lifting the price cap on fees, which is set below the minimum level needed to provide quality childcare, according to the government.[8] However, this might boost the cost of childcare to households, leading mothers to withdraw from the labour force rather than rely on lower-quality, informal care. This concern could be met by providing childcare vouchers directly to households, which may prove to be a less expensive approach than the plan to build public childcare facilities.[9] Concerns about quality should be met by requiring that public support for parents be used for childcare provided by licensed facilities.

Further extending the length of maternity leave beyond 90 days would also boost female participation. One study found that around five months is the optimal length (measured in full-time equivalents) from a labour supply perspective (Jaumotte, 2003). At the same time, it is important to increase the scope for women to take maternity leave. One key is to expand the coverage of the EIS, which plays a major role in financing maternity leave. The revision of parental leave in 2007, which raised the eligible age of children to three-years-old, boosted the monthly allowance to 0.5 million won and allowed parents to take the leave on a part-time basis, should help make this programme more attractive to parents.

In sum, while the Korean tax and social benefit systems are characterised as pro-growth (Chapter 3), women still receive little public support to help them reconcile work and family responsibilities. While policies that are more favourable toward female employment are important, the impact would be limited by workplaces that are not family-friendly, not least due to exceptionally long working hours.[10] Family-friendly workplaces are essential for the reconciliation of work and family life and also have important implications for the fertility rate (see below). The labour market will have to adjust in order to provide mothers with the hours, jobs, wages and careers that will attract them back into employment. While many of these adjustments will be based on agreements between firms and employees, the government needs to ensure an appropriate framework based on the above recommendations.

Boosting the fertility rate while expanding female participation in the job market

The government's goal is to boost the fertility rate from 1.26 to the OECD average of 1.6. The positive correlation between female labour force participation and fertility rates in the OECD area suggests that it is possible to lift both. However, the positive relationship breaks down when the length of working hours is considered (Figure 5.7). Reducing working hours to the OECD average may significantly boost fertility. Another factor reducing fertility is the low level of public spending on family benefits, which at only 0.1% of GDP, is the lowest in the OECD area and well below the OECD average of 2.4%.

Figure 5.7. An international comparison of working hours and the fertility rate

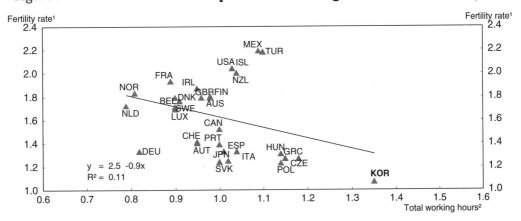

1. The fertility rates are for 2005, except for Canada (2004).
2. The OECD average for total working hours (in 2005) is set at 1.0.

Source: OECD Family Database and calculations by the Secretariat.

StatLink 🖉 http://dx.doi.org/10.1787/514425217766

The government announced a five-year plan in 2006 to boost the fertility rate by alleviating the burden of bearing and caring for children, and creating more family-friendly workplaces to reduce obstacles facing women who wish to combine employment and childrearing.[11] The policies recommended above to lengthen parental leave and increase the availability of childcare to boost female labour force participation should also have a positive effect on fertility, according to OECD research (d'Addio and Mira d'Ercole, 2005). On the other hand, tax and social benefits for families with children, as suggested in the five-year plan, have been found to lower female labour participation in other countries (Jaumotte, 2003). Given the priority to raise female employment, increases in transfers to families with children should be aimed at reducing child poverty, rather than increasing the fertility rate.

Improving the job prospects of young people

The fall in the employment rate for the 15-to-29 age group to a level below the OECD average has raised concern about the integration of youth in the labour market. While the high rate of enrolment in tertiary education partially explains the low rate, there is also a large number of youth who are neither in employment nor in education or training (the so-called NEETs). In 2004, NEETs accounted for 16.8% of the 15-to-29 age group, slightly above the OECD average (Figure 5.8).[12] The share of NEETs among youth with tertiary education is around three times higher than the OECD average, while the share among those with less than an upper secondary education is significantly below the OECD average. This points to a mismatch between the university system and the labour market. Many educated youth are waiting or preparing for job entrance exams in the public or private sector.[13] The high rate of NEETs among tertiary graduates, combined with the relatively low incidence of non-regular employment among this group, suggests that educated youth in Korea tend to stay out of the labour market rather than accept jobs that do not match their expectations. In other words, growing labour market dualism has discouraged employment of educated youth by widening the gap between their reservation wage and the offered wage.

A key way to raise youth employment is to stem the trend toward non-regular employment, which pays far less than regular jobs. In 2007, only 69.6% of new university graduates found jobs (Table 5.5), despite labour shortages in some sectors and 5% economic growth. Although 16.1% accepted jobs as non-regulars, many of the 20.5% that were not working presumably had reservation wages above the pay offered in non-regular employment. Moreover, given limited mobility between regular and non-regular employment, a significant number of graduates prefer to wait for a regular job rather than to be classified as non-regulars.[14] The proportion of new graduates finding employment would be increased by addressing the factors responsible for labour market duality. Another way to boost employment would be to reduce the number of youth preparing for entry exams, primarily for public-sector jobs, a category that accounts for 16% of NEETs. The willingness to accept such opportunity costs suggests that the wage and pension benefits of such jobs are higher than other jobs; an OECD study found a wage premium on public workers in many countries (Strauss and Maisonneuve, 2007).

Improving active labour market policies for youth

Public spending on active labour market policies for youth has increased from 0.02% of GDP in 2002 to 0.09% in 2007. There are 61 public programmes targeting youth through direct job creation, training, employment subsidies and job experience programmes. The large variety of small programmes makes it difficult for youth to find the proper programme, increases administrative costs and complicates monitoring and evaluation (OECD, 2007c). Indeed, classifying programmes by their target group shows a wide variation

Figure 5.8. **Inactive youth: neither in employment nor in education or training (NEET)**

By educational attainment and gender for the 15-to-29 age group in selected OECD countries in 2004[1]

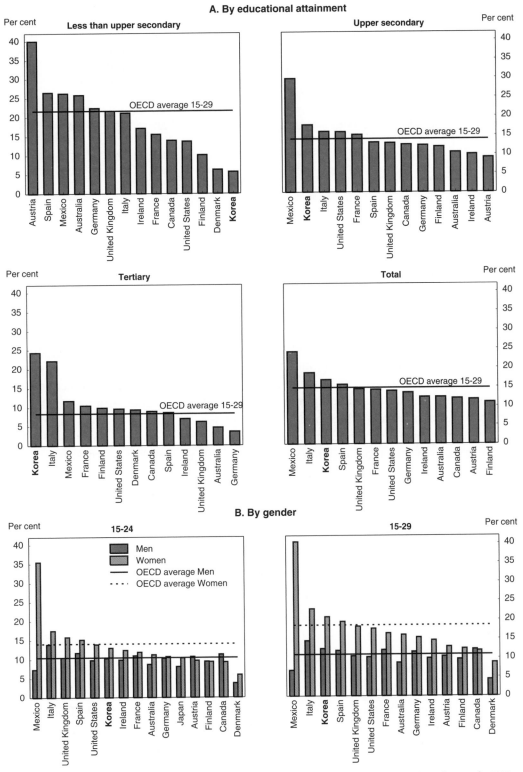

1. Data for Korea and New Zealand are for 2005. For educational attainment in the United Kingdom, they are for 2003.

Source: OECD (2007c), Jobs for Youth: Korea, OECD, Paris.

StatLink ⡃⡩⡅ http://dx.doi.org/10.1787/514438563150

Table 5.5. **Employment outcomes for university graduates in 2007**

	Graduates	Employees	Regular	Non-regular				Self-employed	Not working	Others[4]
				Sub-total	Temporary[1]	Daily[2]	Family[3]			
Total	560 632	390 180	290 907	90 470	60 749	26 633	3 088	8 803	115 073	55 379
		69.6%	51.9%	16.1%	10.8%	4.8%	0.6%	1.6%	20.5%	9.9%
Professional universities	215 040	173 804	132 783	37 678	25 248	11 584	846	3 343	27 527	13 709
		80.8%	61.7%	17.5%	11.7%	5.4%	0.4%	1.6%	15.8%	6.4%
Teacher universities	5 929	4 109	3 680	429	417	12	0	0	1 537	283
		69.3%	62.1%	7.2%	7.0%	0.2%	0.0%	0.0%	25.9%	4.8%
General universities	277 858	168 254	120 618	44 333	28 644	13 608	2 081	3 303	75 842	33 762
		60.6%	43.4%	16.0%	10.3%	4.9%	0.7%	1.2%	27.3%	12.2%
Industrial universities	26 490	19 714	15 701	3 299	2 425	737	137	714	5 354	1 422
		74.4%	59.3%	12.5%	9.2%	2.8%	0.5%	2.7%	20.2%	5.4%
Other universities[4]	282	109	48	57	57	0	0	4	16	157
		38.7%	17.0%	20.2%	20.2%	0.0%	0.0%	1.4%	0.5%	55.6%
Graduate school (general)	35 033	24 190	18 077	4 674	3 958	692	24	1 439	4 797	6 046
		69.0%	51.6%	13.3%	11.3%	2.0%	0.1%	4.1%	13.7%	17.2%

1. Temporary employees include those whose labour contracts are for less than one year.
2. Includes part-time employees who work more than 18 hours a week.
3. Family employees are unpaid workers in establishments owned by family or relatives.
4. Includes those continuing to advanced studies and men fulfilling their military service obligation.
5. Other universities include military schools, Taegu divinity school, etc.
Source: Ministry of Education, Science, and Technology.

in the number of jobs created per won of outlays (Table 5.6). For example, programmes aimed at non-employed university graduates create nearly three times more jobs per won than those aimed at university students. It is important to streamline and consolidate these programmes, thus facilitating more rigorous evaluation to determine which ones should be terminated and which should be expanded. For example, wage subsidies in OECD countries have high deadweight costs, while training programmes in Korea tend to be supply-driven rather than responding to labour market needs (OECD, 2007c).

Table 5.6. **The number of jobs created by employment programmes and their efficiency**

Policy targets	The number of jobs		Jobs per 100 million won	
	2005	2006	2005	2006
Non-employed upper secondary graduates	8 590	13 331	10.3	9.9
Non-employed university graduates	3 719	3 058	15.5	16.5
Upper secondary students	4 023	1 088	15.2	3.2
University students	268	694	4.1	6.5
Unemployed youth	30 793	53 786	19.1	24.1
Total	47 393	71 957	15.7	17.0

Source: Kyu-Yong Lee (2008).

The Youth Job Experience Programme (YJEP), aimed at students and unemployed youth between the ages of 15 and 29, was launched in 1999 to facilitate the school-to-work transition. The 60 000 participants each year are given a training allowance of 0.3 million won per month for two to six months. The programme is available to firms with five or more employees, NGOs, government agencies and public enterprises. Firms are also given subsidies to encourage their participation. This programme is shortening the school to work transition[15] and reducing the share of youth that become economically inactive. The government plans to make the YJEP the main tool for facilitating the school-to-work transition.[16] However, given that the participants are primarily university students, it is necessary to expand the programme to include more lower-educated youth on equity grounds (OECD, 2007c).

Upgrading the education system

Improving the quality of tertiary education through competition and stronger links with firms

Korea has a remarkable record of expanding enrolments at all levels of schooling. The share of the 25-to-34 age group with tertiary education reached 53% by 2006, compared with only 11% for the 55-to-64 age group (Figure 5.9) and will continue rising, given that over 80% of upper secondary students advance to tertiary education, compared to only 33% in 1990.[17] The strong demand for education boosted the number of universities from 148 in 1990 to 211 in 2007, including 161 private ones. A university education is considered almost mandatory by parents. However, the performance of tertiary education is not as good as expected by stakeholders. In an international survey of executives on the effectiveness of a country's education system in meeting the needs of a competitive economy, Korea ranked 53rd out of 55 countries (IMD, 2008), indicating that the university system does not respond effectively to the demands of the business sector. In addition, the large net outflow of students raises questions about quality. The number of students overseas rose by 45% between 2001 and 2007 (Table 5.7), by which time they accounted for 7% of all tertiary students in Korea. In 2006, Korea accounted for 4% of foreign student flows to the OECD area, making it the third-largest source after China and India, while its role as a destination is one of the lowest in the OECD area. Low quality is related to the level of spending: in 2005, spending per student at the tertiary level was $7 606 in Korea (at purchasing power parity exchange rates) compared to an OECD average of $11 512.

Another problem is the mismatch between the skills provided by tertiary education and labour market requirements, which has accompanied the rapid expansion of tertiary education. For example, about 35% of tertiary graduates in natural and social sciences do

Figure 5.9. **International comparison of tertiary education in different age groups in 2006**

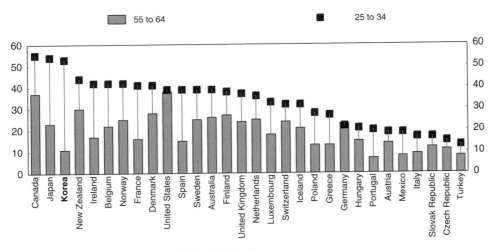

Source: OECD (2008a), *Education at a Glance 2008*, OECD, Paris.

StatLink http://dx.doi.org/10.1787/514442284686

Table 5.7. **The number of students studying abroad**

A. Number of Korean primary and secondary school students who left Korea between 1996 and 2006

	Primary school	Lower secondary	Upper secondary	Total
1996	341	1 743	1 489	3 573
2000	705	1 799	1 893	4 397
2004	6 276	5 568	4 602	16 446
2006	13 814	9 246	6 451	29 511

B. Number of Korean students who studied abroad in university or higher programmes during 2001-07

	Degree programmes			Language study	Total
	Graduate school	University	Sub-total		
2001	37 328	71 823	109 151	40 782	149 933
2004	38 494	67 399	105 893	81 790	187 683
2007	41 993	81 972	123 965	93 994	217 959

Source: Ministry of Education, Science, and Technology.

not find jobs in their field of study (Table 5.8). To reduce mismatch, universities need to provide career-related information and guidance to students. While universities have already launched initiatives to improve their connections with the labour market, greater competition between universities would reward those that are most successful in this regard. This requires an effective institutional arrangement for monitoring the labour market outcomes of each university's students and providing such information to the public (OECD, 2006b). From 2009, universities will be required to conduct self-evaluation of their results. At the same time, they will be evaluated by government-recognised organisations, which will also be responsible for accreditation. Increased transparency about the performance of universities should be accompanied by stronger accreditation requirements. In addition, it is important to implement a May 2008 law requiring public disclosure of key information about universities in 13 areas, such as enrolment rates, employment rates of graduates, faculty ratios, research outcomes, budgets and facilities, to help guide students in their choice of university.

Table 5.8. **Employment rates after graduation and study-job matches of tertiary graduates[1]**

Fields of study	Employment rate (%)	Study-job match rate (%)
All higher educational institutions	76.1	72.3
Education	73.1	86.2
Medical and pharmacy	89.2	92.9
Engineering	78.2	76.8
Social sciences	73.1	62.8
Art and physical education	79.9	77.7
Natural sciences	72.5	67.0
Humanities	68.5	50.2

1. The data are based on a survey by colleges and universities of 560 000 graduates. The employment rate after graduation refers to the ratio of those who found jobs as of 1 April 2007 among those who graduated in February 2007 (including some who graduated in August 2006). The study-job match rate is based on the self-assessment of those graduates.

Source: Ministry of Education, Science, and Technology.

Public universities tend to be heavily regulated, with a large number of ministries applying regulations in a wide range of areas including financing, budget and staffing (OECD, 2007e). Public and private universities are prohibited from using written exams of Korean, English and mathematics, as part of the admission procedure until 2010, at which point universities will be free to introduce such exams. Moreover, there are enrolment quotas for all universities in the capital region and public universities in other areas.[18] In addition, universities were used as "an engine to achieve balanced national development", which may distract them from their fundamental goal. While the government has launched a programme of regulatory reform, further liberalisation of university management would encourage them to better respond to the preferences of students and changes in the labour market. Moreover, it would promote diversity between universities and strengthen competition. Opening the university system to accredited foreign providers would also stimulate competition and upgrade the competitiveness of universities. At present, there is only one foreign graduate school operating in Korea. In sum, greater competition would lead to a more efficient university sector, helping to reduce mismatch problems. In addition, competition is essential to guide the restructuring of the university sector as the university-age cohort begins to shrink.

A second issue related to tertiary education is its high cost for students, reflecting a low level of public funding. Indeed, public outlays on tertiary education amounted to around $1 848 per student (at PPP exchange rates) in 2005 compared to an OECD average of around $8 400. As a share of GDP, it is only 0.6%, half of the OECD average. In contrast, spending on primary and secondary schools, at 3½ per cent, matches the OECD average (Figure 5.10). Consequently, most of the cost of tertiary education is borne by households,

Figure 5.10. **Total public expenditure on education**

As a per cent of GDP in 2005[1]

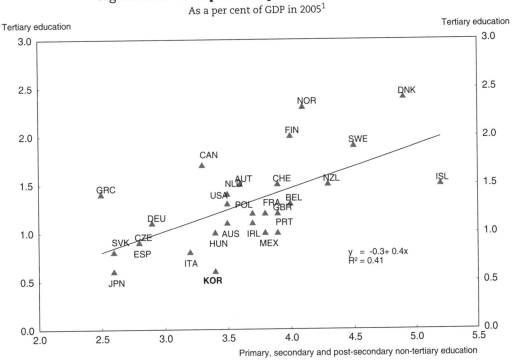

1. Public expenditure here includes public subsidies to households for living costs, which are not spent on educational institutions.

Source: OECD (2008a), Education at a Glance 2008, OECD, Paris.

StatLink ⧉ http://dx.doi.org/10.1787/514455481188

which is generally appropriate given that private returns are higher than social returns. The reliance on private financial resources also helps convey information on costs and benefits of education, thus making possible informed investment decisions (Boarini and Strauss, 2007). In the case of Korea, though, the exceptionally rapid expansion of tertiary education and the low level of public expenditure compared to the OECD average appear to justify increased public spending to reduce the burden on families while improving the quality of the university system. Moreover, limiting the increase in tuition fees by expanding public spending would tend to boost the rate of return on human capital investment and ease financing constraints for individual students (Oliveira Martins et al., 2007). Demographic factors will facilitate a shift in the allocation of funds between levels of education in favour of tertiary education: by 2020, the number of primary and secondary students is projected to fall by one-third while the number of university-age persons declines by only 10.7% (Table 5.9).

Table 5.9. **Projection of the number of students by age cohort**[1]

Number of students in thousands and an index with 2006 = 100

Age cohort	6-11 years	12-14 years	15-17 years	18-21 years	Total	Share (%) of total population
Corresponding school	Primary school	Lower secondary	Upper secondary	College and university		
2006	3 922	2 093	1 907	2 541	10 464	21.7
	100.0	100.0	100.0	100.0	100.0	
2010	3 296	1 961	2 069	2 573	9 901	20.3
	84.0	93.7	108.5	101.3	94.6	
2020	2 510	1 291	1 364	2 268	7 434	15.1
	64.0	61.7	71.5	89.3	71.0	
2030	2 209	1 130	1 174	1 647	6 162	12.7
	56.3	54.0	61.6	64.8	58.9	
2040	2 001	1 074	1 071	1 432	5 580	12.0
	51.0	51.3	56.2	56.4	53.3	
2050	1 525	838	908	1 329	4 601	10.9
	38.9	40.0	47.6	52.3	44.0	

1. The top line for each year shows the number of students in thousands and the second the number as a share of the 2006 level.

Source: Ministry of Education, Science, and Technology.

The financial burden of tertiary education could be reduced by shortening the length of study by streamlining programmes, reducing slack in student timetables, strengthening incentives for studying faster and imposing penalties (higher tuition) for studying longer. Such an approach would also enhance incentives to invest in human capital (Strauss and Maisonneuve, 2007).

Enhancing the quality and efficiency of primary and secondary education

Compared to tertiary education, primary and secondary education is widely praised for its high quality, as demonstrated by international tests: Korean students consistently rank among the top performers in the OECD's PISA tests. With combined public and private spending on educational institutions below the OECD average in absolute amount,[19] both input and output efficiency in Korea are among the highest in the OECD area (Sutherland et al., 2007). However, there are a number of problems in primary and secondary education, as suggested by the rapid expansion in the number of students studying abroad from around 4 000 in 2000 to almost 30 000 in 2006 (Table 5.7).

Reducing the important role of private, after-school tutoring institutes known as *hakwon* is a major government goal and requires better public education. A government survey found that 77% of students in primary and secondary education go to private tutoring for an average of about 10 hours a week (Table 5.10). Each household on average pays about 8% of monthly income for tutoring, with the total cost amounting to 2.2% of GDP in 2007. Adding this amount to public and private expenditures on educational institutions would boost educational outlays to 9½ per cent of GDP, the highest in the OECD area. The large role of private tutoring creates a number of concerns. *First*, it creates very long days for children, thus hindering their full development. *Second*, it competes and overlaps with public education, thus raising total expenditures on education unnecessarily. *Third*, the high cost of private tutoring hinders equal access to educational opportunities, raising equity issues. *Fourth*, it creates problems for the public education system, which has to cope with students of widely differing educational levels. Several studies indicate that the high reliance on private tutoring is related to the low quality of schools (Taejong Kim, 2005) and dissatisfaction with public education (Hyunjin Kim, 2004).

Table 5.10. **Private tutoring in Korea in 2007**

	Participation rate (%)	Average hours of participation per week[1]	Per capita expenditure (thousand won)[1]	Share[2]	Total expenditure (trillion won)	Share of GDP (%)
Total	77.0	10.2	288	8.0	20.0	2.2
Primary school	88.8	10.0	256	7.1	10.2	1.1
Middle school	74.6	11.9	314	8.7	5.6	0.6
General high school	62.0	8.3	388	10.7	3.9	0.4
Vocational high school	33.7	7.4	198	5.5	0.4	0.0

1. Of those attending private tutoring.
2. As a per cent of household income (salary and wage earners) in 2007.
Source: Ministry of Education, Science, and Technology and Korea National Statistical Office.

As in other countries, there is also concern about the system used to allocate students between upper secondary schools. Allowing a wider range of school choice for students at the secondary level would likely be beneficial. Under the residence-based student selection policy – the so-called "equalisation policy" – introduced in 1974, students in urban areas are assigned randomly to schools, both public and private.[20] However, many urban areas are no longer using random assignment, but are instead allowing students the right to choose the schools that they prefer. In addition, Seoul will introduce a new student allocation system based on students' school choices beginning in 2010, another step promoting a wider range of school choice. School selection based on academic record, or to a lesser extent, recommendations from feeder schools, would boost efficiency (Sutherland and Price, 2007), while avoiding standardised entrance exams would limit the need for tutoring. In such a framework, schools would have to compete with each other to improve the quality of education. Such competition requires disclosure concerning the performance of schools and teachers to allow benchmarking. Although Korea has national examinations, follow-up statistics on students' careers and regular inspections of schools, such information has so far not been available to families. However, from December 2008, some key data, including students' academic achievements, are set to become public information.

Competition would also be promoted by permitting more "independent private schools", which were allowed in a pilot project that began in 2002. The government will allow the number to increase from only six in 2008. Another interesting innovation is the creation of four "open-type independent schools" in 2007, in which school management is contracted to a third party in the private sector. Strict regulation, *e.g.* in the areas of curricula and teacher policies, hurts educational performance (Kim *et al.*, 2008). An OECD study found that greater decision-making autonomy at the school level tends to be associated with higher efficiency (Sutherland and Price, 2007). Structural reforms that bring decision-making power and accountability closer to those who teach and manage schools would enhance efficiency without harming quality. In this regard, the recent policy to allow more independent private schools will be beneficial. In addition, 226 high schools have become "autonomous schools" with more independence in management. However, the use of local education governments, which are distinct from local general governments and rely on the central government for more than two-thirds of their revenue, encourages a centralised approach to education (*OECD Economic Surveys: Korea*, 2005). In sum, regulatory reform to expand the autonomous decision-making powers of school would help them meet the needs of students and families.

Increased competition among schools could lead to even higher costs for education. However, there is scope to curb costs and improve efficiency, particularly as regards teachers' salaries. The salary of a school teacher with 15 years of experience averages 2.3 times GDP per capita, as against 1.3 times in the OECD area (Figure 5.11). It is hard to justify such a gap, particularly given that a large part of teaching takes place in private tutoring institutes. Reducing costs would allow schools to employ more teachers and further reduce the student/teacher ratio, which is the highest in the OECD area for both primary and lower secondary schools (Figure 5.12). In addition, levels of efficiency are higher on average in private schools in the OECD area (Sutherland and Price, 2007), which argues for further increasing the number of independent schools.

The quality of secondary education is also affected by the university entrance system. In particular, the ban on written exams as part of the admission process was aimed at standardising secondary education. The heavy reliance on standardised entrance exams

Figure 5.11. **International comparison of teachers' salaries**

Ratio to per capita GDP for a teacher with 15 years experience at lower secondary level in 2006

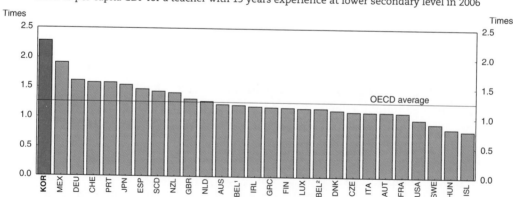

1. Belgium, Flemish-speaking.
2. Belgium, French-speaking.

Source: OECD (2008a), *Education at a Glance 2008*, OECD, Paris.

StatLink 🔗 http://dx.doi.org/10.1787/514465252105

Figure 5.12. **Average class size in primary and lower education**

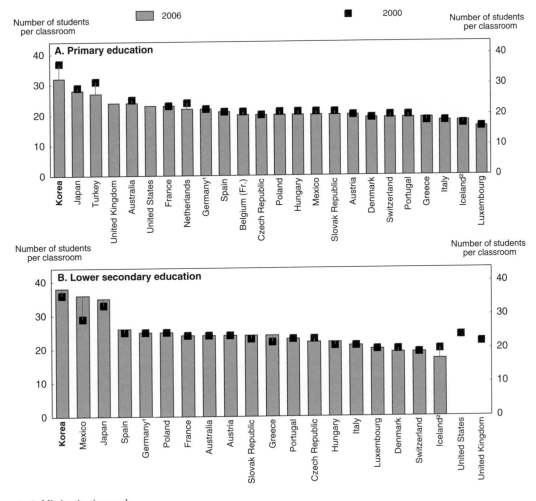

1. Public institutions only.
2. Years of reference are 2001 and 2005.

Source: OECD (2008a), *Education at a Glance 2008*, OECD, Paris.

StatLink ⟐⟐ http://dx.doi.org/10.1787/514465558416

encourages private tutoring to gain admission to the best institutions. Allowing universities more autonomy in selecting applicants would reduce reliance on private tutoring. The revision of the college admission system in 2008 to give more weight to performance in school and less to the standardised test was a step in the right direction. The government is taking additional measures to enhance the autonomy of the admission process: i) a self-regulatory body, the Korean Council for University Education, will take responsibility for supervising the system from 2008; ii) the government will reduce the number of required subjects in the university admission exam in 2012; and iii) universities will be granted complete autonomy in admission procedures from 2013.

Promoting the employment of older workers

Labour force participation in Korea remains high relative to the OECD average for men over 50 and for women over 60 (Figure 5.13). For the over-65 age group, the participation rate is 31% compared with an OECD average of 12%. Moreover the average effective age of

Figure 5.13. **Labour force participation rates for the over-50 age group in 2007**

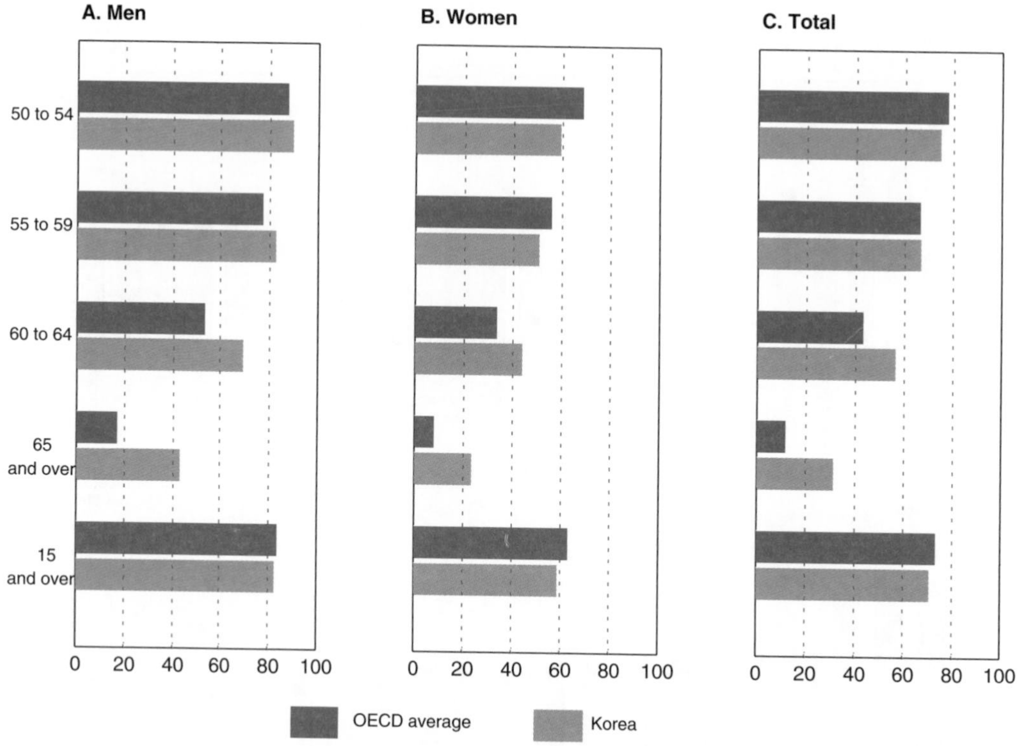

Source: OECD Employment Outlook Database.

StatLink ⟨⟩ http://dx.doi.org/10.1787/514488138368

retirement for men in Korea is 71, the second oldest among OECD countries (Figure 5.14). The early stage of development of the pension system is one factor. For households headed by a person aged 50 or over, public transfers accounted for only 5% of aggregate income in 2006, while the share of wage income was 44%. Transfers from family members or other households accounted for another 46% (Chang, 2008).

While older workers are likely to remain in the labour force, they tend to retire early from their main career, at around 55. Indeed, the average employment tenure peaks at 11 years in the 45-to-49 age group – well below most other OECD countries where the peak is in the 55-to-64 age group – and then falls sharply (OECD, 2005). About three-quarters of departing employees become self-employed, primarily in services with low productivity. Consequently, 34% of workers over 50 are self-employed, as against 13% of those under that age. As for workers who remain employed past 50 more than two-thirds worked in firms with less than 100 workers and less than two-fifths were regular workers in 2007.

Factors explaining early retirement from firms

The early departure of employees reflects the importance of seniority in determining wage levels. Indeed, a worker with 25 years of tenure in a firm earns almost three and a half times more than a newly-hired employee (Figure 5.15) and has less education on average. In 2005, 85% of firms with more than 300 workers set mandatory retirement below the age of 60 recommended by law. Indeed, the average age of mandatory retirement

Figure 5.14. **International comparison of retirement ages in 2007**[1]

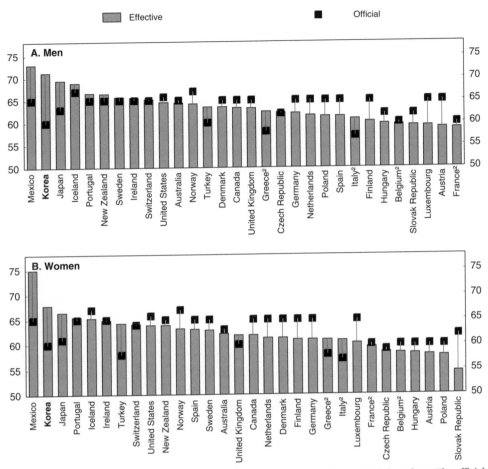

1. The average effective age of retirement is defined as the average age of exit from the labour force. The official age corresponds to the age at which a pension can be received, irrespective of whether the worker has a long record of contributions.
2. Women can retire at age 60 with 40 years of contributions in Belgium and France and at age 55 with 35 years of contributions in Greece and Italy (for manual workers, otherwise at 57).

Source: OECD Live Longer, Work Longer: A Synthesis Report Database (www.oecd.org/dataoecd/3/2/39371902.xls).

StatLink ᴀᴌꜱᴘ http://dx.doi.org/10.1787/514513338178

even fell slightly from 57.2 years in 2000 to 56.9 in 2006. Mandatory retirement enables firms to dismiss workers as seniority-based wages surpass their productivity. Companies in which wages are closely linked to seniority hire fewer older workers (Lee, 2008). Given the difficulty of dismissing regular employees, a mandatory retirement system also helps firms adjust their workforces (Cho and Lee, 2005).

The government has encouraged the use of a performance-based wage system in order to flatten the tenure-wage profile. The proportion of firms including performance as an element in determining wages rose sharply from 1.6% in 1996 to 48.4% in 2005 (Table 5.11), despite opposition from workers. However, the share of regular workers in performance-based wage systems was much lower, at 27.6% in 2005, and would likely be even lower if non-regular workers were included. Moreover, the slope of the tenure-wage profile has not changed much in recent years (Figure 5.15), while the age-wage profile did

Table 5.11. **Use of performance-based wage systems**

	1996	1997	1999	2000	2001	2002	2003	2004	2005
Per cent of workplaces[1]	1.6	3.6	15.1	23.0	27.1	32.3	37.5	41.9	48.4
Per cent of workers[2]	1.3	2.0	7.7	12.0	15.2	19.5	22.6	24.0	27.6

1. Establishments with at least 100 full-time workers.
2. Full-time regular workers in establishments with at least 100 full-time workers.
Source: Ministry of Labour, *Survey on the Annual Salary Scheme* and *Wage Structure Survey*.

flatten between 2003 and 2007 (Panel B). This suggests that firms reduced wages for new hires in the 30-to-50 age group, while maintaining the wage profile for existing workers.

A second factor promoting the early departure of older workers from firms is the retirement allowance. Companies are required by law to pay a lump sum of at least one month of wages to each departing employee for each year worked, although many pay about twice that amount in practice. The lump sum is based on the employee's final wage, which increases sharply with seniority, creating a disincentive to keep older employees. The retirement allowance is not a secure source of income, as it is only partially funded, making payments dependent on the firm's survival. Finally, despite its name, this payment has lost its link to retirement income as most workers receive such lump sums a number of times during their working life, given the short average tenure of employees, and often spend it for housing.

Older workers are also challenged by the skills required in Korea's increasingly knowledge-based economy. The proportion of the 55-to-64 age cohort with tertiary education was only 11% in 2006, compared to 53% for the 25-to-34 age cohort, the third highest in the OECD area (Figure 5.9). The education gap between age cohorts is the largest in the OECD area, leaving older workers at a competitive disadvantage. Indeed, 65% of workers over 50 are in physically-demanding jobs, such as manual work, which tend to be low-paid. Two-thirds of the unemployed over 50 failed to complete secondary school and three-quarters worked previously as daily or temporary workers (Chang, 2004).

Figure 5.15. **Wage profile in Korea[1]**

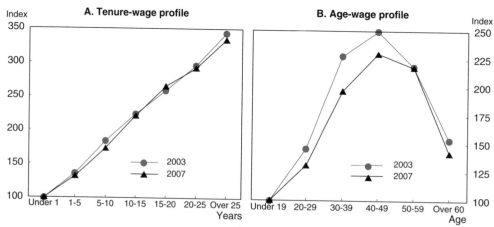

1. Wages for 19-year-olds and younger and for less than a year are set at 100 in each year.
Source: Ministry of Labour, Wage Structure Survey.

StatLink ⟪🎫⟫ http://dx.doi.org/10.1787/514545517208

Policies to promote the employment of older persons

The government's "Basic Plan to Promote Employment of the Aged" aims at increasing the employment rate of the 55-to-64 age group from 59% in 2005 to at least 63%, the level of Japan in 2004 (KDI, 2006). The plan, which will continue through 2021, contains three pillars. First, the government will encourage firms to raise their mandatory retirement age, with a goal of eventually eliminating it altogether.[21] Second, it is providing programmes to support the re-employment of older persons who have left their jobs involuntarily because of retirement ages or dismissal. Third, the government is introducing new wage subsidies. For example, the government subsidises firms for up to five years if they guarantee employment until their retirement age, extend their retirement age or offer re-employment programmes to retirees. In addition, there is a new subsidy for workers whose salary is cut as a result of the introduction of new employment status and type of work in their firm.

The government already offers three different subsidies to encourage firms to hire and retain older workers. The take-up of these grants has nearly tripled since 1996 to ¼ million workers, equivalent to about 7% of the employed over 55. However, the average subsidy per worker is less than 1% of the average wage, suggesting that it does not have a big impact on employment. Real estate service firms account for about two-thirds of the recipient companies, with most concentrated in building maintenance services. The concentration of the subsidies in one business line raises doubts as to their effectiveness in boosting the overall employment of older workers. Indeed, 92% of firms receiving the subsidy responded that they would have hired the same number of workers in the absence of any assistance (Chang, 2004). The government has also provided a subsidy to older workers to promote the introduction of the "peak-wage system", which allows wages to fall after some point in exchange for guaranteed employment to an agreed-upon age. However, the take-up of this subsidy has been very low.[22]

Instead of wage subsidies to reduce the cost of older workers relative to younger ones, it is important to achieve wage flexibility so that older workers remain affordable. Greater opportunities for "continuous employment" at the same firm, rather than self-employment or non-regular work, would encourage older workers to remain in the labour force. Requiring companies to set mandatory retirement at an age closer to the pension eligibility age – or forbidding the use of mandatory retirement altogether – would help change the seniority-based wage system. Firms agree to steep seniority-based wage profiles on the condition that they can force older workers to leave. Without mandatory retirement, firms would insist on wage systems that more closely reflect productivity.

In addition, it is important to abolish the retirement allowance system in order to reduce firms' incentives to retire older workers, as well as to enhance labour mobility. The government launched a company pension system in 2005 to replace the retirement allowance at workplaces with at least five employees, which would provide better income security for retired workers. This requires labour and management to agree on a defined-benefit (DB) or a defined-contribution (DC) scheme. By September 2008, pension plans had been introduced at 8.7% of firms, with large firms taking the lead (21.5%). Overall, company pension plans cover 3.5% of total employees and 9.0% of regular ones. The low coverage reflects different preferences between employers and employees as to which type of plan to introduce. Employers tend to favour DC plans, which account for 79.7% of the company pension plans to date, as they place the downside risk of investment on workers. On the other hand, workers tend to favour DB plans, which are similar to the current retirement

Table 5.12. **Introduction of company pension plans**[1]

	By size of establishment						
	5 to 9 workers	10 to 29 workers	30 to 99 workers	100 to 299 workers	300 to 499 workers	500 or more workers	Total
Establishments with plans	25 459	11 713	5 313	1 128	175	207	43 995
Total number of establishments	292 140	156 304	45 083	8 700	1 018	965	504 210
Per cent with plans	8.7	7.5	11.8	13.0	17.2	21.5	8.7

	By type of company pension plan						
	DB	DC	DB and DC[2]	IRA[3]	DC ratio (%)[4]	DC+IRA ratio (%)[4]	Total
Total	8 911	17 512	386	17 186	40.7	79.7	43 995
500 or more workers	97	53	57		53.1	53.1	207
Less than 500 workers	8 814	17 459	329	17 186	40.6	79.9	43 788

1. Data are for September 2008.
2. A combined defined-benefit and defined-contribution system.
3. Individual Retirement Accounts, a scheme similar to defined contributions, are allowed for workplaces with less than ten workers.
4. As a per cent of the total. DC stands for defined contribution.
Source: Ministry of Labour.

allowance in guaranteeing the benefit paid. The difficult environment for collective bargaining frustrates agreements on the type of pension plan.

At the current pace, it would take more than 15 years to cover just one-half of regular workers in company pension plans. The decision to introduce a company pension while maintaining the retirement allowance reflects the difficulty of phasing out the latter, which is popular with workers. To accelerate the transition to company pensions, the government should remove the preferential tax treatment for retirement allowances, which allow the lump sum to be taxed over a number of years at low rates, a more favourable arrangement than granted to company pension systems. The fact that the retirement allowance does not have to be funded outside the company provides advantages to firms.[23] In addition, the government should encourage DC plans in order to promote pension portability and thereby labour mobility. Given that the average employment tenure is only five years in Korea, a worker may be employed by as many as eight or nine firms during his/her career, making a DB system difficult to manage. To give firms even greater incentives to choose DC plans, the proportion of funds that have to be entrusted to financial institutions under a DB plan (60%) could be raised to 100%, as for DC plans.

Finally, greater emphasis on lifelong learning and training would likely improve the employment prospects of older workers more than employment subsidy programmes. Government expenditures on lifelong learning, including vocational training, amounted to only 0.1% of GDP in 2007 and the participation rate of adults in lifelong education was 29.8% (Table 5.13). The rate rises with the level of education, making it important to target less-educated persons.[24] However, training has to be carefully targeted to be effective (Injae Lee, 2008). The amount of firm-specific and ICT training provided at an enterprise is negatively correlated to its hiring of older workers. This suggests that a lack of firm-specific human capital and ICT skills is an impediment to hiring older workers.[25] Thus, general lifelong education and training may not be effective in raising the employment of older workers, but should be focused specifically on the needs of potential employers. In sum, the allocation of active labour market policies for older workers should

Table 5.13. **Per capita expenditure for lifelong education and participation rate in 2007**

		Participation rate (%)	Per capita expenditure[1]
Total		29.8	142.8
Gender	Male	28.9	181.2
	Female	30.7	106.5
Age	25-34 years old	36.3	299.4
	35-44 years old	29.2	59.2
	45-54 years old	26.5	68.4
	55-64 years old	23.9	34.5
Educational attainment	Lower secondary or below	16.8	10.7
	Upper secondary	24.5	162.3
	University or more	39.4	148.0

1. Out-of-pocket expenditures, excluding public support, in thousand won.
Source: Ministry of Education, Science and Technology.

be carefully based on the longer-run costs and benefits of each programme. While subsidies may provide benefits in the short run, they generally entail high deadweight costs (Martin and Grubb, 2001). Moreover, the continuous provision of wage subsidies may delay structural change and distort the composition of the labour force away from its optimal allocation by changing the relative cost of older workers relative to younger ones.

Conclusion

Korea has considerable scope to expand the use and improve the quality of its human resources. Specific recommendations to reverse labour market dualism, boost the participation rates of women and youth and raise the age when older workers leave firms are summarised in Box 5.2.

Box 5.2. **Summary of recommendations on the labour market and education system***

Reduce labour market dualism

- Liberalise employment protection legislation for regular workers.

- Expand the coverage of social insurance schemes to reduce firms' incentives to hire non-regular workers and provide better protection for such workers.

- Ensure that the newly implemented law to protect non-regular workers does not slow employment growth.

Raise female labour force participation

- Expand the availability of high-quality childcare by relaxing price controls on private-sector providers.

- Lengthen maternity leave and ensure that eligible persons are able to take maternity and parental leave, while encouraging the development of family-friendly workplaces.

- Reduce the use of seniority-based wages and reverse labour market dualism to provide better job opportunities for women.

Improve job prospects for youth

- Reduce mismatches between skills provided in tertiary education and those required in the labour market by strengthening links between universities and companies.

Box 5.2. Summary of recommendations on the labour market and education system* (cont.)

- Improve the quality of tertiary education by strengthening competition, which requires increased transparency about the performance of educational institutions, stronger accreditation procedures and regulatory reform to promote innovation.

- Expand public support for universities as the number of elementary and secondary students decline.

- Reduce the number of NEETs by reversing the upward trend in non-regular employment.

- Improve quality and efficiency of public education to curb demand for after-school tutoring, in part by bringing teachers' salaries more in line with average income.

- Follow through on the plan to allow more independent schools to promote both efficiency and quality.

Promote the employment of older workers

- Abolish the mandatory retirement system, thus helping to flatten the wage-seniority profile.

- Phase out the retirement allowance by accelerating the introduction of company pensions.

- Improve ALMPs by focusing on training rather than wage subsidies and direct job creation.

* Recommendations in each section are ranked in order of their priority.

Notes

1. However, Nam (2007) found that the 37% wage differential decreases to 2.2% if attributes of workers are controlled. Using panel data, he also concluded that there is no difference between the hourly wages of regular and non-regular workers.

2. Expenditures on vocational training for SMEs and non-regular workers increased from 75 billion won in 2006 to 117 billion in 2007, and the number of workers trained from 3 000 to 37 000.

3. According to a survey by the Ministry of Labour in 2008, 16% of firms were planning to turn to temporary worker agencies and outsourcing, while 21% said they had reduced non-regular jobs and 18% planned to do so. About 20% of firms had converted non-regular workers into regular status. Another survey by the Korea Employers Federation reported that about 40% of firms cut or planned to cut non-regular workers while only 19% of them would hire regular workers to fill those vacancies (KOILAF, 2008b).

4. In addition, the World Bank study *Doing Business 2008* ranks Korea 27th among OECD countries in the category "Employing workers", which includes the cost of dismissing a redundant worker.

5. The prevalence of long working hours is also linked to the long-term commitment of regular workers to their firms. Regular employees are trained in-house and receive retirement allowances and other fringe benefits. Wages are essentially seniority-based and strongly linked to certified skills, age and tenure in the firm. In return, regular workers accept flexible adjustment of working conditions and long working hours, including unpaid overtime and, in some cases, taking less leave than granted.

6. The other major obstacles were gender discrimination at establishments (14.4%), burden of housekeeping (13.7%), lack of vision (4.7%) and lack of job information (3.1%). However, low female employment cannot be blamed on the tax system, which unlike those in some countries, does not discourage the employment of second earners in households (see Chapter 3).

7. A subsidy of 0.4 million won per month (a quarter of the average wage) is provided for those with children under one-year-old. The programme also gives a monthly subsidy to the firms of workers taking leave.

8. For example, for children less than one-year-old, the cap is set at 361 000 won per month, with the government providing an additional subsidy of 292 000 won. The combined amount (663 000 won) is well below the 789 000 won that the government calculates is necessary to provide adequate care.

9. A number of countries, including Australia and the United States, have found success in using a system of childcare vouchers. Other countries, such as Canada, Germany and the United Kingdom, use tax credits and cash benefits to reimburse expenses. Shifting government funding from supplying childcare services to providing vouchers to families would foster competition among providers and give more choice to parents, as has occurred in Australia (Pearson and Martin, 2005).

10. The Work and Family Life Compatibility Support Task Force was established in 2008 to address this issue.

11. See Box 5.1 in the 2007 OECD Economic Surveys: Korea for a detailed account of this issue.

12. There is some difference between the OECD definition of NEETs used here and that used in Korea. In Korea, NEETs include youth between 15 and 34 who are not employed, not married, not handling family responsibilities and not attending school or an institution for job preparation (Nam, 2006). In 2007, there were 276 000 youth preparing for job entrance exams in the public or private sector. This group is included in the OECD definition of NEETs, but not in the Korean definition (OECD, 2007c).

13. The NEETs include the 276 000 preparing for job entrance exams, 150 000 who were preparing for college/university entrance exams they previously failed and 196 000 who were "just resting". The remainder cited other reasons such as childcare, housework and disability (OECD, 2007c).

14. According to the 2003 and 2004 EAPS Supplementary Surveys, about 15% of non-regular workers became regular workers while over 20% became economically inactive, unemployed, or unpaid family workers. In contrast, KLIPS data indicate that about one-third of non-regular workers became regular workers in 2005-06. The different definitions of non-regular workers used in the two data sets affects the results. KLIPS data also show about 80% of regular workers retaining their status and less than 10% becoming economically inactive, unemployed or unpaid family workers.

15. Those participating in the YJEP take an average of 9.6 months to move from school to a first job compared with 14.4 months for those without job experience during their studies. Moreover, YJEP participants stayed longer in their first jobs (53% after 24 months) compared with those who did not participate (31%).

16. The YJEP, which was introduced in 1999, is to be improved by strengthening its link to career guidance and training programmes. All participants are to take part in a one-week career guidance programme and are offered employment support by Job Centres after completing the YJEP programme. In order to encourage more opportunities for training at private firms, the proportion of participants in the public sector is to be limited to 30%. In addition, preferential support is provided to companies if they offer places in occupations other than clerical jobs, such as technical and skilled positions (OECD, 2007c).

17. This includes those finishing vocational upper secondary schools. Two-thirds of this group pursue tertiary education.

18. In addition, teachers' universities and medicine and nursing schools face quotas to match supply with labour demand.

19. In 2005, total cumulative expenditure per student during primary and secondary education was $68 424 (at purchasing power parity exchange rates), 22% below the OECD average (OECD, 2008a).

20. As of 2007, there were 2 218 upper secondary schools, of which 995 are private. Despite their name, such schools receive public funds and follow the same curricula as public schools. There are also 129 "special purpose school" offering diversified curricula, such as foreign languages, with special admission criteria.

21. In 2008, the government enacted a law which will prevent unjustified discrimination against older persons in recruitment or employment from 2009 and age discrimination with regard to working conditions such as wages and welfare from 2010 (KOILAF, 2008a).

22. According to the Ministry of Labour, only 226 workers in 37 workplaces in 2006 and 584 workers in 160 workplaces in 2007 received this subsidy.

23. In contrast, firms that adopt DB schemes must entrust at least 60% of the funds to financial institutions and 100% in the case of DC schemes. In both cases, employers must provide payments at least as large as under the lump-sum retirement allowance.

24. The participation rate of those with a lower secondary school or below educational attainment increased from 9.1% in 2004 to 16.8% in 2007, thanks to increased government outlays.

25. The same study showed that firm size is positively correlated with the hiring of older workers, while the existence of a labour union correlates negatively, as they tend to oppose the hiring of new older workers.

Bibliography

Ahn, Joyup (2006), "Nonstandard Work in Korea – the Origin of Wage Differentials", mimeo, Korea Labor Institute, Seoul.

Boarini, R. and H. Strauss (2007), "The Private Internal Rates of Return to Tertiary Education: New Estimates for 21 OECD countries", *OECD Economics Department Working Paper*, No. 591, OECD, Paris.

Chang, Jiyeun (2004), "Grants to Promote Employment of the Elderly in Korea – Introduction and Evaluation", *Korea Labor Institute Issue Paper*, No. 35, Seoul.

Chang, Jiyeun (2008), "The Level and Sources of Income for Older People: Findings from Korean Longitudinal Study of Aging", *JILPT Series*, No. 33, Tokyo.

Cho, Joonmo and Seung Gil Lee (2005), "Labor Market Reform: Issues for Employment Promotion of the Elderly", *KDI Annual Report*, Korea Development Institute, Seoul.

Chung, Jaeho and Byung-Hee Lee (2005), "Flexibility, Turnover and Training", *Korea Labor Institute Issue Paper*, No. 41, Seoul.

D'Addio, A. and M. Mira d'Ercole (2005), "Trends and Determinants of Fertility Rates in OECD Countries: The Role of Policies", *OECD Social, Employment and Migration Working Paper*, No. 6, OECD, Paris.

Grubb, D., J.-K. Lee and P. Tergeist (2007), "Addressing Labour Market Duality in Korea", *OECD Social, Employment and Migration Working Paper*, No. 61, OECD, Paris.

Hwang, Soo Kyeong and Jiyeun Chang (2004), "Female Labor Supply and Labor Policies for Female Workers in Korea", *Korea Labor Institute Issue Paper*, No. 30, Seoul.

IMD (2008), *World Competitiveness Yearbook 2008*, International Institute for Management Development, Lausanne.

Jaumotte, F. (2003), "Labour Force Participation of Women: Empirical Evidence on the Role of Policy and Other Determinants in OECD Countries", *OECD Economic Studies*, No. 37, OECD, Paris.

Jeong, Jin-Ho (2003), "Wages in Korea", *Korea Labor Institute Issue Paper*, No. 25, Seoul.

Kim, Hyunjin (2004), "Analysing the Effects of the High School Equalisation Policy and the College Entrance System on Private Tutoring Expenditure in Korea", *Journal of Educational Policy*, Vol. 1, No. 1, Korean Educational Development Institute, Seoul.

Kim, Taejong (2005), "Shadow Education: School Quality and Demand for Private Tutoring in Korea", KDI School of Public Policy and Management.

Kim, Taejong, Ju-Ho Lee, and Young Lee (2008), "Mixing *Versus* Sorting in Schooling: Evidence From the Equalization Policy in South Korea", *Economics of Education Review*, forthcoming.

Korea Development Institute (KDI) (2006), "Government Initiative to Promote Employment of the Aged", *Economic Bulletin*, August, Seoul.

Korea Employers Federation (2006), *2006 Industrial Relations and Labour Market of Korea*, Seoul.

KOILAF (2008a), "Prohibition of Age Discrimination From Employment to Dismissal", *Korea Labor Review* Vol. 4, No. 19, Korea International Labor Foundation, Seoul.

KOILAF (2008b), "Non-Regular Work Laws, One Year After Its Introduction; Evidence and Prospect", *Korea Labor Review*, Vol. 4, No. 21, Korea International Labor Foundation, Seoul.

Lee, Kyu-Yong (2008), "Evaluation of Fiscal Job Support Programs", e-Labor News No. 77, Korea Labor Institute, Seoul.

Lee, Injae (2008), "Factors Determining Recruitment of Older Persons in Korea", *JILPT Series*, No. 33, Tokyo.

Martin, J. and D. Grubb (2001), "What Works and for Whom: A Review of OECD Countries' Experience with Active Labour Market Policies", *Swedish Economic Policy Review*, Vol. 8, No. 2.

Ministry of Labour (2008), *Survey on Gender Equality in Employment*, Seoul.

Nam, J. (2006), "The Trends and Factors of Youth NEET", Paper presented at the 7th Conference on KLIPS, Korea Labor Institute, Seoul.

Nam, J. (2007), "Wage Differentials between Non-Regular and Regular Works – A Panel Data Approach", *Korean Journal of Labor Economics*, Vol. 30, No. 2.

OECD (2005), *OECD Economic Surveys: Korea*, OECD, Paris.

OECD (2006a), *Live Longer, Work Longer: A Synthesis Report*, OECD, Paris.

OECD (2006b), *Thematic Review of Tertiary Education: Korea*, OECD, Paris.

OECD (2007a), *Babies and Bosses – Reconciling Work and Family Life: A Synthesis of Findings for OECD Countries*, OECD, Paris.

OECD (2007b), *Facing the Future: Korea's Family, Pension and Health Policy Challenges*, OECD, Paris.

OECD (2007c), *Jobs for Youth: Korea*, OECD, Paris.

OECD (2007d), *OECD Economic Surveys: Korea*, OECD, Paris.

OECD (2007e), *OECD Reviews of Regulatory Reform: Korea*, OECD, Paris.

OECD (2008a), *Education at a Glance*, OECD, Paris.

OECD (2008b), *Going for Growth*, OECD, Paris.

OECD (2008c), *OECD Employment Outlook*, OECD, Paris.

Oliveira Martins, J., R. Boarini, H. Strauss, C. de la Maisonneuve and C. Saadi (2007), "The Policy Determinants of Investment in Tertiary Education", *OECD Economics Department Working Paper*, No. 576, OECD, Paris.

Pearson, M. and J. Martin (2005), "Should We Extend the Role of Private Social Expenditure?", *OECD Social, Employment and Migration Working Paper*, No. 23, OECD, Paris.

Strauss, H. and C. de la Maisonneuve (2007), "The Wage Premium on Tertiary Education: New Estimates for 21 OECD countries", *OECD Economics Department Working Paper*, No. 589, OECD, Paris.

Sutherland, D. and R. Price (2007), "Linkages Between Performance and Institutions in the Primary and Secondary Education Sector", *OECD Economics Department Working Paper*, No. 558, OECD, Paris.

Sutherland, D., R. Price, I. Joumard and C. Nicq (2007), "Performance Indicators for Spending Efficiency in Primary and Secondary Education", *OECD Economics Department Working Paper*, No. 546, OECD, Paris.

World Bank (2008), *Doing Business 2008*, (*www.doingbusiness.org*), Washington D.C.

OECD PUBLISHING, 2, rue André-Pascal, 75775 PARIS CEDEX 16
PRINTED IN FRANCE
(10 2008 21 1 P) ISBN 978-92-64-05425-7 – No. 56585 2008